Parenting Through
Pop Culture

Parenting Through Pop Culture

Essays on Navigating Media with Children

Edited by JL Schatz

McFarland & Company, Inc., Publishers

Jefferson, North Carolina

ALSO OF INTEREST

The Image of Disability: Essays on Media Representations,
edited by JL Schatz and Amber E. George (2018)

LIBRARY OF CONGRESS CATALOGUING-IN-PUBLICATION DATA

Names: Schatz, J. L., editor.
Title: Parenting through pop culture : essays on navigating media
with children / edited by J L Schatz.
Description: Jefferson : McFarland & Company, Inc., Publishers, 2020. |
Includes bibliographical references and index.
Identifiers: LCCN 2020005065 | ISBN 9781476676944 (paperback) ∞
ISBN 9781476639796 (ebook)
Subjects: LCSH: Mass media and children. |
Internet and children. | Parenting.
Classification: LCC HQ784.M3 P37 2020 | DDC 302.23083—dc23
LC record available at https://lccn.loc.gov/2020005065

BRITISH LIBRARY CATALOGUING DATA ARE AVAILABLE

ISBN (print) 978-1-4766-7694-4
ISBN (ebook) 978-1-4766-3979-6

Front cover image © 2020 Rawpixel.com/Shutterstock

Printed in the United States of America

*McFarland & Company, Inc., Publishers
Box 611, Jefferson, North Carolina 28640
www.mcfarlandpub.com*

To Ezra and Seralena,
and to everyone who helped me grow
into the parent I am today

Table of Contents

Introduction

Making Sure Media Matters

JL Schatz

Purpose and Intent of This Book

This book arose out of my brother's suggestion to write a book on how to talk with kids about the media since I am both a parent and an academic who writes on cultural studies. My biggest hesitation was that, despite talking to my two kids extensively about the media we watch, it seemed like many of the ways I tried to talk to my kids weren't successful. While I had learned some tricks, I certainly didn't presume to have the solution on how to talk with children about the media. The one thing I did know was to keep trying and learning from my kids in the process. So instead I decided to put together a collection from various perspectives on how to parent alongside pop culture given its growing inevitability. There is a need for parents to figure out ways to effectively talk with kids about representations throughout the media in order to navigate it productively. The essays within this book are designed to help with precisely this process. Unlike many other books on parenting and media, this one doesn't focus its question squarely on "how much time" or "what kind." Instead, it is designed to discuss how to talk and unpack representations found within the media in order to challenge its hegemonic rhetorical foundations.

Naturally, part of my and my brother's desire for a book to approach parenting and media differently arose from the fact that the amount of media available for children to consume has exponentially increased in recent years, occupying some kids for more than nine hours per day (Tsukayama 2015). Nevertheless, it is no longer adequate to understand media as simply the few hours of television during the day since the existence of social media and advertising has become ever-present in many lives. This requires parents to develop a more nuanced understanding of how the media operates, the power of it to influence lives, and their children's interactions in both their fictional encounters and the real world. In short, it requires parents to engage in not only the amount and type of media their children consume but also unpacking the representational norms that inform society and one's sense of being (Gauntlett 2002; Borgerson and Schroeder 2005). To this end, regardless of how much one believes children should consume media, and how strictly parents should limit the types consumed, there is a need to engage in dialogue with one's kids given the inevitability of media consumption and the representational consequences with the world beyond the screen. Different essays throughout this collection take up different examples of how parents can conduct such conversations with their children, how to parent through media to promote progressive activism, and the way certain pieces of the media break down or reconstruct hegemonic norms. Taken together, they serve to demonstrate the various ways parents can navigate media with their children to produce active political practices to make for a better world.

This reorientation from viewing media consumption as politically neutral can advance parental conversations with kids since it broadens the conversation beyond the simple binary of yes/no on what types and how many hours one consumes. Instead, it causes parents and children to talk about what it means to be a consumer and the consequences of that consumption. This understanding of politics requires understanding political decision making as much more than what happens at the voting box, or even what specific policies individual governments should pass. Rather, it requires understanding how each choice one makes both consciously and unconsciously connects to the larger macro-socioeconomic structures in which that choice takes place. For instance, whether one intended to support animal cruelty, or their individual support for the humane treatment of animals in the media, the use of live animals in entertainment furthers a form of speciesism that hurts animals in the real world (Orabona 2013; Wildlife Rescue and Rehabilitation; PETA). This can be seen in films like *The Hobbit* where, despite animals dying and being harmed during the course of the training and housing conditions, it was still able to get the American Humane Association's seal of approval for no animals being harmed during filming (Schatz 2016, 4–6). At the same time, by looking toward representations of countless children's classics like *Bambi* or *Finding Nemo* it can be possible to teach children to have compassion for animals, reality, and difference in the first place (Militz and Foale 2017; Preston 2010; Halberstram 2011). The same can be said for a number of other -isms that are taken up in the media and are perpetuated in its creation.

Several of the essays in this collection expose how representations of race, class, gender, sexuality, and speciesism perpetuate hegemonic values in the media. In each instance, what remains important is investigating how these intersections between consumption and representation can serve as nexus points for becoming better parents and help provide the necessary springboard for our kids to produce a better tomorrow. As Douglas Kellner and Jeff Share (2007) write,

> The critical component of media literacy must transform literacy education into an exploration of the ideological role of language and communication to define relationships of power and domination. […] In addition to these elements, critical media literacy brings an understanding of ideology, power, and domination that challenges relativist and apolitical notions of most media education in order to guide teachers and students in their explorations of how power and information are always linked. This approach embraces the notion of the audience as active in the process of making meaning, as a cultural struggle between dominant readings, encompassing oppositional readings or negotiated readings (Hall, 1980; Ang, 2002). Critical media literacy thus constitutes a critique of mainstream approaches to literacy and a political project for democratic social change [61].

Ultimately, uncritically consuming any amount of media produces a form of consumption that leaves the worst aspects of media and society unchallenged by representing itself as value neutral. Furthermore, by taking up critical conversations with our children we can learn to grow ourselves as we challenge internalized norms about many of the representations we readily consume as parents. To this end, "critical media education is a process that requires planting seeds and scaffolding the steps for transformative pedagogy" (Kellner and Share 2007, 62).

All too often parental approaches to the media is viewed exclusively through the lens of negativity and limitation. Study after study has been conducted on how media creates negative consequences for children from violence, to social isolation, to feelings of inadequacy, and so on (Bickham and Rich 2006; Agliata and Tantleff-Dunn 2004; Hawkins et al. 2010; Grabe, Ward, and Hyde 2008). No doubt, these concerns should be taken seriously. However, only focusing on these negative outcomes ignores the societal influences that creates the inspiration for media's production in the first place. Like Kellner and Share (2007),

> we are not saying that media do[es] not contribute to and at times cause many social problems, we take issue with this approach because of its decontextualization and anti-media bias, which over-simplify the complexity of our relationship with media and take away the potential for empowerment that critical pedagogy and alternative media production offer. When the understanding of media effects is contextualized within their social and historical dynamics then issues of ideology are extremely useful to media education to explore the interconnections between media and society, information and power (Ferguson, 1998, 2004) [60].

Coming to understand how media representations are fashioned out of the real-world desires that become reflected back to us creates a more nuanced view of how to interact with the media. Just like in the real world, where society can and does make changes, media can also change and can help create important nexus points for critical reflection.

By taking media as power, and its consumption as politics, it is possible to shape the world around us and alter the representations that are fed back to children and adults alike. As Foucault (1978) reminds us, where there is power there is resistance. Through critical conversations with our children over the media, our dialogue can serve as a starting point to larger conversations on what it means to be a parent, and the change we want to see our children be a part of. Thus, being critically informed and using that knowledge to guide conversations can help us better navigate the politics of consumption and enable children to make better choices by understanding the implications of what they watch and consume on the screen (Thoman 2003). Simply put, as parents we can no longer afford to be indifferent about what media our children and their peers consume since it very much shapes their identities and our relationships to them as parents (Nichols and Good 2004). Ultimately, this is why we must seek to engage our kids where they are instead of just setting out to establish limits.

Of course, there may be instances where prohibiting specific shows or social media sites is prudent. However, even in these instances it is critical to unpack the representations and issues with your kids over the reasons. Doing so will help them have a better understanding of those things their friends might be consuming. This is crucial since it could help one's own children figure out how to help other children navigate what they might be going through or thinking about. For example, regardless if one lets their own elementary and middle school children watch Netflix's *13 Reasons Why*, which resulted in a sharp increase in suicide, there are kids in their classroom who will have watched it, or have talked with older siblings who have watched it (Schwartz 2019). In turn, helping one's own children understand how a show that glorifies suicide, like *13 Reasons Why*, is inappropriate viewing material can help one's children watch for signs in their friends, who might start talking about why suicide is cool after watching the show. In fact, these conversations and pressures helped cause Netflix to replace the suicide scene so as to no longer explicitly show the suicide directly (Chiu 2019). And, while this does not decrease the risk of the show valorizing suicide, it still serves as an additional place for discussion for further change. Regardless of the specific example, what is important is that even when parents feels a certain element of media consumption is inappropriate, the reasons for why should still be communicated to their children to help them understand the politics behind the motivation to prohibit something specific in the first place. This helps children understand media consumption, and consumption in general, as a political choice as well as helps to inform them of the issues surrounding the representations at hand. As a result, children will be more informed about how to interact with the world, enabling conversations over media to spill out into reality.

Ultimately, the intent of this collection is less an authoritative guide on how to parent, as it is a series of suggestions and reflections on how to navigate the ever-changing media and representational landscape in the process of parenting. During the course of the book, many authors attest to the fact of not knowing it all and having learned themselves in the process of parenting their kids. No doubt, there is a large philosophical tradition calling for radical openness instead of moral absolutism (hooks 1989; Abel 2016; Peters 2013). At the same time, this doesn't mean a world without limits and boundaries altogether when it comes to children and media representation. Thus, other essays in this book attempt to productively confront some of the negative representations that are put out there. Taken together this collection seeks to widen the discussion over how to resist the dangerous patterns that are replicated by the media, how to navigate positive paths forward in conversations with children, as well as how to grow as parents who must learn to adapt to changes in media representations and consumption patterns.

Overview of Book and Outline

In order to achieve the objectives of this collection, this book is divided into two parts. The first is geared explicitly around the question of parenting and how to guide children through conversations on the media and social networks. Various authors take up different positions in relation to how to be a parent and how to navigate these discussions. Some explore specific elements of the media in order to frame their examples, while others talk more broadly about social media or television at large. What they all have in common is that they help to provide suggestions to the reader over varying tips and strategies on how to parent. And, while no one essay claims to be the end-all-be-all of parenting, taken together the hope is to provide the reader with useful ways to interact with children over the media.

The first essay, by Ryan Vaughan, traces the history of how parents have been portrayed in relation to their kids through television sitcoms over the past several decades. This essay serves to provide a background on how hegemonic depictions of parenting have been represented and have changed over time in the context of the United States. In so doing, he traces how the traditional upper-middle class white family, with the breadwinning father and loving wife who took care of the kids who would have episodic antics, changed into dealing with drama that disrupted those antics and then eventually into an era where parents were erased altogether. In response, he urges us to watch and talk about these shows together by using a communal tone that is expressed in his writing style. Beginning the book in this way is designed to ease the reader into understanding how parenting is represented and what a world without parents might look like.

In her essay, Charity Gibson explores the negative ramifications of severing parent-child relationships in the media. In this way, her essay builds upon the first essay by going into more depth in the current media moment, where parents are increasingly portrayed as absent from children's lives. She argues that these parentless representations directly harm parent-child relationships and advocates that parents should urge their children toward media that depicts better portrayals of the benefits of parenting. In doing so, this essay helps to outline what beneficial representations can look like and what types of media might best enhance those relationships to forge better connections with one's children.

Amber E. George and Jacob E. Gindi cover a specific example of how to talk with young children about environmental destruction and other social issues using the movie *Cloudy with a Chance of Meatballs*. Their essay works as testimony of their experience on how movie night at home with the kids can serve as something more than mindless entertainment, while breaking down complex real-life issues in a way that can be digested by children through using animated fiction. While this essay is about a specific film, its suggestions on how to have these conversations are applicable to a wide range of issues and other movies that can be used as a backbone for talking about larger social and political concerns.

Anne Bialowas and Ryan Cheek also take up specific media examples in order to explore how fatherhood and masculinity functions in regard to superheroes in their essay. Together they come up with a funneling system to guide conversations with young children and teenagers over issues of gender and sexuality by starting with broad questions about the film and characters into more specific instances in the media and the real world. To do so, they look at the popular movies *The Incredibles* and *Ant-Man* to show how hegemonic masculinity is often caught up with representations of fathers in ways that reinforce violent gender norms. Again, while they navigate the issue of gender through specific examples, the strategies for conversation with kids are readily exportable to other issues and media representations.

The last essay in this part, by Mike Catello, takes up the question of social media and activism. In his essay, he explains how the recent increase of social media as an avenue for activism requires parents to approach conversations over their political orientations differently than in the past where hashtags and Facebook didn't exist. Encouraging children to learn how to engage in Internet activism meaningfully and responsibly can better help them find their voice and figure out why social and political politics matter. This requires parents to be aware of how quick social media activism happens as well as what sorts of activism are now available. By having conversations with their children early, parents can help forge the conditions where their children can be the leaders of tomorrow and the spearheads for change today.

Part two of this book is designed with specific readings and interpretations in mind. Unlike the previous part where the essays are geared around giving some sort of advice, even if they lack a sense of absolute authority, this part is more specifically geared toward philosophical interventions with children's media. As a result, the essays in this part seek to unpack the hegemonic representations within specific examples in the media in order for readers to understand how these norms operate and reread them to deconstruct their prevalence. Taken together these essays are meant to provide readers with the necessary analytical and rhetorical tools to intervene against problematic media representations and how to read politics in the media.

In her essay, Rae Lynn Schwartz-DuPre looks at how the *Curious George* stories have normalized colonial representations through George's capture from Africa and the civilizing lessons he learns at the end of each story when his antics reach their conclusion. Instead of censoring these stories for their racialized representations, she encourages readers to reread these texts as a form of rhetorical intervention that can help undermine the colonialist underpinnings of the *Curious George* series by exposing what the Man in the Yellow Hat truly represents. These interventions are necessary lest we forget the legacy of violence that colonialism has perpetuated throughout the world in the name of progress.

Kevin D. Kuswa looks at the PBS show *Odd Squad* and explores how it outlines a pedagogy of learning together and being a team. In doing so, he explores some of the benefits of what it means for kids to work together to solve problems and highlights some of the positive representations that exist in children's programming in relation to race and gender. And, while he claims there is certainly a ways to go, the fact that certain shows are providing a path forward in developing relationships between kids and what it means to be a parent is desirable. Ultimately, this essay helps encourage parents to take away from children's programming new ways of being open to their kids through the specific messages *Odd Squad* represents.

Amar Singh looks at how *Calvin and Hobbes* serves as a way of understanding the value of imagination even if it comes across as a lie. As a result, he grapples with what it means to violate a moral maxim for the benefit of the child alongside how the imaginative creation of Hobbes by Calvin can create a form of self-worth that is desirable. This philosophical discussion is meant to serve as a way for the reader to understand the value in approaching fiction as a means to engage with truth in both ethical and instructive ways. While this essay doesn't resolve the question in each media instance, it does take up the acceptance of imaginary friends and the real-world consequences of what could happen based upon a parent's response to the truth.

Debaditya Mukhopadhyay returns to the question of gender and sexuality this time in relation to Disney's most recent live-action film *Beauty and the Beast*. This reading looks at how masculinity and femininity are portrayed within the film in order to provide entry points to understanding the hegemonic representations within this popular remake of a classic tale. Naturally, these representations are not isolated to this one film, or even Disney in general. As a result, this analysis is useful in coming to identify what it means for characters to be labeled as a beast and what it means to be the hero in any individual tale.

In the last essay of the book, I look at how scientific neutrality has dangerous consequences even if science itself can be neutral. To do so, I look at Netflix's remake of the 1980s popular kids' cartoon *She-Ra*. Unlike in the original, Netflix's version has a lot more to do with science than its predecessor that relied on mystical powers, scantily clad women, and poorly animated fight scenes. This essay exposes how the show cautions against the acceptance of science for science's sake since it is precisely that belief that enables the creation of increasingly destructive weapons, which threaten the very existence of the planet. My hope in concluding the book in this way is that it will leave readers with an understanding of why neutrality in relation to science, politics, or media isn't an option. Rather, this essay's goal is to show how technology can be used as a force of social good or as an instrument to solidify violence and domination, just like the media.

Ultimately, by the end of the book, readers should realize the need to engage with the media thoughtfully as individuals as well as parents since its presence necessarily impacts the world in which it is created. Understanding the importance of media, beyond just a question of limitation, is necessary for individuals and parents since its consequences can't be understated. Beyond shaping how people understand the world, and things like gender, media production has immediate implications on the resources used to produce it and the way its effects ripple throughout the world. Figuring out ways to navigate these issues with children is essential for creating a better world and altering the media landscape of tomorrow. Hopefully, this will aid in the production of more caring and thoughtful kids who can envision the solutions to the global and social problems they are unfortunately inheriting from the representations and reality of today.

Works Cited

Abel, Mark. 2016. "Radical Openness: Chord Symbols, Musical Abstraction and Modernism." *Radical Philosophy*. https://www.radicalphilosophy.com/article/radical-openness.

Agliata, Daniel, and Stacey Tantleff-Dunn. 2004. "The Impact of Media Exposure on Males' Body Image." *Journal of Social and Clinical Psychology* 23(1): 7–22.

Animal Protection Institute. n.d. "Animas in Entertainment." https://wildlife-rescue.org/services/advocacy/animals-in-entertainment/.

Bickham, David, and Michael Rich. 2006. "Is Television Viewing Associated with Social Isolation?" *Arch Pediatrics Adolescent Medical* 160: 387–392.

Borgerson, Janet, and Jonathan Schroeder. 2005. "Identity in Marketing Communications: An Ethics of Visual Representation." In *Marketing Communication: New Approaches, Technologies, and Styles,* edited by Allan Kimmel. Oxford, UK: Oxford University Press.

Chiu, Allyson. 2019. "A Graphic Suicide Scene in '13 Reasons Why' Drew Outcry. Two Years Later, Netflix Deleted It." *The Washington Post,* July 16, 2019. https://www.washingtonpost.com/nation/2019/07/16/reasons-why-suicide-scene-pulled-netflix/?utm_term=.faa9f17e6cb9.

Gauntlett, David. 2002. *Media, Gender and Identity: An Introduction.* New York: Routledge.

Grabe, Shelly, Monique Ward, and Janet Hyde. 2008. "The Role of the Media in Body Image Concerns Among Women: A Meta-Analysis of Experimental and Correlational Studies." *Psychological Bulletin* 134(3): 460–476.

Halberstram, Jack. 2011. *The Queer Art of Failure.* Durham, NC: Duke University Press.

Hawkins, Nicole et al. 2010. "The Impact of Exposure to the Thin-Ideal Media Image on Women." *The Journal of Treatment and Prevention* 12(1): 35–50.

hooks, bell. 1989. "Choosing the Margin as Space of Radical Openness." In *Yearnings: Race, Gender and Cultural Politics.* https://sachafrey.files.wordpress.com/2009/11/choosing-the-margin-as-a-space-of-radical-openness-ss-3301.pdf.

Kellner, Douglas, and Jeff Share. 2007. "Critical Media Literacy: Crucial Policy Choices for a Twenty-First-Century Democracy." *Policy Futures in Education* 5(1): 59–69.

Militz, Thane, and Simon Foale. 2017. "The "Nemo Effect": Perception and Reality of Finding Nemo's Impact on Marine Aquarium Fisheries." *Fish and Fisheries Journal* 18(3): 1–11.

Nichols, Sharon, and Thomas Good. 2004. *America's Teenagers—Myths and Realities.* New York: Routledge.

Orabona, Bob. 2013. "Animals in Entertainment." *Friends of Animals,* August 20, 2013. https://www.friendsofanimals.org/program/animals-in-entertainment/.

PETA. n.d. "Animals in Entertainment Factsheets." *People for the Ethical Treatment of Animals.* https://www.peta.org/issues/animals-in-entertainment/animals-used-entertainment-factsheets/.

Peters, Michael. 2013. "The Concept of Radical Openness and the New Logic of the Public." *Educational Philosophy and Theory* 45(3): 239–242.

Preston, Daniel. 2010. "Finding Difference: Nemo and Friends Opening the Door to Disability Theory." *English Journal,* 100(2): 56–60.

Schatz, JL. 2016. "The Brown Wizard's Unexpected Politics: Speciesist Fiction and the Ethics of *The Hobbit*." In *Screening the Nonhuman: Representations of Animal Others in the Media,* edited by Amber E. George and JL Schatz, 3–16. New York: Lexington Books.

Schwartz, Matthew. 2019. "Teen Suicide Spiked After Debut of Netflix's '13 Reasons Why,' Study Says." *National Public Radio,* April 30, 2019. https://www.npr.org/2019/04/30/718529255/teen-suicide-spiked-after-debut-of-netflixs-13-reasons-why-report-says.

Thoman, Elizabeth. 2003. "Materials for Teachers 9A: Skills and Strategies for Media Education." *Center for Media Literacy.* https://www.living-democracy.com/pdf/en/V4/V04_P03_U09_TM_9A.pdf.

Tsukayama, Hayley. 2015. "Teens Spend Nearly Nine Hours Every Day Consuming Media." *The Washington Post,* November 3, 2015. https://www.washingtonpost.com/news/the-switch/wp/2015/11/03/teens-spend-nearly-nine-hours-every-day-consuming-media/?utm_term=.27378c35e624.

Part One

Parents? We Don't Need No Stinking Parents

A Discussion of Television's Pursuit of a Parentless Society[1]

Ryan Vaughan

There are certain things that you just can't say to people, no matter how comfortable you might be with your relationship to them. Through trial and error, I have learned that you can tell people they're fat or ugly, you can tell people they're sexist or racist, but under no circumstances can you tell someone they're a bad parent. The mere implication that you disagree with someone's parenting choices is generally met with either "the finger"[2] or months if not years of passive-aggressive retaliation. There's just something about the parent/child relationship that makes any criticism or suggestion feel like a personal attack. No one wants to be a bad parent, but every parent is from time to time. You would think that this shared realization that all parents are basically winging it—using techniques gleaned from the strengths and weaknesses of their own parents, cues from television and media, and their own personal interpretation of what is good or bad for their kids—would allow for a more open and less defensive cultural dialogue about parenting. Luckily for me, there are things I can yell at about parenting (the litany of TV shows I will reference in this essay) without someone taking a swing at me. For generations, the media, specifically television sitcoms, has had a hand in shaping the way people parent (Muller 2014). No doubt, the media is constantly fluctuating between reflecting and dictating culture. Using parenting as an analytic, we're[3] going to find out what kind of role television has played in shaping argument and discussion, and to what end.

This essay will attempt to make sense of a televisual family structure and aesthetic that has seemingly gone awry. It will also take a crack at tracking the concept of family as represented by TV shows over time and with respect to cultural change, and how we as parents can adapt to these changes and use them to further our own definition of family. Contrary to popular belief, television has the ability to strengthen relationships and the understanding of concepts like culture and family. The audience needs to see television as a site for creating meaning and identity in addition to entertainment and pleasure.[4] My admission that I don't have all the answers, but continue to seek them, should give me some credibility.[5] Parenting should not be an edict handed down from some overlord. It's not *Leave It to Beaver* or *Father Knows Best*. It should be an ongoing discussion based on the universal understanding that none of us is any better than another, that there are an infinite number of ways to raise a child.[6] "Infinite" is a lot, and parents should be open to all of it.

I'm going to assume that anyone reading this understands what "traditional parenting" means from a televisual perspective (Douglas 2008), and if not, other essays in this book by Charity Gibson among others can help shape your own personal definition. The aforementioned *Leave It to Beaver* and *Father Knows Best*, in addition to *The Adventures of Ozzie and Harriet* and *The Donna Reed Show*, are prototypes that set the standard of parenting on television against which all others would eventually be compared. Everyone in the family knew their place, and those "places" didn't leave too much room for interpretation or individuality. Father: stoic, authoritative, all-knowing, crushingly middle-class breadwinner, with just enough misogyny and repressed rage to keep everyone on their toes. Mother: doting wife, somewhat ditzy, wears heels around the house even though all she is meant to do in the house is cook and clean, mostly relates to kids by saying, "Ask your father," and pretty enough to keep everyone interested.[7] Kids: cute and precocious, getting into innocuous trouble every week like throwing a rock through the neighbor's window or getting a "C" on an algebra test, and usually have some defining feature; a dimple, freckles, an odd haircut to keep everyone watching. These shows, and many others like them from the 1950s and 60s established a baseline of parental relationships that became one of the first in a litany of viewer conundrums (Morreale 2003). They offered the idea that "this is how it's done," when so many weren't doing it that way. That puts an audience in a precarious position. If I'm not like Ward or June Cleaver, am I a bad parent? If my family doesn't look or act like The Andersons from *Father Knows Best*, am I doing it wrong? There are certain times and subjects that arise when I don't "know best," does this preclude me from being a father? It was essentially the birth of modern day "parent shaming" in which television *reflects* a very specific idea that exists minimally in reality (the perfect family) and tacitly *dictates* that we should all live that way. Our differences became inadequacies. Our diversions from this evolving standard of parenting became our failures that needed to somehow be made great again.[8] One idea was made abundantly clear, however, and that was the idea that parents are essential to a functioning family and society.

As the "family sitcom"—at least "family" in the sense that there were kids still in the throes of being raised—all but disappeared in the wake of the Civil Rights movement and the onset of the 1970s, the dominant parental voice from television came from a bigot and a dingbat in the form of Archie and Edith Bunker in *All in the Family*. With Norman Lear created shows (*All in the Family, Good Times, Maude, The Jeffersons*) the intent was to reflect and hope that the reflection might dictate a shift in approaches to parenting, along with race, gender, sexuality, politics, and a multitude of other pertinent issues churning in American culture at the time. Archie and Edith cling to the "traditional" parenting models established by programs that came before them in a culture that was changing and demolishing those norms. They pined for simpler times in the theme song that opened every episode. Essentially evoking images of the white middle class male's greatest hits which, at the time included: doing largely what they wanted with little repercussion in a binary world they dominated without Civil Rights and gender identity issues, among other things that now constitute the MAGA movement.

Even as their daughter Gloria and her boyfriend Mike[9] are, quite literally, screaming at them for being so closed-minded and backward, *All in the Family* is less about parenting than it is about a generational culture clash. The show begs viewers to embrace the clash[10] rather than repress it. Embracing this kind of discourse and discord is how cultures change, adapt, and grow.[11] Set against contemporary television families, the Bunkers offer lessons in humility and respect that are largely foreign to younger modern audiences. The show is intentionally disruptive, often cacophonous. However, the fact that Archie and Edith's parenting style yielded a strong, thoughtful, intelligent, and compassionate daughter should say something about "traditional" approaches to parenting, or at least hint that there is something worth saving from that 50s way of thinking.

If *All in the Family* was hinting at it, *Happy Days* was yelling it at us through a bullhorn. The 70s era sitcom set in the 50s was a show created to remind American culture where it came from in parenting terms and rose to meet and resist the more challenging ideas and attitudes toward parenting and culture that *All in the Family* represented. *Happy Days* quite blatantly ignored the cultural tumult that it was born amidst, as if in some sort of denial that anything had changed, while Norman Lear's stable of shows that dominated television in the 70s both accepted the cultural circumstances as well as embraced and examined them in insightful and interesting ways (Marc 1997). Archie Bunker is really just Howard Cunningham (the dad from *Happy Days*) after a significant cultural upheaval that he thinks threatens everything that was once good (white, heteronormative).

Good Times was another of Lear's creations that was decidedly, not white.

If nothing else, *Good Times* was a poignant look at a life often overlooked, the life of a black family in the ghetto, and not a glamorized or sensationalized version of that life.[12] *Good Times* thrust the plight of the working class minority into the national conversation and provided a pointed and humorous commentary on lives previously unexplored by television. James (father) and Florida Evans (mother) added a new, colorful wrinkle to the timeline of traditional parenting on television, marking a change that the industry itself was trying to ignore by its relative lack of traditional family sitcoms through the entire decade. James and Florida are more hands on, more essential and relevant to their children's day to day lives than any parents before them. Both parents work, both parents contribute relatively equally to raising the children and disseminating advice, and both parents clearly exhibit the stresses and agony of raising children.[13] It's arguably the first admission by a televisual entity that parenting isn't all picnics and picket fences. It's often dirty business that can at once fulfill and overwhelm you. It has always been this way for a majority of parents, and the more authentic representation of parenting in *Good Times* resonated with audiences for the very reason that they could relate. The parental standard set by 50s and 60s television was outdated, unrealistic, and virtually impossible to live up to, despite the attempt by *Happy Days*[14] to remind us how simple it was. One thing that cannot be denied is the importance of the role parents play in the day to day lives of their children. Archie has his way, but he is the portal through which any and all discourse is routed, and Lear sets him up more as a cautionary tale than a hero. Howard Cunningham has all the saccharine trappings of a devout 50s dad—despite his eventual affinity for the cheesy rebel, Fonzie. His intervention into his children's lives is largely superficial.

If nothing else, according to the entertainment media of the time, the 1980s was a decade that prided itself on progress,[15] and the family television shows that ruled the land were indicative of that progress. If the shows of the 70s acknowledged and grappled with the fallout of the Civil Rights movement, the 80s seemed to focus on the second wave of feminism that sought legal and social equality for women. In fact, virtually every sitcom produced in the era featured a mother who deftly managed her work and home life with aplomb. Shows like *The Cosby Show* (Clair), *Family Ties* (Elyse), *Growing Pains* (Maggie), and *Who's the Boss?* (Angela) tried, however successfully, to bring together the traditions of 50s TV parenting, the wrought conflict of post–Civil Rights family dynamics, and the most burgeoning movement at the time, gender equality. Ratings and viewership indicated that audiences responded positively to this movement within the genre[16] since these shows, at least on the surface, showed a willingness to adapt to changing times while essentially sticking to the traditional formula of father/mother/kids hierarchy that they were comfortable with. Fathers became softer, less stoically intimidating figures, while mothers were represented as tougher and more intellectual than their simpering forebears. It was as if some genius said, "Hey, why don't we make the mothers more like the fathers, and the fathers more like the mothers, but not too much. Just enough, like give the mom a job and have the dad be a good listener" without even realizing the impact a statement as flippant as that would deliver. As a result of these new parental archetypes the role of the children in these programs became more consequential. They were no longer silly props to be manipulated by their parents for our delight and amusement. They now had a seat at the table, and while sitting, they could say more than just "May I be excused?"

The children in 80s sitcoms began to develop a voice and figure into discussions with parents/adults on more equal footing. They certainly had more freedom to voice their opinion without being abruptly dismissed as "just a kid." The political arguments and discord between conservative Alex P. Keaton and his parents, liberal/progressive Steven and Elyse (*Family Ties*),[17] are what made the show worth watching, often driving the narrative. The outspoken and eclectic attitudes of Denise Huxtable and her more traditional parents Cliff and Clair (*The Cosby Show*)[18] were engaging enough to yield a spin-off show (*A Different World*). The disparate personalities of lovable cad Mike and nerdy goody-goody Carol Seaver gave their parents Jason and Maggie (*Growing Pains*) everything they could handle, and shed light on the concept of parenting each of your children differently according to the child, as opposed to the more traditional "my way or the highway" approach.

We were used to TV kids "knowing their place" or "being put in their place," and 80s TV parents and kids certainly still understood these concepts, but the places they knew and into which they were being put, were changing.[19] There was nothing disrespectful or inherently irreverent about these new parent/child representations. The children were becoming more active participants in their rearing. Their characters were given more depth. The situations they went through each episode became more significant and less trivial, more meaningful and less cutesy. As a result, TV parents were becoming less demanding and more understanding as the emotional gulf between them and their TV children began to diminish. The idea that children were gaining ground or making valuable strides toward equal footing in the parent/child relationship had its origins in 1980s family sitcoms.[20] This is where the idea of a parent being as much a friend to their child as an authority figure began to spread. The children talked to their parents differently and with more confidence. The parents listened and generally gave their children a voice. A more functional family unit became the byproduct of the changes in both our society and the pretend society audiences tuned in to watch every night.

Without function, there can be no dysfunction, and the 80s with all its suburban hunky-dory functionality set up the 1990s to be a dysfunctional circus. The sitcom went in one of two directions as the 90s unfolded: (1) Sitcoms tried to mimic the 80s formula and ride it out until even the last fan of the genre kicked in their TV out of frustration/mercy (*Step by Step, Home Improvement, Family Matters, The Fresh Prince of Bel-Air,* etc.) or (2) Sitcoms avoided the traditional family altogether, choosing instead to concentrate on makeshift "families" in either the workplace or an urban setting (*Seinfeld, Frasier, Friends, Murphy Brown, News Radio,* etc.). Many of the programs mentioned here enjoyed a great deal of success, but it was hard to deny that the concepts of family, parenting, and childhood on television were rapidly changing.

Enter three shows that redefined "family" for audiences in the 1990s: *Roseanne, Married… with Children,* and *The Simpsons.* These three programs made dysfunction the new function in direct response to what some would deem unrealistic portrayals of family established in the 80s and, before that, the 1950s. In retrospect, *Roseanne* plays like a *Good Times* for lower class, white, middle America. It accurately illustrates the struggle to make ends meet for two parents (Roseanne and Dan Connor) who *have to* work, who *have to* pinch pennies, who *have to* move their daughter's boyfriend into the basement because his birth mother is abusive. These kinds of things are inconceivable to the Huxtables (*The Cosby Show*) or the Seavers (*Growing Pains*),[21] and all too cruel realities to the Connors. There's a feeling of desperation that pervades every episode and it permeates into their home, their furniture, their clothing, and the way they relate to their kids (Becky, Darlene, and DJ). There's no time for sugarcoating things. Everyone in the family, even the kids, speaks boldly and to the point. Everything about the series is blunt, and this bluntness is how *Roseanne* distinguished itself from the family shows that came before. *Roseanne* went out of its way to avoid glamorizing family life, and there's a sweetness and feeling of unity among the Connors that challenges the lingering desperation every episode. After all, the kind of family *Roseanne* represented was far closer to that of its typical viewer than were most of its predecessors, they were far from perfect (Morreale 2003).

Married… with Children used many of the same tactics as *Roseanne* to establish itself as the new normal. The Bundys are dysfunctional to a fault. Parents Peg and Al certainly hate each other, but they may hate themselves more considering they each settled for the pathetic excuse for a human being that is their spouse. The children, Bud and Kelly, have a frighteningly similar relationship, both with each other and their parents. The way they act toward each other and communicate with each other makes them a family in name only, and it seemed to coincide with a movement in Western culture away from traditional conceptions of family. These shows were a definitive reaction to the shows of the 80s. Television is nothing if not reactionary. When a show is successful, new shows pay attention and sprout up around it, including everything that works while addressing criticisms that may have plagued the original.

The Simpsons went to distinct and overt lengths to establish dysfunction as the new function. In the reality created by *The Simpsons*, their family is considered normal. Oafish father, Homer; stay-at-home stalwart, Marge; rascal son, Bart; brilliant daughter, Lisa; and other daughter, Maggie. It's who they are set against, and subsequently live next to that marks this shift in the definition. The Flanders family is, by all accounts, "normal" according to the more traditional notion of family that we understand or were taught to believe in. Neighborly, God-fearing, sweater-wearing, obedient, churchgoing, vanilla, mustachioed, repressed, family. The fact that audiences looked at *The Simpsons* all through the 90s and to this day, and fingered the Flanders as the oddball family, is indicative of how far from the "norm" our understanding of family has progressed. The members of the Simpson family are all parodies of very specific tropes in television, and it is through this parody and similar deviations from the norm that *Roseanne* and *Married... with Children* embody that give value to alternative approaches to family and parenting.

At first glance, it would be easy to conclude that the Bundys, the Connors, and the Simpsons are "bad" parents, but that conclusion is one that can only come after comparison to the "perfect" parents, which is rather unfair as those don't actually exist. Their children are healthy, mostly intelligent, opinionated, generally kind, well-adjusted, human beings, just like the "perfect" ones. They urged us to start making distinctions between the multitude of different parenting styles and the relationships that can grow from them, as opposed to the "good" and "bad" paradigm that we had been referencing for so long.

The 90s highlighted the evolution of the American family to include a breadth of definitions, but it was a hastily drawn animated show on MTV that would change the stakes drastically. *Beavis and Butt-Head*[22] told the story of two teenagers left to their own devices in a parentless world. This turns out to be a horrible yet hilarious situation, as you can likely imagine. *Beavis and Butt-Head* was the first to give us children without parents. Every family show before it, with the possible exception of *The Little Rascals*, had different things to say about family, but they all seemed to agree that parents or guardians were an essential entity. Whether the family is father/mother/children (most of them), father?/father?/daughter (*My Two Dads*), mother/two daughters (*One Day at a Time*), father/mother/furry alien/children (*ALF*) father/uncle/weird friend/three daughters (take a guess),[23] each includes an authority figure/parent to provide guidance and support to the children. Beavis and Butt-Head have no such guidance or support and what ensues is rather predictable, considering everything television and culture has been telling us about parents and children. The boys trudge, episode after episode, through a swamp of never-ending nuisance, disrespect, abject stupidity, negligence, delinquency, and sloth. They watch and mock music videos all day before venturing out into the world only to make it a worse place than when they found it. They are creatures that have no regard for life or basic human decency, true mouth-breathing dirt bags who contribute nothing to anything but their desire to see naked women and eat nachos (Kellner 1995). It counts as somewhat of a victory for traditional parenting models. Beavis and Butt-Head were proof that kids need parents lest we all be subjected to legions of frog baseball-playing, TP for bunghole-needing kids. The lives that Beavis and Butt-Head lived were so bad and headed nowhere that even the teenagers that made up the majority of their audience, who may be susceptible to this kind of glorified vagrancy (me and my friends), had no interest in living without parents. Children not only need guidance, a vast majority desire it, and want to be held to a standard and to be challenged.

The steady move away from the family sitcom, and to some degree, sitcoms in general in the 90s came about with the proliferation of reality television, the expansion of cable and satellite providers (and with it, niche channels for seemingly every demographic), and once the 2000s hit, the development of Internet based streaming services. What defense did it have, after all? When you compound these factors that led to family sitcoms drowning in a sea of "reality" and diversification, with the fact that most homes now had multiple televisions operating, it was bound to happen. With a TV not only in every home, but in every *room* in many cases, audiences changed their viewing habits. Gone were the days of having to watch what Dad wanted because he had the remote. You could now go virtually anywhere to watch whatever you wanted, and it should come as no surprise that there was a plethora of programming just for you to not only make this possible, but also desirable.

Subsequently, families were watching television in very different ways, and that is to say, "not as families." One of the appeals of the family sitcom that sustained its success for so long was that, in most cases, families were tuning in together. As that drastically changed and family members began to separate and go to their respective corners of television, the family sitcom was down for the count. It was both a physical (watching in different rooms) and an ideological (watching shows specifically "for" you) departure from the traditional family relationship with television. You can think about it this way: the 90s marked a move away from family and toward the individual, in both its television (workplace and urban sitcoms) and culture (Casey 2008).

It was also filled with a generation of kids who were being told by their 80s TV watching parents that "they could be anything they wanted to be." This movement was only exacerbated by market research and the concept that there's a show and a network specifically for you, no matter your age, race, gender, or sexuality.

This confluence of circumstances was directly responsible for a sort of authority vacuum, to use a term I just made up. The only things families were watching together were *American Idol* and other reality contests like *So You Think You Can Dance with the Stars on Ice*.[24] Sitcoms were littered with shiftless 20–30 somethings trying to have sex with each other. Parents had, for the most part, been eradicated from the airwaves and this allowed the children to fill that vacuum with irreverence, unearned hubris, and chicanery. As parents and families began to breakdown all over television, kids' networks like Nickelodeon and the Disney Channel were there to capitalize, comfort, and console child audiences by initiating the next logical step in this evolution: a parentless utopia. In much the same way as the children were props for the adults in the sitcoms of the 50s and 60s, parents were props for the children in programs in the 2000s and 2010s, and in some cases they weren't even props. They were discarded altogether. Useless in a world where children were so teeming with confidence and hubris that their awesomeness could barely be contained. It amounts to a legitimate and very not-made-up affront to the institution of parenting that we as a culture have worked for so long to cultivate. The number of programs designed to neuter or eliminate parents on these two networks alone is staggering and should indicate that this isn't merely a "back in my day" old man observation. Please refer to the accompanying chart as support:

The Parentless Utopia

Show	Network	Explanation
iCarly	Nickelodeon 2007–2012	Lives with doofus brother. Only parent is openly mocked as an overprotective hypochondriac.
Jessie	Disney Channel 2011–2015	Teenage nanny (Jessie) and buffoonish butler preside over gaggle of kids.
Hannah Montana	Disney Channel 2006–2011	Tween pop-star (Hannah) lives double life. Billy Ray Cyrus is actual parent.
Victorious	Nickelodeon 2010–2014	Kids are oozing with so much talent, they have to go to a special school to harness it. Teachers are lunatics.

Show	Network	Explanation
Wizards of Waverly Place	Disney Channel 2007–2012	Kids are so special they actually have super powers.
The Thundermans	Nickelodeon 2013–2018	More super powers.
Drake and Josh	Nickelodeon 2004–2007	One of the trailblazers. Parents are tangentially involved, but firmly establishing the "moron parent who exists only to be duped by clever children" type.
Sam & Cat	Nickelodeon 2013–2014	Live action, girl version of *Beavis and Butt-Head*, but like that's a good thing.
That's So Raven	Disney Channel 2003–2007	Sassy girl has psychic powers that she often misinterprets. Parents help her in no discernable way.
The Suite Life of Zach and Cody	Disney Channel 2005–2008	Pre-pubescent twins marauding around a luxury hotel harassing everyone, most notably the hapless concierge.
The Suite Life on Deck	Disney Channel 2008–2011	See above … on a boat.
Zoey 101	Nickelodeon 2005–2008	Britney Spears' sister is at a special middle school that might as well be a college.
A.N.T. Farm	Disney Channel 2011–2014	More kids so incomprehensibly fantastic that they need their own school.
JONAS	Disney Channel 2009–2010	Famous kids don't need parents.

The generation of children that were raised on this barrage of parentless programming are widely considered to be selfish and entitled. This is a broad generalization culled from years of experience in classrooms and my own home but being inundated with either images of dimwitted or altogether absent parents and authority figures would certainly help support this kind of sweeping statement. Though television has become more specialized with specific networks dedicated entirely to every demographic imaginable, not only "Children," but "Children 3–5 Years Old," "Children 6–10," and "Children 11–14 from Single Family Homes with Brown Hair Born on a Wednesday," it still doesn't account for the shift away from family. If anything, these networks had an opportunity to uphold a strong familial identity for the demographic that arguably needs it most—kids—with the rest of television sharply moving away from the family sitcom (*Friends, Will & Grace, It's Always Sunny in Philadelphia, How I Met Your Mother*, etc.).

In virtually every example outlined in the chart, the parent or authority figure is an entity to be avoided rather than engaged. If kids need help or guidance, why go to a parent? Parents are obstacles to overcome in these programs and will likely be ridiculed for not understanding the problem in the first place. These shows promote the notion that if a character needs advice or assistance, he or she need look no further than the kid sitting next to them, or the kid sitting next to the kid sitting next to them. When every kid is exceptional and wise beyond their years, help is only a Snapchat away. This rarely works out in real life. It's a far cry from the parentless world suggested by *Beavis and Butt-Head*. In fact, Beavis and Butt-Head would objectively hate every one of these pumped up, obnoxious, overachievers.[25] It's borderline irresponsible for these networks and individual programs to advance this "anti-parent agenda" that can so easily contribute to the perpetuation of the stereotype of the millennial generation. Or is it? Too often in our relationships with media and television, people conflate the concepts of responsibility and opportunity. This ultimately leads to scapegoating and blaming television for all of culture's ills. Television creators have no responsibility to parents and children alike, but they do have an opportunity to offer them programing that is both entertaining, socially conscious, and meaningful, so why not seize that opportunity.[26] On the contrary, it is absolutely a parent's responsibility to raise their children, but the opportunity to use television to help in doing so, is often overlooked.

The future of parenting and the family on television is unclear. There have been shows that have taken up the charge of filling the authority vacuum. Shows like *The Goldbergs, F Is for Family*, and *That '70s Show* harken back to family days of yore in much the same way as *Happy Days* did in the 70s. *F Is for Family* certainly has an *All in the Family* vibe to it, with creator, star, and curmudgeonly comedian Bill Burr using every creative breath he has to admonish the current state of family by illustrating the way he was raised in the 70s. We get to see a version of Archie Bunker raising young children and it's eye-opening to an audience not accustomed to seeing or hearing those kinds of familial relationships. *Modern Family, Everybody Loves Raymond*, and *The Middle* all attempted to connect audiences to an idea of family, which followed many of the conventions set forth by their predecessors along with timely cultural adaptations to try and establish a new foothold. There will always be programs like these, but do they have the influence to shift American culture back toward more traditional incarnations of family and do we even want that kind of change?

Modern Family first aired when my oldest son was ten years old. At the time, I was searching for something on television that could provide for my family what television had provided for my parents and me in my youth (the 80s): an opportunity to come together and engage each other through art[27] with the capacity to reach adults and children alike. The search inevitably brought me to *Modern Family* and its array of family definitions. The show gives depth and breadth to the notion of family (Cam and Mitchell—homosexual, Phil and Claire—traditional, Jay and Gloria—multi-generational and multi-cultural) and addresses some topics that may be considered too controversial for "family" viewing. I was caught between the idyllic conventions of the shows I grew up with and a culture that had advanced far beyond those conventions. Once I stopped complaining that there were no "good family sitcoms anymore" and realized that "good family sitcoms" meant addressing pertinent issues within American culture that were largely ignored within the shows of my youth, I started to watch *Modern Family* with my family in order to foster an open dialogue about homosexuality, multiculturalism, and the concept of family. Not surprisingly, our individual relationships with television changed. We wanted to watch more together. I developed a certain affinity for the silliness of Disney Channel and Nickelodeon shows but watching them with my kids gave me an opportunity to point out their shortcomings when it came to family. Conversely, I was able to use the proliferation of television across mediums and demographics to my advantage by introducing the shows from my youth to "my youth." Turns out, they love *The Cosby Show* and *Saved by the Bell*[28] as much as I do, and we can trace the developments outlined here, together. As a result, my kids started to realize that they don't have all the answers, and it doesn't matter what's on TV because every show is an opportunity for a conversation when you watch it with your parents. I can only speculate about the reasoning behind this most recent move into parentlessness. For content producers, corporations, and networks it most likely comes down to the bottom line, but I've chosen to answer the "to what end" question by taking the opportunity to be the "real" parent that fills the void in the "parentless society."

So, what are you supposed to do with all this information? There are so many options. You can (1) skip ahead to other, more insightful essays in this book[29]; (2) think about the role that television plays in your life with your children and how it may be contributing to/detracting from a healthy relationship; (3) develop your own theory about parenting and television and challenge me to a debate to the death; and (4) be aware.[30] What I have stressed to my own children through the years (they are all teenagers now) is media literacy. Media literacy is something that many media consumers, television watchers chief among them, are severely lacking. Be aware: Television is always trying to tell us something, but are audiences interested in or even equipped to interpret what it's saying? Be aware: Media is like government, if you passively take it for granted and let it run unchecked, it will manipulate you and bend you to its will. If you engage it critically as an active participant in the relationship, however, progress becomes the end result. Be aware: Rather than being one of the extremes represented by TV parents, today's parents should seek to incorporate the best of what each extreme has to offer to impart to their children. Be aware: Knowledge of the past has never been more crucial to the understanding of the present. I have used, both in the classroom and at home with my kids, these very shows that seemingly perpetuate much of what ails Western culture to illuminate and inform that culture's current zeitgeist. While the televisual timeline provided here may seem like nothing more than a categorical list of family sitcoms and TV nick-names[31] and how those shows reflected or dictated *actual* parenting, it is also somewhat of a harbinger of things to come.[32] Be aware.

NOTES

1. Writing should be entertaining and enlightening. These notes will be equal parts context, levity, and scholarship.
2. An underused gesture, in my opinion.
3. The "we" in this essay is an intimate "we." It's me and you, the reader, not some presumptive, universal "we."
4. Because things can be more than one thing.
5. I have three children. They are not perfect. Parenting is a process.
6. It takes a village?
7. Also, with a dead-eyed yearning to feel something. Anything.
8. Wink, wink.
9. Mike was not so affectionately referred to as "Meathead," one of the greatest nick-names in television history (along with "Boner" from *Growing Pains*). It was levied against Mike by Archie out of fear of a changing and more open-minded culture overtaking him.
10. Not the legendary punk band, The Clash.
11. Exposing millennials to *All in the Family* is one of the great subtle joys of teaching television.
12. Yes, it's still a sitcom with all the inherent silliness and catchphrases (Dy-No-Mite!!), but it made great efforts to marry those conventions with legitimate cultural critique.
13. Not everything is hunky and/or dory.
14. "The Fonz" and "Chachi" were great nicknames too.
15. The cultural ethos of "greed is good" as put forth in the movie, *Wall Street*, Reagan-omics, and women trading their aprons for pantsuits, both in real and pretend (television and film) defined the 1980s.
16. Family sitcom ratings in the 1980's remained strong in the midst of changing demo-graphics and landscape. https://en.wikipedia.org/wiki/Top-rated_United_States_television_programs_by_season
17. "Skippy" from *Family Ties* is another nickname worth noting.
18. "Cockroach," Theo's pal on *The Cosby Show*, has to be a top 10 TV nickname.
19. The traditional hierarchy of authority was still intact, but kids were starting to ques-tion that hierarchy.
20. It also gave birth to the "Very Special Episode" trend in sitcoms. https://tvtropes.org/pmwiki/pmwiki.php/Main/VerySpecialEpisode
21. "Inconceivable" until they realized the success of *Roseanne* amidst their own rapidly diminishing relevance. Both shows (*The Cosby Show* and *Growing Pains*) added underprivi-

leged characters that moved in with their families in their final years of production. The latter played by a young Leonardo DiCaprio.

22. You may think "Butt-Head" would be on the awesome nickname list, but it's not. As far as I know it's his given name. "Cornholio," however, is a different story.

23. If you guessed *Full House* you win the prize.

24. Not an actual show … yet.

25. In fact, they did. Mike Judge brought *Beavis and Butt-Head* back to television in 2011 in order to mark the stark contrast between the eras. Could the youth of today even remotely relate to the youth of the 90s?

26. Much like this essay.

27. Yes, television is art.

28. Which brings us to "Screech." The greatest sitcom nickname of all time.

29. If you haven't already.

30. That looks so much like "Beware," which would make just as much sense as "Be aware" in this statement.

31. I can provide you with this, upon request.

32. What we do when presented with a harbinger will define us for eternity.

Works Cited

Casey, Bernadette, and Neil Casey. 2008. *Television Studies: The Key Concepts*. London: Routledge.

Douglas, William. 2008. *Television Families: Is Something Wrong in Suburbia?* London: Routledge.

Kellner, Douglas. 1995. *Media Culture*. London: Routledge.

Marc, David. 1997. *Comic Visions: Television Comedy & American Culture*. Oxford, UK: Blackwell Publishers.

Morreale, Joanne. 2003. *Critiquing the Sitcom: A Reader*. Syracuse, NY: Syracuse University Press.

Muller, Treion. 2014. *Reality Parenting: As NOT Seen On TV*. Springville, UT: Plain Sight Publishing.

Un-Parented Children

Media's Message to Combat

CHARITY GIBSON

Introduction

We all know that children are impressionable. It is for this reason that countless studies have been conducted to uncover how exposure to media influences children (Strasburger 2006; Buckingham 2001; Holland 2001). Arguments claiming that media inhibits youth's creativity or serves as a hindrance to sustained attention spans are now somewhat common concerns (Clement and Miles 2017; Duncley 2015; Kardaras 2017). Some worry about media's influence on families. Media can impede upon quality family time, as it is a rather solitary enterprise, even if the family watches the same show. Some studies explore representations of families in film and television and critique the patriarchal, white, middle class, heterosexual values that a lot of media endorses (ter Bogt 2010; Venzo and Hess 2013; Shome 2000). However, a little explored area is the role that representations of parents and the parent-child relationship play in media. These relationships often fall into two camps. Either the parents are unengaged with their children and the storyline is somehow contingent on the necessity of "un-parented children," or the parents and children are somehow pitted against one another. Although one could argue that such tropes exist for the sake of an entertaining plotline and are harmless, children and even teens interpret these messages as normative and often imitate them. William Douglas (2003) explains that "television families influence family cognition" (1). Many negative messages about parents exist in "kid friendly" shows and films. These messages divide children and adults, teaching youth that they should not desire a close relationship with their parents, that their parents are oblivious or even ridiculous, and that it is only their peers and not their parents who truly understand them and to whom they should go for advice.

Previous generations often endorsed a family dynamic in which the parents ruled according to authoritarian principles. According to Kathy Hardie-Williams (2014), within this parenting style, "there is no room for discussion, options, alternatives, or negotiation between parents and their children." However, after World War II, culture began moving away from rigid forms of parenting positing performance for its own arbitrary sake over relationships and obedience. Authoritative parenting emerged (though certainly individuals had been practicing this before it was a cohesive movement) as a way for parents to maintain authority in the home while simultaneously nurturing their children. Hardie-Williams (2014) maintains that "an authoritative parenting style responds to the emotional needs of children while setting limits and boundaries." Much research advocates the benefits of authoritative parenting, springing from Diana Baumrind's work started in the late 1960s. In it, she presents authoritative parenting as a balanced approach between authoritarian parenting, which emphasizes parental control over child agency, and permissive parenting, which sacrifices all parental control for the sake of total child autonomy. As Nancy Darling and Laurence Steinberg (2007) note, "This work on authoritativeness and its beneficial effects builds on half a century of parenting and parenting style" (488). However, media today resists positive portrayals of parent-child relationships, including positive portrayals of authoritative parenting.

This contemporary distrust of authoritative parenting has influenced a large genre of mainstream media that children readily consume, which challenges the idea that parents are wise and able to properly guide their offspring. Steven D. Greydanus (2018) calls this trope of flawed and laughable parents "Junior Knows Best." He says, "At their worst, parents can be incorrigibly [lacking in wisdom …] or they can be woefully misguided" (Greydanus 2018). It may be that due to the harmful effects of authoritarian parenting, the pendulum has now swung in the opposite direction, known as permissive parenting. Rather than finding and endorsing a style of parenting such as the authoritative model, in which parents simultaneously are in charge but also encourage children to become autonomous, media today seems to have lost its faith in parents serving as guides for their children altogether. Instead, media should strive to depict parents who appropriately interact with their children, who consequently flourish. Rather than removing parents from the plotline, suggesting that their presence is a nuisance or even a detriment, media needs to show how an authoritative type parenting style, according to Tracy Trautner (2017), "allows children to be independent thinkers [and] self-regulate their emotions," which results in them being "successful and happy."

Parents today are aware of many potentially negative impacts media can have on children and consequently monitor programs due to issues such as violence, sexuality, substance use, and language. However, the subtle (and sometimes even blatant) message depicted in many shows and films that parents are unnecessary or a killjoy and that their children are better off without them is being accepted unquestioningly by many families. After all, even if it is apparent, it can be laughed off as "just a movie." Nevertheless, narrative is powerful. This is just as true for books as media. According to Peggy Alber (2016), stories "convey values, beliefs, attitudes and social norms which, in turn, shape children's perceptions of reality." While it would be almost impossible for parents to completely censor their children's exposure to ideologically challenging and even harmful content, one of the most effective strategies parents can utilize regarding media monitoring is being aware of exactly what their children are watching. Parents should look for not only the blatant messages but also the underlying ones that their children are internalizing from the media. Parents should seek to engage their children regarding the validity of such messages, offering meaningful conversations about the shortcomings of many of the portrayals.

Problematic Parental Representations

One can see media's disillusionment regarding effective authoritative parenting through the common portrayals of fathers. Sitcom and film dads serve as fodder for lampooning. One theme that has developed is that of the silly daddy. As David McGee and Brye Hantla (2013) explain, "Buffoonish, ignorant, self-centered, and inept television dads must be shown their proper places in the home […] at worst, they are relegated to the intellectual level of the family pet" (36). While the Pew Research Center reports that today's fathers are more involved in family life and share more in family duties than did the previous generations' fathers, their portrayal in media shows no appreciation for the progress made (Parker and Livingston 2018). When fathers are portrayed in the home, they are not presented as smart or capable. "It must have reflected our own discomfort with dads being competent," said Hanna Rosin on a panel about the future of fatherhood (Madrigal 2014).

In children's television and film, fathers' failure is usually comic relief. Disney's popular sitcom *Good Luck Charlie* contains many scenes showing the ineptitude of the father. The pilot episode for the series sets the tone for an incompetent father, Bob. Amy, his wife and the mother of four, is returning back to work after maternity leave, and he is supposed to be in charge while she is away. During the course of the episode, Bob falls down the stairs while carrying his infant son. Fortunately, he manages to catch his son but bruises his own tailbone and has to be driven to the hospital by one of his older children. Once Amy arrives at the hospital, she claims she is a horrible mother; however, the implication is that this is untrue and, in fact, she stands out like a beacon of perfection in contrast to her incompetent husband. When Bob responds that it is he who is the horrible father, Amy respond with "I know" (Baker and Vaupen 2010). Based on the evidence given, the children viewers are bound to agree to Bob's ineptitude. However, parents also notice. Mother and librarian Rosemary (2011) comments on the show, in her blog *Mom Read It*, that Bob "seems to be lucky he can function on his own, as he comes across dim-witted beyond belief." While the movement away from presenting homes as patriarchal institutions is commendable, the loss of competence that media fathers have suffered suggests to children that there is little to be gleaned from their fathers. He exists to provide for them but not to lead them or serve as an example. Although this pattern can be traced back to earlier shows such as *The Flintstones* and *The Simpsons*, contemporary media including *Peppa Pig* and *The Incredibles* continues the trend. It is positive that the father is no longer typically portrayed as an authoritarian figure; contemporary media does not present this style of heavy-handed parenting as normative or worthy of emulation. However, an additional reason for moving away from the presentation of authoritarian fathers may simply be that, in many programs, the children viewers are supposed to like the father because his role in the story is to function as the light-hearted character who often contrasts a serious character or situation. Portraying fathers as authoritarians is un-useful because not only is this parenting method ineffective, but it also results in an unlikeable father character. Yet, the pendulum has swung so far in the opposite direction that today, although media fathers are likeable, they are so non-threatening that they provoke no respect. This occurs through the representation of permissive parenting in fathers, which showcases them as being loving but unable or unwilling to offer clear guidelines and expectations. Such permissive parenting actually harms the parent-child relationship. As Laura Markham (2019) explains, "When children can't trust that parents can help them with the full range of their emotions, they don't feel connected to the parent. When a child doesn't trust that parents will enforce rules that keep the child healthy and safe […] the child disrespects the parent." As a moderate blend rather than an extreme on either side (be it authoritarian or permissive), an authoritative father gives respect to his children while simultaneously garnering it for himself. Sadly, "the current American generation of television consumers sees the role of dad as something to be mocked, leading to the implication (conscious or not) that traditionally authoritative, kind, loving, and wise fathers are no longer essential (or possibly even existent)" (McGee and Hantla 2013, 14). This portrayal in media has negative repercussions on the family lives of its viewers when internalized.

Portraying fathers negatively in media can impact how fathers interact with their families, as well as how boys will grow up to father their own children. As McGee and Hantla (2013) posit, "Perhaps watching […] programs where the role of the father is minimized affects the way men are expected to behave as fathers, which subsequently affects the way men behave in a certain culture" (39). However, little attention has been given to how farcical portrayals of fathers impact children's view of and relationship with their fathers. Contemporary media's fear of giving authority and competency to fathers may stem from feminists' justifiable disapproval of patriarchal parenting. However, presenting television and film fathers as mostly permissive parents teaches children that dads do not have a backbone. Of the permissive parenting style, Trautner (2017) explains, "There are very few demands of a child in this situation and parents have a difficult time saying 'no' as they avoid asserting authority and confrontation. They also avoid punishment at all times." This style of parenting results in children who hold little respect for their parents because they function more like peers who lack jurisdiction to enforce boundaries than authority figures. The one redeeming element of silly daddies in media is that, despite all their flaws, they typically love their children. While love is indeed essential, we should seek ways to present children with multifaceted fathers, capable of simultaneously being loving as well as competent and wise. This role should not hark back to older times in which this father figure supersedes the mother's role, but rather it should be complimentary to the positive mother portrayals that serves as stark contrasts in "doofus daddy" entertainment. The National Fatherhood Initiative encourages parents to discuss portrayals of negative father figures with their children when they encounter them in the media and expose children to TV shows "that portray fathers as competent and nurturing" (Steward 2015). While these shows may not be easy to find, they do exist. Older shows such as *Seventh Heaven, The Andy Griffith Show*, and *Little House on the Prairie* contain positive father figures, though, hopefully, media will begin introducing new positive father characters in current entertainment, as the current lack thereof speaks to the contemporary misnomer of what defines a good father.

Whereas negative father portrayals can be defended as all in good fun, negative mother portrayals have a much less lighthearted association. Mothers often attain villain status in media. Kathleen Rowe Karlyn (2011) describes media's tendency to celebrate female agency for girls and young women by pitting them against the antagonism of oppressive mothers. There is "ambivalence around mothers that persists in widely consumed forms of popular culture today" (Karlyn 2011, 4). She acknowledges the "hysteria" and "monstrosity" that movies specifically endorse regarding mothers (Karlyn 2011, 8). While negative fathers are typically just clueless, negative mothers are well aware of their carefully calculated actions. They are manipulative, narcissistic, and even power hungry. Due to the immense amount of mother-blame in contemporary Western culture, these representations are often received and internalized without much criticism. Mothers are blamed by both children and culture as well as by themselves. As Adrienne Rich (1995) persuasively argues, "The institution of motherhood finds all mothers more or less guilty of having failed their children" (223). The villainizing of mothers adheres back to fairy tales, in which Sandra Gilbert and Susan Gubar (2000) point out that mothers are often evil stepmothers, queens, and other forces to be overcome. "Sweet, dumb Snow White and fierce mad Queen are major images literary tradition offers women" (Gilbert and Gubar 2000, 46). In an interview with Terry Gross (2018), Rich criticizes "the legends that always depicted the step-mother as cruel, the bad mother" whose continuation speak to "the myths in popular psychology of the evil mother" that abound even today.

Even contemporary retellings of classic stories often continue to portray mothers as impediments to their children's agency and success. A good exam-ple is Mother Gothel in *Tangled*, which is Disney's rendition of the Brothers Grimm Rapunzel story. The story is modernized: Rapunzel herself is royalty rather than her love interest being a prince, as occurs in the traditional tale; also, her lover is not temporarily blinded. However, one element that remains constant is that the mother figure is the antagonistic force in the story. At one point, Mother Gothel explains why Rapunzel should trust her, literally singing from her villainous lips, "Mother knows best, […] it's a scary world out there. Mother knows best. One way or another, something will go wrong, I swear. […] Me, I'm just your mother, what do I know? I only bathed, and changed, and nursed you. Go ahead and leave me, I deserve it. Let me die alone here, be my guest! When it's too late, you'll see, just wait. Mother knows best."

While Disney is correct in showing Mother Gothel's abusive parenting to be negative, they draw from a longstanding stereotype that mothers are likely to be manipulative and narcissistic. Rapunzel is only able to achieve autonomy by distancing herself permanently from her mother (who dies be-cause she can no longer retain her youth which she has maintained through the power in Rapunzel's hair). While certain elements, such as Rapunzel's premarital sex, pregnancy, and birth to twins, is eliminated from Disney's ver-sion, the villainous mother remains in the story because she is not perceived as inappropriate content for children. Natalie Wilson (2010) recognizes that "Gothel is presented as a passive-aggressive nightmare–the tyrannical sin-gle mother so overbearing [that] Rapunzel must beg for the opportunity to leave the tower." If this model of a mother existed in a vacuum specific to only this story, there would be less danger of an overarching message being sent to children. Unfortunately, the dark and dangerous mother is a staple throughout much of children's entertainment. Although this theme can be traced back to Disney's classic fairy tales such as *Cinderella* and *Snow White and the Seven Dwarfs*, more recent films beyond *Tangled* such as *The Parent Trap*, *Ella Enchanted*, *Enchanted*, and *Happily N'Ever After* also portray the evil stepmother. The television series *Once Upon a Time*, though geared to-ward a teenage and adult audience, does the same.

Some may argue that media villainizing stepmothers does not fall into true mother blame, as it is not a "real" mother who is being critiqued but rather a stepmother. However, because so many blended families exist, critiquing a stepparent impacts just as many families as does critiquing a biological parent. According to the Stepfamily Foundation (2018), "50% of the 60 million children under the age of 13 are currently living with one biological parent and that parent's current partner." The trend of outright villainous mothers does not stop at step parents either; it continues with biological ones. The film *Leap!* (entitled *Ballerina* in Europe) continues with the trope of an evil mother, though this time she is not royalty. Régine lives vicariously through her daughter and harasses others who serve as competition to her daughter's success as a dancer. Régine's villainy escalates to the point of chasing someone up the Eifel tower with the intent of committing murder, though she, ironically, becomes trapped herself on the tower, and her fate is unknown at the film's end. All of the mentioned films give children the message that their mothers do not know or care about what is best for them. Emphasizing how a lack of positive mother role models affects girls, Karlyn (2011) claims that "girls have been hard pressed to imagine what female collectivity might look like among women of their own generation or across time" (8). Girls cannot be empowered by having the choice to become influential mothers if media only portrays the mother role as one that disempowers others. Mothers are too often presented as practicing authoritarian parenting in which they not only rule with an iron fist but also in which their discretion is unwise or unfounded. It is also noteworthy that when a monstrous mother exists within the plotline, the father is almost always absent or portrayed as weak or powerless. There is typically little, if any, indication of where he is, but if the father is incompetent when paired with a capable wife, he is completely missing when an overly powerful mother is present.

In media, adults in general and fathers and mothers specifically are often portrayed negatively, though for different reasons. However, an equally, if not more common, trope is the case of the absent parents, be they dead, working, out of town, or simply never introduced to the plot. This is especially prevalent regarding mothers. Sarah Boxer (2014) challenges, "Show me an animated kids' movie that has a named mother in it who lives until the credits roll." She lists off a myriad of movies that do not pass this test, ranging from classics such as *Bambi* and *The Great Mouse Detective* to more recent films such as *Finding Nemo* and *Mr. Peabody and Sherman*. While there are also movies that contradict Boxer's claim, there are enough that support it for one to recognize that there is indeed a trend regarding missing mothers. In many scenarios, the mother's absence is never even a consideration for children, as the characters in the story easily manage without her. If losing the mother is important to the plotline, the mother may be valorized, but she serves as more of a symbol than a realistic representation. Boxer (2014) argues that the removal of the mother is emblematic of a patriarchal culture in which "mothers are killed in today's kids' movies so the fathers can take over." While there is certainly room for a feminist critique within this discussion, one should note that, contrary to Boxer's claim, fathers are also often absent. The father dies early on in *Quest for Camelot, Lion King,* and *The Princess and the Frog*; both parents die early in *Frozen*; and the mother in *Toy Story* is a single parent. In the sitcom *Fuller House,* DJ Tanner is a widow. The absent mother motif is almost ludicrous in its contradiction of reality, as Megan Gannon (2013) reports that two-thirds of homes include married parents and that, regarding single parent homes, "single parent dads are still greatly outnumbered by single moms." Gannon's study also reveals that single dads are more likely to live with a partner; thus, even if a single father is unmarried, he is likely to introduce his children to his romantic partner who will likely serve as some type of mother figure. Media's rampant portrayal of absent mothers is simply unrealistic. In contrast, the number of father absent homes continues to rise. According to Dawn Lee's (2018) research from the U.S. Census Bureau, "Today 1 in 4 children under the age of 18—a total of about 17.2 million—are being raised without a father." However, the portrayal of missing fathers in media, though often not untrue, perhaps downplays the severity of the situation. David Blakenhorn (1996) argues, "As our society abandons the fatherhood idea, we do not simply become more aware of children growing up without fathers, we also become accepting of that. In a culture of fatherlessness, fatherhood becomes irrelevant" (75). When children see fathers being portrayed as irrelevant in media, it is only a matter of time before this ideology begins manifesting itself in their own interactions with their parents. Children and youth who seek separation from their parents are not going to receive the full benefits of being parented beyond the economic security the parents provide. In families that value the parent-child relationship, children benefit from the mentorship, guidance, and emotional stability of a strong relationship with their parents. Not only do children not receiving these benefits miss out themselves, but they are likely to repeat the pattern of shallowness in their own future relationship with their children.

The absent parent motif is not specific to media; it has a longstanding tradition in literature, which has a pronounced legacy of presenting children as parentless. Novels ranging from *Oliver Twist* to *Jane Eyre* to *Anne of Green Gables* capitalize on a youthful underdog who makes his or her way in the world without the guidance of parents. Carolyn Dever (2006) emphasizes the absence of the mother, saying that "the maternal ideal within narrative fictions is a rule honored more often in the breach […] in terms of maternal death or desertion" (xi). Dever (2006) suggests a literary pattern in which children are viewed as dependent on their mothers and can only blossom as characters if their mother, who asserts herself too heavily or on whom children rely too fully, is removed. If one recognizes that not only mothers but also fathers have important roles to play in the nurturing and raising of children, then Dever's (2006) ideas can also be applied as a rationale for missing fathers. Analyzing parental absence, Nicola Alter (2017) notes something similar regarding the logic for unattached children, saying that absent parents allow for children to learn how to problem solve for themselves. Yet, this suggests a false sense of independence in which children create their identity apart from their familial history as opposed to as an extension of it. While media often suggests that success depends on children leaving their family behind, celebrating their own individuality, and branching out on their own, research suggests the opposite, showing that it is strong family bonds that best help nurture children to become capable adults who will eventually function independently. Speaking to parents who have spent adequate time cultivating a strong bond with their children, Gail Gross (2016) explains, "Your child will approach everything with a stronger sense of self […] and a strong central core[. …] As a result, he will learn to depend on his own resources and capacities, which allows him to be independent and self-actualized."

An example of a current children's show that contrives unrealistic autonomy is *PJ Masks,* a cartoon targeting an impressionable preschool through early elementary school audience. In this show, three kids become superheroes and fight crime at night. This world of good guys and bad guys (and girls) is comprised solely of children, though it is made clear that they still live with their families. There is no explanation of where the parents are, why they are allowing their kids to leave their house in the middle of the night, why they are not helping take care of the problems, or why some parents are raising their children so poorly that they are turning into supervillains. Ty Kulik (2015) compares and contrasts these bad parents to others and finds them worse due to their complete lack of presence: "At least in *Charlie Brown* and *The Simpsons* the parents are there. They may not be the best people in the world, but they are there and that's more than I can say for the adults and parents in *PJ Masks.*" Shows like *PJ Masks* are the next logical step after the ideology showcased so well in *Charlie Brown.* The "wa-wa-wa" language of adults suggests that grown-ups speak a different language than their children, cannot be bothered by their children, or do not have any useful direction to offer. Therefore, it is not surprising that in media portrayals, the children's adventure typically happens without their parents' awareness and from a proximal distance.

While shows such as *PJ Masks* suggest that children who will soon embark into adolescence need to go off on their own, without their parents' knowledge, to cultivate their individuality and contribute to society, Kathy Weingarten (1998) suggests that parents can and should be involved in helping children mature. A strong parent-child relationship should not inhibit children's autonomy; instead, it should give them the confidence they need to venture out in incremental, age appropriate ways. Rather than internalizing the message that they should sneak out at night to have adventures their parents would never allow, children should be given examples of families where the parents help cultivate their children. While it is impractical and unwise to attempt to shield children from all the negative portrayals of parents within media and entertainment, parents can and should seek to converse with their children about the errors in these portrayals, especially in relation to their own family. Parents can ask their children questions about where the characters' parents may be, why many parents they know act differently than the drastically flawed parents in the show/film, or how children characters might benefit from having some assistance or guidance from their parents.

Showing positive parent-child interactions does not mean that media must sidestep the reality that the parent-child relationship does include conflict. Some level of friction will exist in even the best of relationships. If it does not, this may be due to a parents' authoritarian parenting style in which children are not allowed to voice their own opinions or act of their own accord. Parent-child conflict should be portrayed in order for restoration to occur. However, in many films, this restoration is basically the parents coming to realize that their children were right all along. In *The Little Mermaid*, King Triton must learn to accept his daughter's decision and come to her rescue so that she can continue with her decision to leave her life and people behind in order to become human and be with her love, Prince Eric. Something similar occurs in *Mulan*; her father realizes she has been right in impersonating him and going to war, since her intentions were pure. Greydanus (2018) lists a variety of films that follow in this pattern, including titles such as *How to Train Your Dragon* and *Moana*. He notes, "In the end, the child's aspirations are vindicated, leading not only to a paternal change of heart, but to a revolutionary breakthrough in the social status quo" (2018). In this pattern, the child serves as a beacon of youthful wisdom, though thwarted by archaic parenting. The problem with this formula is that it does not teach children viewers effective ways to resolve conflicts with their parents. It teaches children that the conflict is actually their parents' fault and given enough time, if they are good people, they will come around.

Alternative Representations

There are television shows and films that resist absent and/or awful parent tropes and instead provide positive portrayals of simultaneously wise, involved, and fun parents who cultivate and maintain strong relationships with their children. Parents should seek out these resources and expose their children to them. One decent example is *Happy Feet Two*. In this movie, when the penguins are trapped by ice, Mumble, the father penguin, argues that even children can help everyone gain their freedom, which inspires teamwork within the penguin colony. They free themselves by recognizing that both children and parents can work together and positively contribute to a shared goal. This ending is especially powerful because earlier in the film, Erik disregards the advice his father Mumble and mother Gloria try to give him, only later seeing that they had always been invested in him. Due to these details within the plotline, the *Australian Council on Children and the Media* (2019) has maintained that the film shows value in "the importance of family" and that the "movie could also give parents the chance to talk with your children about what can happen when you don't listen to your parents." Because Mumble has experienced the same feelings of anxiety his son feels, he is an effective mentor for his child.

Disney Pixar's *Brave* shows progress of a sort because in it, the mother-daughter relationship is restored. As Caitlin Flynn (2015) points out, "Most Disney princesses don't even have mothers." Merida, a teenage princess, does indeed have a mother with whom she regularly interacts; however, she has been at odds with Queen Elinor, who expects her daughter to adhere to traditional femininity fitting for a royal. Only after Elinor is changed into a bear, due to a spell, do the mother and daughter bond. In the end, Elinor rescinds her claim that Merida must marry, and the two mend their relationship. Furthermore, throughout the story, Merida has a strong relationship with her father, and King Fergus is portrayed, though humorously and perhaps as an overly doting parent, as an apt ruler and insightful husband and father. Thus, at the end of the film, Merida is restored to a positive parent-child relationship within a nuclear family, which serves as a stark contrast from the myriad of films which only show healthy relationships between a child and one parent in the end. Merida continuing to live at home also differs from films in which the child must "leave the nest" to achieve autonomy. Thus, there is much to praise regarding *Brave*. The film has been lauded by many for emphasizing the mother-daughter relationship rather than a romance. However, the means through which parent-child reconciliation comes is not without its flaws: similar to *The Little Mermaid,* the parent-child relationship still largely adheres to the theme of parent-blame in which the parent is misguided for adhering to tradition and, in the end, sees things appropriately from his or her child's perspective. Of course, forcing Merida into an arranged marriage is problematic. The issue is not with critiquing this patriarchal practice; rather, the fact that the script was written in such a way as to have the mother endorse such a foolish view reinforces the interpretation that parents are misguided in their traditional beliefs. Thus, there is a continued need for films and television programming that presents conflict as normative within the parent-child relationship, but which shows the resolution as something in which both parent and child are willing to learn from the other. Furthermore, children are often in need of guidance and, at times, do need to learn how to change their attitudes and behaviors to morally and socially appropriate practices. There is also a time and place for showing this in media, though the challenge is in not making the program so didactic that children lose interest or find the story too contrived.

Another positive example in media of effective parents is Amazon Studios' original two season series *Wishenpoof*. This program has been highly recommended by educational expert Angela C. Santomero (2017), who categorizes the series as a "kid empowerment show" in which the "goal is for kids to learn executive functioning skills" (139). Though Santomero (2017) does not identify the role that parental figures play in the show, her endorsement highlights that the main character, Bianca, exemplifies a child who is learning how to achieve agency and independence. Yet, this is accomplished through present parents (both mother and father appear in every episode) who encourage Bianca to master her magical powers (wish magic that grants wishes) that her mother also has. Additionally, much of Bianca's growth occurs via social situations in which magic is peripheral to the topic at hand. As opposed to the film *Frozen,* in which the parents are responsible for encouraging Elsa to bottle up her emotions and hide her true self from world (in the short amount of time they are alive before a tragic shipwreck), in *Wishenpoof,* the parents encourage Bianca by orienting her within their family system while simultaneously encouraging her to have some experiences apart from them. The show strikes an effective balance of parent-child interaction and child autonomy. Furthermore, Bianca's parents employ authoritative parenting, directly addressing behaviors and thought processes in a loving and constructive way. Shows like *Wishenpoof* model for children ways that adults' experiences can be useful for children. They show the wisdom that comes from experience and the value of multigenerational relationships.

Ultimately, laughable fathers (that children viewers laugh at rather than with), villainous mothers, absent parents, and dumb parents should not be the norm. Certainly, there are children who have each of these types of parents in their own life. This must be acknowledged, and there is a time and place for seeing one's own experience and identifying with it, as well as for being exposed to situations different from one's own. However, overall, media should offer children edifying examples of the family unit. This should especially continue in portrayals of parenting, allowing children to see in narrative format the rationale behind authoritative parenting and the effective result it has on the characters they know and love.

Works Cited

"Adrienne Rich on the Powerful, Powerless Mother." 2012. Interview by Terry Gross. *NPR*, March 30, 2012. https://www.npr.org/2012/03/30/149678681/adrienne-rich-on-the-powerful-powerless-mother.

Alber, Peggy. 2016. "Why Stories Matter for Children's Learning." *The Conversation*, January 2016. http://theconversation.com/why-stories-matter-for-childrens-learning-52135.

Alter, Nicola. 2017. "Must Fictional Parents Always Be Absent?" *Thoughts on Fantasy*, August 14, 2017. https://thoughtsonfantasy.com/2017/08/14/must-fictional-parents-always-be-absent/.

Australian Council on Children and the Media. n.d. "Happy Feet Two." *The Australian Parenting Website*. https://raisingchildren.net.au/guides/movie-reviews/happy-feet-two.

Blankenhorn, David. 1996. *Fatherless America: Confronting Our Most Urgent Social Problem.* New York: Harper Perennial.

Boxer, Sarah. 2014. "Why Are All the Cartoon Mothers Dead?" *The Atlantic*, July/August 2014. https://www.theatlantic.com/magazine/archive/2014/07/why-are-all-the-cartoon-mothers-dead/372270/.

Clement, Joe, and Matt Miles. 2017. *Screen Schooled: Two Veteran Teachers Expose How Technology Overuse Is Making Our Kids Dumber.* Chicago: Chicago Review Press Incorporated.

Darling, Nancy, and Laurence Steinberg. 2018. "Parenting Style as Context: An Integrative Model." In *Interpersonal Development*, edited by Brett Laursen and Rita Zukauskiene, 487–496. New York: Routledge.

Dever, Carolyn. 2006. *Death and the Mother from Dickens to Freud: Victorian Fiction and the Anxiety of Origins.* Cambridge, MA: Cambridge University Press.

Douglas, William. 2003. *Television Families: Is Something Wrong in Suburbia?* London: Routledge.

Duncley, Victoria L. 2015. *Reset Your Child's Brain: A Four-Week Plan to End Meltdowns, Raise Grades, and Boost Social Skills by Reversing the Effects of Electronic Screen-Time.* Novato, CA: New World Library.

Flynn, Caitlin. 2015. "Fact: Merida from 'Brave' Is Disney's Most Feminist Princess." *Bustle*, September 2015. https://www.bustle.com/articles/107099-fact-merida-from-brave-is-disneys-most-feminist-princess.

Gannon, Megan. 2013. "Record Number of Single Dads Head US Households." *Live Science*, July 2013. https://www.livescience.com/37918-record-number-of-single-dads.html.

Gilbert, Sandra, and Susan Gubar. 2000. *The Madwoman in the Attic: The Woman Writer and the Nineteenth-Century Literary Imagination.* New Haven, CT: Yale University Press.

Good Luck Charlie. 2010. Episode 1, Season 1 "Study Date," created by Phil Baker and Drew Vaupen, aired April 4, 2010 on Disney Channel.

Greydanus, Steven D. 2016. "We Need to Talk about Cartoon Parents." *Decent Films*. http://decentfilms.com/articles/junior-knows-best.

Gross, Gail. 2016 "A Stable Home Equals a Successful Child." *Let's Talk: Dr. Gail Gross*, April 12, 2016. http://drgailgross.com/a-stable-home-equals-a-successful-child/.

Hardie-Williams, Kathy. 2014. "Authoritarian and Authoritative Parenting Styles: Which Is Best?" *Good Therapy.org*, May 2, 2014. https://www.goodtherapy.org/blog/authoritarian-and-authoritative-parenting-styles-which-is-best-0502144.

Holland, Patricia. 2001. "Living for Libido: or, 'Child's Play IV': The Imagery of Childhood and the Call for Censorship." In *Ill Effects: The Media Violence Debate*, edited by Martin Barker and Julian Petley, 78–86. London: Routledge.

Kardaras, Nicholas. 2017. *Glow Kids: How Screen Addiction Is Hijacking Our Kids—and How to Break the Trance.* New York: St. Martin's Griffin.

Karlyn, Kathleen Rowe. 2011. *Unruly Girls, Unrepentant Mothers: Redefining Feminism on Screen.* Austin: University of Texas Press.

Kiladitis, Rosemary. 2011. "TV Show Review: Good Luck Charlie (Disney Channel, 2011-Present.)" *Mom Read It*, November 28, 2011. https://momreadit.wordpress.com/2011/11/28/tv-show-review-good-luck-charlie-disney-channel-2011-present/.

Kulik, Ty. 2015. "Where the Hell Are the Responsible Adults on *PJ Masks*?" *Seedsing*, December 8, 2015. https://www.seedsing.com/seedsing/2015/12/8/where-the-hell-are-the-responsible-adults-on-pj-masks.

Lee, Dawn. 2018. "Single Mother Statistics." *Single Mother Guide*. July 2018. https://singlemotherguide.com/single-mother-statistics/.

Madrigal, Alexis C. 2014. "Attitudes Toward Men and Childcare." *The Atlantic*, June 29, 2014. https://www.theatlantic.com/entertainment/archive/2014/06/dads-on-sitcoms/373673/.

Markham, Laura. 2019. "What's Wrong with Permissive Parenting?" *Aha! Parenting*. https://www.ahaparenting.com/parenting-tools/positive-discipline/permissive-parenting.

McGee, David, and Bryce Hantla. 2013. "The Portrayal of Fathers in Popular Media." *The Journal of Discipleship and Family Ministry* 3(2): 36–46.

Parker, Kim, and Gretchen Livingston. 2019. "6 Facts About American Fathers." *Pew Research Center*, June 12, 2019. http://www.pewresearch.org/fact-tank/2017/06/15/fathers-day-facts/.

Rich, Adrienne. 1995. *Of Woman Born: Motherhood as Experience and Institution*. New York: W. W. Norton.

Santomero, Angela C. 2017 "Is Preschool Programming Educational?—Commentary on Chapter 7." In *Media Exposure During Infancy and Early Childhood: The Effects of Content and Context on Learning and Development*, edited by Rachel Barr and Deborah Nichols Linebarger, 135–140. Switzerland: Springer International Publishing.

"'Shake It Baby, Shake It': Media Preferences, Sexual Attitudes, and Gender Stereotypes Among Adolescents." *Sex Roles* 63(11–12): 844–859. https://doi.org/10.1007/s11199-010-9815-1.

Shome, Raka. 2000. "Outing Whiteness." *Critical Studies in Media Communication*, 17(3): 366-71.

"Stepfamily Statistics." *The Stepfamily Foundation*. 2018. http://www.stepfamily.org/stepfamily-statistics.html.

Steward, Melissa. 2015. "How Mass Media Portrays Dads and What You Can Do About It." *National Fatherhood Initiative*, July 2, 2015. https://www.fatherhood.org/fatherhood/americas-fatherhood-problem-mass-media-and-how-we-can-fix-it.

Strasburger, Victor. 2006. "'Clueless': Why Do Pediatricians Underestimate the Media's Influence on Children and Adolescents?" *Pediatrics* 117(4): 1437-1421. http://pediatrics.aappublications.org/content/117/4/1427.short.

Trautner, Tracy. 2017. "Permissive Parenting Style." *Michigan State University*, January 19, 2017. http://msue.anr.msu.edu/news/permissive_parenting_style.

Venzo, Paul, and Kristy Hess. 2013. "'Honk Against Homophobia.' Rethinking Relations Between Media and Sexual Minorities." *Journal of Homosexuality* 60(11): 1539–1556.

Weingarten, Kathy. 1998. "Sidelined No More: Promoting Mothers of Adolescents as a Resource for Their Growth and Development." In *Mothering Against the Odds: Diverse Voices of Contemporary Mothers*, edited Cynthia García Coll, Janet L. Surrey, and Kathy Weingarten, 15–36. New York: The Guilford Press.

Wilson, Natalie. 2010. "Disney's Gender Roles Remain Un-Tangled." *Ms. Magazine*, November 29, 2010. http://msmagazine.com/blog/2010/11/29/disneys-gender-roles-remain-un-tangled/.

Cloudy with a Chance of Ecological Justice

Creating Alternative Storylines for Children

Amber E. George *and* Jacob E. Gindi

The animated children's film *Cloudy with a Chance of Meatballs* (2009) holds immense potential for teaching young people about various ecological issues such as food insecurity, reliance on animal-based food sources, sustainability, overconsumption, and environmental degradation. However, the film falls incredibly short of providing any meaningful social commentary that could positively impact children. In some respects, it even contributes to the narrative that ecological injustice and consumerism are inevitable, and thus acceptable. Suffice to say that this film reinforces the idea that most people do not think about where their food and water originates. Despite these shortcomings, there are still some valuable lessons to be gleaned from *Cloudy with a Chance of Meatballs*. This essay presents techniques to teach our children media literacy skills and critical environmental issues. Media literacy provides children and parents "a framework to access, analyze, evaluate, create, and participate with messages in a variety of forms—from print to video" (CML 2019). It is imperative for children to develop methods for sociological inquiry and self-expression since they are necessary for being functional, contributive members of society (CML 2019).

The analysis presented here emphasizes the power media literacy can have on children's worldview, especially when analyzing popular visual texts. We also suggest that learning media literacy is best combined with spending time in nature. Environmental education that combines both hands-on play along with media analysis is especially crucial to children who tend to spend more time inside with their televisions and devises. For many children and adults, nature has become something to "watch, consume, wear, and ignore" (Louv 2005). Thus, nature benefits children because "unlike television, nature does not steal time, it amplifies it[. … N]ature inspires creativity in a child by demanding visualization and the full use of the senses" (Louv 2005). Through frequent and positive childhood experiences with nature, empathy for nature develops and has a healthy impact on children's mind, body, and spirit

(Arnold et al. 2009). Hands-on play time outdoors has proven to decrease symptoms of ADD and improves resistance to negative stress and depression (Louv 2005). Therefore, children will cultivate a sense of wonder about the Earth by employing a combined pedagogical approach of using familiar cultural examples such as the *Cloudy* film, combined with direct experience outdoors. Ultimately, this can lead to children becoming environmentally informed and ecologically active adults that can productively negotiate, and even contest, ecological injustice (Chawla 2001). Since these are issues that current and future generations will encounter at one time or another, it is imperative that we instill children with a sense of moral responsibility to the natural world; to care about people, nonhumans, and nature, as their happiness and wellbeing could very well depend on it.

Using Movies to Inspire Social Change

Many children look to characters in movies as role models, and entities that they can emulate (Addis 1996). However, not all characters or storylines present our children with information that is emulation worthy. Furthermore, discussing adult-like themes such as climate change, human-made environmental disasters, and obesity with children can be difficult. Moreover, the number of kid-friendly films that adequately deal with these issues are in short supply. Studies have proven that impactful learning about environmental issues is generally possible when the child perceives the subject matter as important and relevant (Kola-Olsuanya 2005). As parents and informed social justice activists of the natural world, we selected *Cloudy with a Chance of Meatballs* for its perceived relevance to the everyday lives of our children. The children referred to the characters, scenery, and plot as being similar to their own, or people they know. However, like so many things our children consume, we must go beyond what is on the screen to ensure they receive accurate messages. To do this, children must learn media literacy so that they can think critically about the media they are passively consuming, resist faulty advertising, and become smarter consumers of media sources.

Many parents want to have conversations with their children about issues related to nature, nonhuman animals, and each other but hesitate for lack of knowing where to start (Pratt et al. 2013). We want to inspire our children to have a positive impact on the world, and in order to inspire change, we needed activities that would nurture their cognitive, social, and emotional development. Screening films with our kids is an excellent tool for developing verbal, social, and emotional skills about specific topics through media that is relevant in our children's lives (Hébert 2002).

Parents face an endless amount of questions and challenges concerning how to navigate media. Some parents approach the issue of media and technology by being what Alexandra Samuel (2015) calls "limiters." These parents put strict limits on what and how long their children watch and play with media, most especially when they are very young. Other parents who allow their children to control the amount of time and content are called the "enablers." As with just about everything in life, moderation might be the key to navigating our children's media usage. The middle ground of media use is what Samuel (2015) calls "media mentors." Parents who consistently engage with their children tend to nurture children who are more media savvy (Samuel 2015). Media mentors watch movies, download apps, and play video games with their children, sharing their interests and criticisms. Thus, "the same parenting rules apply to your children's real and virtual environments" (Brown et al. 2015). Parents should still play with their children, know their friends, and teach kindness during online interactions to promote positive experiences (Brown et al. 2015). Furthermore, a study by the American Academy of Pediatrics (2013) suggests that "the quality of content is more important than the platform or time spent with media." Parents who do their research by reading reviews, asking friends, and exploring the content themselves are more likely to find high-quality content. When parents embrace technology and show interest in the media their children consume, it is easier to have dialogues about what they are watching. It also helps to know what interests your child so that you can support positive engagement with media. The National Association for the Education of Young Children agrees that when parents use media "intentionally and appropriately, technology and interactive media are effective tools to support learning and development" of children (Ashbrook 2015).

Some of the best philosophers on this planet are children. Children ponder the "who, what, when, where, and whys" of information daily and also live in an ongoing state of wonder about the world. If philosophy begins in wonderment as Plato suggests, then childhood is when the riddles of the world are most intriguing to young minds (Plato *Theaetetus*, tr. Jowett, 155c-d). What Plato meant by wonderment is wonder in the sense of "puzzlement" or "perplexity" (Plato *Meno*, tr. Guthrie 2016, 84c). Philosopher Gareth Matthew (1996) agrees that philosophy is naturally enjoyable for most children because it is "motivated by puzzlement" and "conceptual play." This type of philosophical play is important: "Parents and teachers who […] refuse to play this game with their children impoverish their own intellectual lives, diminish their relationships with children, and discourage in their children the spirit of independent intellectual inquiry" (Matthew 1996, 21). If Plato is correct that philosophy is best discussed via dialogue, then who better to engage in such matters than children for whom speech is a wonderful abyss of discovery.

Children also tend to be clear of some of the hardened adult traits that can prohibit the free flow of philosophical ideas. Prejudice, dogma, and negativity typically do not sour the young mind as it does for most adults. Children are more inclined to freely investigate ideas and situations on their terms, or a priori, without preconceived notions about how the world should operate. Even the most absurd hypothesis is open to analysis within a child's mind, and they are willing to work through it until a natural conclusion emerges. Adults tend to work their way through an absurd hypothesis by quickly dismissing it because it does not conform to conventional wisdom or scientific "truths" (Matthews 1996). Furthermore, "[t]here is a certain innocence and naivete about many [...] philosophy questions. This is something that adults, including college students, have to cultivate when they pick up their first book of philosophy. It is something natural to children" (Matthews 1996, 73). At their core, children are open, curious, and inquisitive, perfectly embodying the traits of a philosopher (Haynes 2008).

While wonder is the raw material of philosophy, it is not philosophy itself. We need to do philosophy; actively use our reason to solve riddles and make sense of the world around us. Knowing how brilliant children are at philosophy, we have begun hosting what we call "philosophy night" at home. We seek to give our children space not only to consider whether something is "right" but also why it exists in the first place through exchanging ideas freely, politely, and reasonably. Taking a cue from child psychiatrist Robert Coles (1986), we believe that children are quite capable of tapping into their moral intelligence to self-reflect. Coles (1986) states that children have a "keen moral sensitivity to ideals and values" and "no one teaches children sociology or psychology; yet children are constantly noticing who gets along with whom and why" (24). Thus, providing children with the opportunity to nurture these experiences can help them discover greater depth and meaning in their lives. It also provides parents with the opportunity to enter the children's world through their perspectives.

The ancient Greek philosopher Socrates was famous for insisting he was never anyone's teacher. Instead, he likened himself to a midwife; he helped people give birth to ideas (Plato *Theaetetus,* tr. Jowett 1990). Many times, using the Socratic method of questioning helps our children examine ideas and determine the validity of those ideas. Socrates, known for professing his ignorance on various topics, engaged others in dialogues to scrutinize thoughts until the truth emerged. Disciplined practice of thoughtful questioning through the means of "acting dumb" is a useful method for helping our children develop independent thinking while giving them ownership of what they are learning. Questioning coupled with fruitful dialogue promotes children's discussion, debate, evaluation, and analytical skills. They come to understand the strengths and the weaknesses in the story and gain an appreciation for how others might perceive the film as well. As parents, the authors of this essay act as facilitators or collaborators rather than authority figures in our dialogues. We actively participate in these discussions alongside our children and encourage them to consider alternative viewpoints, listen attentively and respectively, and share in an orderly, honest, and fair manner with each other. Ultimately, facilitated discussions that use philosophy to enhance critical thinking allows us to learn about ourselves and each other, all the while gaining valuable media literacy skills. This enables us to explore insightful philosophical ideas with our children such as truth, justice, beauty, and friendship along with the more specific ethical themes related to sexism, racism, animal rights, and environmental justice.

As with most children in early adolescence, we sometimes encounter roadblocks when doing philosophy. One roadblock encountered from time to time involves their go-to answer when faced with a puzzling question: "I don't know." This simple phrase can relay valuable information as it could mean they do not want to talk to us, or want to avoid engaging in thoughtful discussion, or they have no answer. Our instincts as parents might be to let them off the hook, change the subject, demand they answer, or launch into lecture mode by answering the question for them. The problem with all of these responses is that children learn that such a response automatically opts them out of doing the hard work of personal reflection and critical thinking. We stress to our children that the deliberation of their thoughts, feelings, and beliefs is fun, freeing, and imperative to their development. There are times when such shallow responses as "I don't know" are acceptable, but during movie night we try to stay focused on learning rather than consuming empty entertainment. A follow-up question we often use is "If you did know, what would your answer be?" By demonstrating genuine care and patience, and giving children the time to consider their response, they will often respond more thoughtfully.

Other tactics to help children think critically involves brainstorming and allowing plenty of time to think of a response. Sometimes they do not know how to answer the question, so we help by offering possible replies. By modeling possibilities, this assists children with putting into words what they were thinking or feeling but found difficult to express. Also, allowing them plenty of time to answer, it shows that we genuinely care what the child thinks and want to understand their thoughts. If they say, "I don't know" we will respond, "That's OK, take a minute to think about it. We are willing to wait." With the pressure on, they may sit and stare all the while we remain open and encouraging, perhaps even saying something like "What you think is important," but doing nothing to fill the uncomfortable silence. From our experience, this process demonstrates to the children that their thoughts are worth knowing which empowers them to think of something to share.

Screening Cloudy with a Chance of Meatballs

Children can learn media literacy by using just about any narrative. *Cloudy with a Chance of Meatballs* (2009) was chosen for this analysis because it is a lighthearted film that conveys some useful messages to children while also appealing to adults using subtle, mature humor. It also presents a parody of a disaster film genre that can be used to learn about climate change, food, and water sustainability, among other notable issues. Exploring stories helps children bridge the gap between their interior life and life outside of the home in nature or public spaces (Collins 1997). Furthermore, studying the *Cloudy* film in particular, with its focus on a young scientist's adventures in saving the planet, helps make science more accessible to young minds. For many children, science can be abstract and, therefore, it should be made "part of their own personal world if it is to be understood and remembered" (Butzow 1989).

We begin movie night by sharing with the children a basic plot outline of the film. This way, they are primed to enter the world of the characters. We also share with them who created the film, as we believe this also helps with their understanding of the overarching scope of the plot. *Cloudy* (2009) is a computer-animated film loosely based on the children's picture book of the same name published by Judi and Ron Barret (1974). The original story depicted edible meteorological phenomena randomly falling out of the sky, three times a day, to the point where it caused natural disasters much the same way that the film depicts it. However, in the film adaptation, filmmakers Phil Lord and Chris Miller of Sony Pictures Animation created a young, socially awkward, publicly ridiculed inventor named Flint Lockwood who develops a magical machine to deal with his town's lack of food sources. Both the film and the storybook do not shield children from social and environmental ills but rather "show kids the world and its problems, instead of a purely sunny untainted one" (Pollack 2000). Furthermore, the film version takes moralizing to a new level by going beyond just saving the people's lives, to save the life of the whole planet. After we discuss the plot and origins of the film, we begin the movie. There are times when we will pause the film and ask the children questions along the way. We sometimes ask about the messages as they arise in the story or save some until the end.

Flint Lockwood and his father live in what appears to be an American island on the Atlantic Ocean called Swallow Falls. It appears that most people in the community have fallen on tough times because their primary source of food and income, a sardine cannery, was shut down. The film suggests the global market for sardines has collapsed because "everyone realized that sardines are gross." At this point in the film, we stop the film to discuss what is going on and how it relates to real-life situations. As adults, we know that exploring environmental issues can often be a complex and sometimes a depressing task. So, we needed to determine how to communicate ecologically just principles in an upbeat, and comprehensible way. Without scaring the children by giving them too much doom and gloom, we present the issues of environmental degradation as straightforward as possible. Even if parents shelter their children from learning about environmental destruction, it is likely they would still learn about it elsewhere but lack an outlet to explore their feelings. Thus, we believe our children deserve to know all sides of a given issue since it expands their knowledge and allows them to develop solutions. By presenting them with all sides, they use their intellectual capacity to think through the issues to foster growth.

We start by asking the children if they know of any situations that are similar to the problems arising in this town and whether there is any way that this crisis could happen here. This brings to mind the genuine issues that people encounter globally when their environments have either been saturated or depleted of natural resources. Overfishing continues to be an issue in several communities that lack proper management and restrictions on fishing. One well-known fishing crisis took place in Newfoundland, Canada, in 1992. Decades of overfishing cod led to ecological disaster for the ecosystem and 40,000 fishers losing their jobs and livelihood abruptly (Environmental Defense Fund 2018). We discuss whether the absence of habitat protection, unvaried agriculture programs, and destructive fishery practices that ruin Swallow Falls could occur in our community (Environmental Defense Fund 2018). The children consider how the townspeople should not take more than they are allowed. Some towns have social systems that monitor and enforce fishers, like Lockwood's father Tim, from only taking their fair share. Another solution encourages the townspeople to engage in sustainable agriculture that moves away from animal-based food sources toward practices that do not destroy the waterways or land. After much discussion, our children realize that humans must take responsibility for the activities that are damaging, altering, and disrupting natural ecosystems.

Flint, feeling quite compassionate about the devastating impact that food insecurity, joblessness, and hopelessness has had on his town, devises a creative scientific solution. He invents a machine called the "Flint Lockwood Diatonic Super Mutating Dynamic Food Replicator" (FLDSMDFR) that turns water into food. Since his house cannot supply enough electricity to run the machine, he foolishly taps into the nearby power plant that supplies an overabundance of energy. The jolt of electricity sends the machine destructively rocketing through town, smashing things and ultimately ends up permanently stuck in the sky. Soon after, the machine rains food on the town.

At this point in the film, we pause to discuss the nuts and bolts behind the FLDSMDFR machine. In particular, we focus on how Flint's decision to build a machine that only works by using an abundance of water and electrical sources, fails to consider how this might affect the eco-community in which he lives. We facilitated an interesting discussion about how water is a vital entity as a biological necessity for all life on Earth. Children learn that "water management" is an approach to providing humans, nonhumans, and land with appropriate water sources to maintain their well-being. Flint does not consider how water influences the character of the land, nor how overfishing and damaging agricultural practices have altered the land in such a way as to disrupt ecosystems. Garett Hardin (1968) suggests that humans often fall victim to a "tragedy of the commons" regarding water resources. Individuals may believe that oceans, lakes, and rivers are "common" places to be shared by all. However, if we all were to act on personal interest without concerns for others, it could lead to a decreased water supply. Each person gets trapped into a cycle that compels them to seek out more and more water, without limit. Therein lies the tragedy; the world's water supply is not infinite (Hardin 1968). Thus, Flint acts upon his belief in the freedom of the commons, and ultimately, this leads to his and the community's demise. When Flint's machine reconfigures the molecular structure of water to turn it into food, it potentially robs animals, the land, and humans from accessing clean, fresh water to live. Furthermore, we assume it uses fresh water, just as agriculture and industry uses almost 90 percent of fresh water worldwide, both of which are also a massive source of pollution (Boylan 2015). One might implicitly assume that there is a never-ending supply of viable fresh water readily available in Shallow Falls. In some areas of the world, fresh water is not equally distributed; some areas have shortages while others have too much. This is a concern of scientists, philosophers, politicians, and economists who recognize that water resources are used unfairly and inefficiently (Cominelli 2009). People must realize that water is a precious resource and that a large portion of the world lacks potable water and proper sanitation. Thus, creating a machine that uses one precious resource, potentially to the detriment of other natural recourses, is not a sustainable solution despite the *Cloudy* movie suggesting otherwise (Boylan 2015).

It seems little thought is given to how water will be harnessed to power the FLDSMDFR machine. In reality, such a massive harboring of water would require constructing dams to control irrigation and electricity. Dams often disrupt the natural flow of water and significantly impact the animal and plant life that depend on them (Roy 1999). In environmental policy, it is a well-established fact that large water management projects must proceed with as much caution as possible because of the unintended harmful consequences it can cause to ecosystems. This is known as the principle of precautionary reason (Boylan 2015, 210). Any interruption in the natural order of things should meet the burden of proof that the intervention will create a sustainable outcome. If a large amount of water were artificially removed from the land of Swallow Falls, it could cause long-term damage that interrupts and degrades the natural flow of water, and potentially pollutes it. Our overarching theme with this discussion is that the children understand that environmental systems are worthy of respect and the principle of precautionary reason should be applied when tampering with any ecosystem, biome, watershed, or water source.

In theory, having the ability to create food out of thin air should eliminate the environmental concerns attached to food production, including the sustainability of harvested food, animal agriculture, and destruction of threatened habitats. If one could create any food source imaginable, we should promote the production of healthy and nutritious foods for everyone in an environmentally sustainable and safe manner. However, the real issues surrounding global food security and health are not at all addressed within the town of Swallow Falls. None of the societal costs, including those that impact the health of the environment and the beings that live within it, are even remotely on the radar of observation. Instead, we witness the townsfolk mesmerized by the big, juicy hamburgers that start dropping from the sky. Eventually, the machine rains bacon and eggs for breakfast. Flint receives requests for ice cream at birthday parties and T-bone steaks for special occasions. People become so greedy and gluttonous, wanting more and more and bigger and bigger portions, that Flint invents a communication tool that allows individuals to order any food they want. News about the Swallow Falls food machine travels fast, leading the town to become the hot new food tourist destination renamed "Chewandswallow."

Once the children get a proper perspective on the foods that are raining from the sky, we pause to discuss food ethics. First, we discuss what food insecurity is by explaining that it is a lack of consistent access to nutritional food for an active, healthy lifestyle (USDA 2018). Food insecurity is easily solved by Flint whose machine rains animal-based, unhealthy, processed food sources with unfavorable results. With a near constant supply to food, the townspeople become belligerent and greedy consumers, never satiated, and demanding that Flint produce the unhealthy foods they want such as ice cream and candies. The characters delight in playing in (and eating) palaces made out of Jell-O, snowball fights using ice-cream snowballs, and rivers of candy. Despite the images of light-hearted fun, the imagery of unlimited consumption provides the children with capitalistic undertones of domination of nature. Flint's passion for becoming a famous scientist while simultaneously saving the town perpetuates materialistic values that fuel capitalism. Flint manipulates nature in such a way as to overproduce food sources that when left to litter are harmful to the environment, create extreme weather situations, require the killing of nonhumans, and also poisons humans' bodies as well. This is a clear example of what ecofeminists suggest leads to the destruction of nature, nonhuman animals, and people for the main purpose of creating wealth and fame through capitalism (Gaard and Gruen 1993). Even Flint's dad recognizes that people should not always get what they want and hints that food raining down from the sky will cause greed, laziness, and will not be good for people.

One theme that we consistently discuss in our household is that eating is an ethical act (Terry 2009). We teach our children that through the act of eating, we make a moral decision not to consume foods that depend on the suffering of others. Our food choices are intertwined with our values and relationship to where food sources originate (Twine 2017). The horrors of factory farming, which requires animal abuse to produce that juicy hamburger and dairy-based ice cream, are as absent in the imagination of most meat eaters as when some magical machine turns water into food for the people in Chewandswallow (Miller 2012). Despite being a significant part of the plot, food sustainability and outsourcing is sadly not dealt with in any analytical fashion in the film.

Americans account for just 4.5 percent of the world's population but eat approximately 15 percent of the meat produced globally (Stokstad 2010). Overconsumption and escalating demand for animal-based products have severe effects for the environment, nonhuman animals, and humans (World Bank 2010). The processing of animal-based food sources is resource-intensive, placing an incredible strain on the environment and causes horrific abuse to animals in the process (Walker et al. 2005). Furthermore, one-third of global cereal crop production is fed to animals, while the world still faces severe famines and annual hunger periods. Thus, movement away from animal-based foods toward other sources like high protein plants including nuts could mean nutritional values are improved while leaving a smaller ecological footprint and less animal abuse on factory farms. Alternate sources of nutrient-rich foods such as tofu can be obtained from plants as compared to consuming the flesh of animals (Macdiarmid et al. 2011). In fact, a 30 percent reduction in production and adult consumption levels of animal-source foods would meet national greenhouse gas emission targets and would at the same time, reduce years of life lost from human heart disease by 15 percent (Wilkinson et al. 2009). Ultimately, the health of human beings and nonhuman animals cannot be separated from the health of our ecosystems (Johnston et al. 2014). Americans must pursue sustainable diets that promote ecological stability through improved nutritional health, low environmental impact food production, and no reliance on animal-based food sources to meet the needs of the global population.

The townspeople of Chewandswallow are so obsessed with consuming unhealthy snacks and gorging themselves that they do not consider the health impact of their actions. Their happiness seemed predicated on whether they could get Flint to make the foods they wanted and maintain a continual supply. Interestingly, Flint does notice that people's food requests get bigger and increase in frequency, but no one mentions any concern for health issues. Other than the mayor, whom we can see grows exponentially in size, no one else grows obese which is not very realistic given the images of what the town folks are eating. Regardless, our spineless hero, unable to reject requests, keeps up with the demand to please the people. In reality, a staggering 2.1 billion people are overweight globally (Ng et al. 2014), and of that number, an estimated 41 million children under five years of age are overweight (World Bank 2010) due to eating junk foods. There is no doubt that obesity is a major problem that contributes to many of the health issues humans endure today.

While obesity is often the result of uncontrollable factors related to heredity and illness, the environment in which one lives also plays a role (Gostin 2010). Transnational food corporations have powerful marketing strategies that target children with appealing images of unhealthy foods and drinks. These ads tend to displace healthy choices to encourage heavily processed food sources, which ultimately undermine parents and public health efforts aimed at getting children to eat well (Pechmann et al. 2005). The food industry claims that their efforts at aggressive advertising are merely giving the consumers (read: children) what they want, and it is up to the consumer to make their food choices. We know that children, however, are sometimes limited in their ability to make sound nutritional choices and are especially vulnerable to marketing agendas that tempt their pallets with high sugared over processed foods (Pechmann et al. 2005). Resisting advertisements requires the ability to weigh long-term health consequences of consumption against short-term rewards, an ability that is difficult for young children (Pechmann et al. 2005).

Watching a film like *Cloudy* in which unhealthy food is falling to the ground with no limit presents an ethical issue—how parents encourage healthy eating within a medium that promotes gluttony and excess? Consider for a moment that in the town of Chewandswallow there is so much food produced that they simply dump the surplus of over-processed food into a nearby reservoir. The excessive overconsumption, food choices, and gluttony presented in this film for comedic effect may leave children confused about their food choices. After all, if it was okay for the townspeople of Chewandswallow to consume those types of food in that amount, why is it not okay for children to do the same? They made gluttony and eating junk food look like fun. Without strong values and ethical standards that set nutrition as a high priority, rates of childhood obesity could remain unchecked, and progress in achieving global food security will be difficult to secure.

Soon after our discussion of consumption and gluttony, we move into discussing the natural food disasters that occur as a result of the machine going rogue. Eventually, Flint realizes that his invention has morphed into a dangerous, cataclysmic deluge that creates unsightly food storms such as a torrent of spaghetti tornadoes, run-away meatballs, and other gigantic food-stuffs that crashes to the ground and threatens to obliterate the town. Over-sized pickles smash into buildings and a giant pancake completely covers the local school. Once the storms hit, we pause to discuss with the children what the characters may be thinking. It is interesting to see how children relate the food storms to the human-made disasters from the news. Overall, we have found it difficult to prevent children from learning about several national and global calamities including natural or human-made disasters indirectly through media. These tragedies can be disturbing to our children, and when exposed to catastrophic events they often display anxiety as a result. For in-stance, "the first response phase after a disaster is marked by emotions of fear, shock, anxiety, grief or relief that other family members survived" (About Kids Health 2010). A few weeks after the disaster, children can be clingy, needy, irritable, hostile, revert to fears of the dark, or even physical symp-toms that include a change in appetite or poor sleeping patterns (About Kids Health 2010). Thus, we use what happens in *Cloudy* to discuss the impact that human-made events can have not only on individuals but also on entire towns. This discussion helps foster resiliency coping with traumatic disasters when they occur and supply the tools needed to process these issues should they arise in real life.

Initially the children did not realize that the storms in the film were human-made, which makes them different than other natural environmental disasters. We discuss how events such as hurricanes and tornadoes, which can strike suddenly and without warning, are powerful natural disasters that hold incredible destructive potential to humans, animals, and the environ-ment. Then there are disasters caused by humans that can include chemical spills, fires, and in the case of *Cloudy*, mega food storms that cause significant property damage, environmental contamination, and potentially loss of life. The disasters apparent in *Cloudy* are due to human carelessness and mishan-dling a dangerous piece of scientific equipment.

When things spiral out of control, and the food weather becomes dan-gerous, masses of surplus food piling up in that reservoir reach the breaking point. As the dam bursts, food floods the town in an avalanche of excess food, burying them in giant hamburgers and hot dogs. In an era of global warm-ing and climate change, a story where a weather disaster is brought on by human interference and a scientist whose inventions keep having unforeseen consequences is enlightening. We pause the film to discuss the ethical role that scientists play in the creation of new technologies. For this discussion, we reference another family favorite, *Jurassic Park* (1993), when Ian Malcolm says emphatically, "Your scientists were so preoccupied with whether or not they could, they didn't stop to think if they should." Thus, just because you *can* make it, doesn't necessarily mean that you *should* make it. Humans may believe that science can solve all of humanity's problems. However, we must remember that the solutions we think of must include ethical, environmental, and community-based considerations. Scientists do not have all the answers and they must be open to exploring the limitations of their research. Thus, the weather-related giant food storms, which neatly parallels the effects of other human-made disasters, serves as a backdrop for discussing scientific ethical responsibility.

This analysis would be remiss if neglected to analyze some of the broader relationships and character development in the film. In particular, we question the budding romantic relationship between Flint and Sam Sparks, the weather channel meteorologist. We highlight the differences in how Flint and Sam's scientific knowledge, confidence, and identities are portrayed. Our daughter noticed right away that Sparks is an attractive, young girl who is intelligent but afraid to demonstrate her smarts for fear of rejection. Our son suspected that Flint is especially drawn to her because he recognizes that she is hiding a superior intellect under her "dumb blonde" exterior. Sparks is not what one might consider to be a strong female character because she is far more intelligent than what is required for her job, and she feels she must play stupid to get ahead in her career. There are some glimmers of her intelligence throughout the film. However, only after she assists Flint in saving the town does the audience come to understand Sparks is scientifically knowledgeable. Unfortunately, Spark's willingness to reinforce the notion that women cannot possibly be talented or interested in science, technology, engineering, and mathematical (STEM) fields suggests she fell prey to the devastating effects of gender bias (Bian et al. 2017).

There is currently a movement in the United States to disrupt two commonly held prejudices about women in STEM; the first is that men outnumber women in these fields, and the second is that women are socialized to avoid careers in STEM because they are perceived as unsuitable for women (Valla and Ceci 2014). Gender bias holds women like Sparks back from pursuing a more prestigious career and also being true to herself. Should Sparks demonstrate that she is an intelligent young woman, and step outside of the rigid gender roles, it could jeopardize her career advancement and even a relationship with Flint. It is not until Flint, using his white male privilege in STEM, encourages her to be proud of her nerdy identity that she seems to gain self-acceptance. This relationship sends the message that only through a male's acceptance can women see themselves as capable. Flint shows some hope for being an impactful male ally to Sparks when he encourages her at the end of the film to embrace her nerdiness. A male ally is defined as "building relationships with women, expressing as little sexism in their own behavior as possible, understanding social privilege conferred by their gender, and demonstrating active efforts to address gender inequities at work and in society" (Johnson and Smith 2018). However, Flint's character lacks the type of development to suggest that gender bias is unacceptable.

We praise the action of characters who resolve their conflicts peacefully, are compassionate and nurturing, and act ethically. For the characters who behave poorly, we talk about their behavior and explain why their actions are problematic. We also discuss the importance of social acceptance along with the idea that one should never compromise who they are just to be popular. Furthermore, seeking fame and fortune should not be pursued lightly, especially concerning scientific undertakings that can have grave consequences on communities. Flint eventually seems to discover that one should invent things for the right reasons, not for parental acknowledgment or celebrity glory.

Conclusion

Flint and Sam eventually defeat the defunct machine, however, leftovers falling from the sky ruin the town. With the machine destroyed, the food storm subsides, and everyone returns safely to Chewandswallow. Flint's father, Tim, finally shows his appreciation for his son and his inventions, and Flint and Sam celebrate with a kiss. Meanwhile, the obese mayor is seen stranded in the middle of the sea, having eaten nearly all of his peanut butter and jelly sandwich boat, while muttering that his plans were not well thought out.

To wrap up our discussion, and address any lingering questions, we use some questions that can be adapted for any film and used to hone media literacy skills. These questions may include the following.

- What is left out of the story, and why?
- Does the film present information using a balanced view or does it present information about only one side?
- Do you need more information to understand the full message of the film? Why do you think this?
- Was there anything about the film that confused or surprised you?
- How did the message of this film make you feel?
- Do you think others might feel the same way as you?
- Would some people disagree with the message in this film? Why do you think this?

With this particular film, we concluded by asking: "Do you think they made this film to inform you of something that is happening in the world?"

"Did they make this film to change your mind or behavior?" Our children, being the beautifully naive optimists that they are, believed this film was made so that they could "become better human beings." They talked about being a hero like Flint but to do more to save the planet such as boosting the level of sustainability at home, at school, and in their lifestyle. Some of their lifestyle solutions included creating backyard farms to grow local healthy foods, including questioning how they would keep bugs and deer away from their crops without the use of harmful chemical repellents. Their solutions considered the interests of not only humans but also nonhumans and the environment.

The children also discussed how important it is to not only critique media, but to also become part of nature by going outside and exploring. As was stressed at the beginning of this essay, "we need to allow children to develop their biophilia, their love for the Earth, before we ask them to academically learn about nature and become guardians of it" (White et al. 2008). We encouraged the children to develop long-term solutions that involves a family type of project. Their solution was planting a garden to grow fruits and vegetables that was sure to have identifiable results and is something that they can regularly do, for an indefinite period. They understood that this is only one of many ways that they can make a difference in creating food sources that are nutritious, affordable, and good for animals and the environment.

Furthermore, Matthews (1996) suggests that we can do philosophy with children, or anyone else, by reflecting "on a perplexity or a conceptual problem of a certain sort to see if one can remove the perplexity or solve the problem. Sometimes one succeeds, often one doesn't. Sometimes, getting clearer about one thing only makes it obvious that one is dreadfully unclear about something else" (83). We witnessed this happening with our children when they came to understand that overconsumption is an issue, but perhaps even worse is the excessive amounts of packaging on process foods that equates to extra garbage. They realized they can conserve garbage by drinking water from the tap instead of buying bottled water and consume less single-serve junk food items by buying in bulk.

Ultimately, the *Cloudy* film served as an appropriate case example for encouraging our children to take decisive ecological action while learning media literacy. Passively watching the film is not enough to cultivate their burgeoning environmental sensibilities. Ultimately, alternative readings of the story are necessary since the film fails at providing practical ideas for eco-action and Flint falls short of being the sort of ecological hero that children can, in good faith, emulate. These alternative readings of *Cloudy* can help convey serious environmental issues while instilling ecological values that will stick with children into adulthood.

Works Cited

Addis, Adeno. 1996. "Role Models and the Politics of Recognition." *University of Pennsylvania Law Review* 144(4): 1377–1468. doi:10.2307/3312617.

Arnold, Heather E., Fay G. Cohen, and Alan Warner. 2009. "Youth and Environmental Action: Perspectives of Young Environmental Leaders on Their Formative Influences." *The Journal of Environmental Education* 40(3): 27–36.

Ashbrook, Peggy. 2015. "Thinking About Technology and Young Children." *NSTA*, November 16, 2015. http://nstacommunities.org/blog/2015/11/16/thinking-about-technology-and-young-children/.

Barrett, Judi, and Ron Barrett. 2009. *The Complete Cloudy with a Chance of Meatballs.* New York: Atheneum Books for Young Readers.

Bian, Lin, Sarah-Jane Leslie, and Andrei Cimpian. 2017. "Gender Stereotypes About Intellectual Ability Emerge Early and Influence Children's Interests." *Science* 355 (6323): 389–391. DOI: 10.1126/science.aah6524.

Boylan, Michael. 2015. *Environmental Ethics.* Somerset: Wiley.

Brown, Ari, et al. 2015. "Beyond 'Turn It Off': How to Advise Families on Media Use." *AAP News*, 36(10): 54. DOI: https://doi.org/10.1542/aapnews.20153610-54.

Butzow, Carol. 1989. "Science Through Children's Literature: An Integrated Approach." Colorado: Teacher Ideas Press.

Center for Media Literacy. 2019. "Media Literacy: A Definition and More." https://www.medialit.org/media-literacy-definition-and-more.

Chawla, Lisa. 2001. "Putting Young Ideas into Action. The Relevance of Growing Up in Cities To Local Agenda 21." *Local Environment* 6(1): 13–25.

Cloudy with a Chance of Meatballs (film). 2009. Written and directed by Phil Lord and Christopher Miller. Distributed by Sony Pictures.

Coles, Robert. 1986. *The Political Life of Children.* Boston: Houghton Mifflin Company.

Collins, Rives. 1997. *The Power of Story: Teaching Through Storytelling.* Arizona: Gorsuch Scarisbrick.

Cominelli, Elenoria et al. 2009. "Water: The Invisible Problem. Access to Fresh Water Is Considered to Be a Universal and Free Human Right, but Dwindling Resources and a Burgeoning Population Are Increasing Its Economic Value." *EMBO Reports* 10(7): 671–676. http://doi.org/10.1038/embor.2009.148.

Council on Communications and Media. 2013. "Children, Adolescents, and the Media." *Pediatrics* 132(5): 958–961.

Environmental Defense Fund (EDF). 2018. "Overfishing: The Oceans' Most Serious Environmental Problem." https://www.edf.org/oceans-most-serious-problem.

Gaard, Greta, and Lori Gruen. 1993. "Ecofeminism: Toward Global Justice and Planetary Health." *Society and Nature* 2: 1–35.

Gostin, Lawrence O. 2010. *Public Health Law and Ethics: A Reader.* Berkeley: University of California Press.

Guthrie, William K.C. 2016. *The Greek Philosophers, from Thales to Aristotle.* London: Routledge.

Hardin, Garrett. 1968. "The Tragedy of the Commons." *Science* 162 (3859): 1243–1248.

Haynes, Joanna. 2008. *Children as Philosophers: Learning Through Enquiry and Dialogue in the Primary Classroom.* New York: Routledge.

Hébert, Thomas, and Kristie L. Speirs Neumeister. 2002. "Fostering the Social and Emotional Development of Gifted Children Through Guided Viewing of Film." *Roeper Review* 25(1): 17–21.

Johnson, Brad & David Smith. 2018. "How Men Can Become Better Allies to Women." *Harvard Business Review*, October 12, 2018.

Johnston, John et al. 2014. "Understanding Sustainable Diets: A Descriptive Analysis of the Determinants and Processes That Influence Diets and Their Impact on Health, Food Security and Environmental Sustainability." *Advances in Nutrition* 5(4): 418–429.

Jurassic Park (film). 1993. Based on the screenplay written by Michael Crichton and David Koepp. Directed by Steven Spielberg. Distributed by Universal Pictures.

Kola-Olusanya, A. 2005. "Free-Choice Environmental Education: Understanding Where Children Learn Outside of School." *Environmental Education Research* 11(3): 297–307.

Louv, Richard. 2005. *Last Child in the Woods: Saving Our Children from Nature-Deficit Disorder.* Chapel-Hill, NC: Algonquin Books.

Macdiarmid, Jennie et al. 2011. "A Balance of Healthy and Sustainable Food Choices: Project Report of Livewell." *World Wildlife Fund-UK.* http://assets.wwf.org.uk/downloads/ livewell_report_jan11.pdf.

Matthews, Gareth. B. 1996. *The Philosophy of Childhood.* Cambridge, MA: Harvard University Press.

Miller, John. 2012. "In Vitro Meat: Power, Authenticity and Vegetarianism." *Journal for Critical Animal Studies* 10(4): 41–63.

Ng, Marie, et al. 2014. "Global, Regional, and National Prevalence of Overweight and Obesity in Children and Adults During 1980–2013: A Systematic Analysis for The Global Burden of Disease Study 2013." *The Lancet* 384(9945): 766–781.

Pechmann et al. 2005. "Impulsive and Self-Conscious: Adolescents' Vulnerability to Advertising and Promotion." *J. Public Policy Mark* 24(2): 202–221.

Plato, and Benjamin Jowett. 1990. *Theaetetus.* Raleigh, N.C: Alex Catalogue.

Pollack, Michael. 2000. *Hearts and Minds: Creative Australians and the Environment.* New South Wales: Hale & Iremonger.

Pratt, Michael W., Joan E. Norris, Susan Alisat, and Elise Bisson. 2013. "Earth Mothers (and Fathers): Examining Generativity and Environmental Concerns in Adolescents and Their Parents." *Journal of Moral Education* 42(1): 12–27.

Roy, Arundhati. 1999. "The Greater Common Good." http://www.narmada.org/gcg/gcg.html.

Samuel, Alexandra. 2015. "Parents: Reject Technology Shame: The Advantages of Helping Kids Learn to Navigate the Digital World, Rather Than Shielding Them from It. *The Atlantic,* November 4, 2015. https://www.theatlantic.com/technology/archive/2015/11/ why-parents-shouldnt-feel-technology-shame/414163/.

SickKids Staff. 2010. "Psychological Effects of Disaster on Children." *About Kids Health,* May 7, 2010. https://www.aboutkidshealth.ca/Article?contentid=302&language=English.

Stokstad, Erik. 2010. "Could Less Meat Mean More Food?" *Science* 327(5967): 810–811.

Terry, Bryant. 2009. *Vegan Soul Kitchen—Fresh, Healthy, and Creative African American Cuisine.* New York: Perseus Book Group.

Twine, Richard. 2017. "A Practice Theory Framework for Understanding Vegan Transition." *Animal Studies Journal* 6(2): 192–224. http://ro.uow.edu.au/asj/vol6/iss2/12.

USDA. 2019. "The Definition of Food Security." https://www.ers.usda.gov/topics/food-nutrition-assistance/food-security-in-the-us/definitions-of-food-security.aspx.

U.S. Global Change Research Program. 2017. "Climate Science Special Report." https:// science2017.globalchange.gov/downloads/CSSR2017_FullReport.pdf.

Valla, Jeffrey M., and Stephen J. Ceci. 2014. "Breadth-Based Models of Women's Underrepresentation in STEM Fields: An Integrative Commentary on Schmidt (2011) and Nye et al. (2012)." *Perspectives on Psychological Science* 9(2): 219–224.

Walker, Polly et al. 2005. "Public Health Implications of Meat Production and Consumption." *Public Health Nutrition* 8(04): 348–356.

White, Randy, and Vicki L. Stoecklin. 2008. "Nurturing Children's Biophilia: Developmentally Appropriate Environmental Education for Young Children." White Hutchinson Leisure & Learning Group. www.live-learn.org/resources/teachers/A_Sense_of_Place_Conference/ Biophilia.pdf.

Wilkinson, Paul et al. 2009. "Public Health Benefits of Strategies to Reduce Greenhouse-Gas Emissions: Household Energy." *The Lancet* 374(9705): 1917–1929.

World Bank. 2010. "World Development Report 2010: Development and Climate Change." http://documents.worldbank.org/curated/en/201001468159913657/World-development-report-2010-development-and-climate-change.

Funneling Fatherhood, Masculinity and the Super-Dad Through a Critique of Mr. Incredible and Ant-Man

Anne Bialowas *and* Ryan Cheek

Introduction: Why Parents Should Talk to Kids About Media

Media provides abundant examples from which to understand patriarchal behaviors and hyper-masculine norms. Superhero films, in particular, contain copiously gendered characters and plotlines to begin conversations with children on issues such as who gets to be a hero—men or women (Coyne, Linder, Rasmussen, Nelson, and Collier 2014, 418). Additionally, there are the nuanced layers of identity when a superhero is also a parent. Two film franchises, *The Incredibles* and *Ant-Man*, exemplify archetypical superhero fathers negotiating their roles as masculine protectors of both family and society. Bob Parr (Mr. Incredible) struggles with the outlawing of his superhero identity and the mundaneness of taking on the role of a traditional provider in a less than exciting career selling insurance. Hank Pym (the first Ant-Man) is a father haunted by the loss of his wife and ends up alienating his daughter in a patronizing attempt to protect her from her mother's fate. Scott Lang (the second Ant-Man) is a previously incarcerated convict motivated by the desire to reconnect with his daughter. All three encounter distinct challenges to their super-dad roles yet are similarly presented through the pernicious imagery of masculinity and stock patriarchal tropes of absentee and overprotective fathers.

Both *The Incredibles* and *Ant Man* are rich media texts to critically analyze fatherhood and masculinity while also being established in popular culture. The original *Incredibles* won the 2005 Academy Award for Best Animated Film and Sound Editing, as well as being nominated for Best Screenplay (Hochwald 2018, 8). In addition to critical acclaim, *The Incredibles* films are also commercially successful with the 2018 release of *Incredibles 2* becoming the best animated opening of all time, the biggest PG-rated opening, and the eighth highest film launch overall (Bahr 2018). According to Disney, "adults made up 31 percent of the audience, families accounted for 57 percent and teens 11 percent" (Bahr 2018). Brad Bird the writer and director of both *Incredibles* said, "These films major in family and minor in superheroes" (Hochwald 2018, 8). This underscores the power of the franchise to mediate children's understanding of family through the superhero genre.

Ant Man (2015), as part of the Marvel Cinematic Universe, does not have quite the same draw as *Incredibles*. However, it did top the $500 million worldwide box office threshold and can be considered a big hit (Mendelson 2015). The sequel, *Ant-Man and the Wasp*, debuted strong with solid reviews and earned $76 million in its opening weekend (Mendelson 2018), while ultimately topping the $600 million worldwide mark (Hughes 2018). Additionally, the franchise is popular among young demographics, as *Ant Man* was nominated for Nickelodeon's Kids' Choice award for favorite movie (*The Hollywood Reporter* 2016).

The impact of our analysis is twofold: first, parents can and should engage their children in critical conversations about the media they consume. We demonstrate the workability of a particular process for such conversations and the necessity of turning children away from passive consumption to active engagement. Second, the representations of fatherhood in the superhero genre support problematic gendered ideologies that promote patriarchal understandings of familial dynamics in general and parenting specifically. Our use of the term "patriarchy" is informed by Fixmer-Oraiz and Wood's (2019) highlighting of patriarchy as the "rule by fathers" which "generally refers to systems of ideology, social structures, and practices created by men, which reflect the values, priorities, and views of men as a group" (265). By analyzing two artifacts with sequels released around Father's Day 2018 showing superheroes actually as fathers, we note the ways dominant cultural understandings of fatherhood are represented in film. It is our goal to empower parents with a strategy for helping children critically analyze the popular media they already consume (superhero films) in a relatable context (family dynamics).

Funneling Strategy: How to Talk with Kids About Media

Real's (1996) concepts of reception theory and co-authoring, which assumes that audiences are active receivers of media who help construct meaning, guides our understanding of media culture. By co-authors we mean that viewers create meaning alongside the creators of media. Co-authors are active participants whose "interaction incorporates both text and viewer to generate meaning and immediate experience" (Real 1996, 44). Parents need to unpack how their children engage and create understanding from media texts. Combined with co-authorship is the assumption of reception theory and the notion that "how we as subjects perceive and interpret text of media culture" can and will vary (Real 1996, 92). It is important to remind parents of co-authorship and reception theory as texts are polysemic and can be interpreted in multiple ways as evidenced by the encoding and decoding model (Hall 1980, 131). This model demonstrates that even if media creators encode a particular meaning into a text (movie, advertisement, song, etc.) that audiences can decode it in a variety of ways.

The strategy based on these theoretical assumptions is for parents to start a critical engagement with their children by asking general questions first that help guide a discussion to more specific critical questions later. This strategy can be thought as a funneling process, proceeding through three layers: content, value, and critique (see Figure 1). Decades of research has demonstrated that talking to your children about media "is consistently one of the most effective ways to reduce the media's negative effect on children" (Coyne et al. 2014, 419). As a result, we propose that our funneling process is a helpful strategy parents may employ to engage their children about the media they consume (see also Austin, Hust, and Kistler 2009; Bauer and Dettore 1997; Nathanson 2001). The purpose of the first layer is to capture a breadth of content and basic understanding of the text. One content question is: Who are some of your favorite characters? Why? As children begin answering these questions, then parents will get an idea what is resonating and connecting with their child. Often a character that will be a favorite is based on humor and seen as funny by a child. A follow up question could guide a parent to ask if the humor is based on farts, poop, or burps and how that could vary as opposed to the humor being based on making jokes at the expense of another character and being a mean person.

The second layer unpacks the types of values and value systems represented. For older children, they may engage with more in-depth questions in this second layer that go beyond content. One question is "What value and/or belief systems are represented? How so?" The many iterations of *Annie* (film, television, cartoon, theater) show an orphan taken in by a billionaire and seemingly having a better and happier life with more material wealth. A child may recognize that wealth seems to be a cultural value and a parent could unpack by asking follow-up questions: How much wealth is needed to be happy? Why do we value monetary possessions over relationships? Character behavior, dialogue, and motivations can be operationalized as a window into the value systems embedded in a media text. With some question planning, a parent can help a child discern and interpret values that media may rely on. Depending on the age of the child, the discussion of values within the text will vary from the parent pointing out values to the child or the child identifying the values themselves.

The third layer and most narrow point of the funnel home in on critique and are specific to questions focused on problematic or positive aspects based on such critical issues of race, gender, sexuality, disability, and class. While this critique layer may have some overlap with values and value systems in layer two, it is important to have a separate layer for these relevant issues. Extending the *Annie* example, parents could begin the process of getting a child to reflect on how media can support societal power structures such as the social service industry and capitalism. Questions could be: How does Miss Hannigan's character make you feel about the orphanage? Is it fair for Warbucks to have a lot of money while others like Annie have almost nothing? Outside of *Annie*, another film a parent could ask about is *Moana* and issues of gender: What did you think about the scene where Moana pointed out to Maui that she was not a princess? Does this seem different from other movies where most of the main female characters are princesses? The depth of questions will depend on the child's age. If a parent does not start with such a specific critique layer question, then the parent can first learn what is resonating and how their child interacts with a text. Over time the funneling phase may increase from general to specific questioning more quickly as a child may be able to first point out problematic and positive aspects based on critical issues like race without the parent providing questions. The questions from this third layer set up a conversation that is ripe for myth-busting with the potential to significantly enhance a child's media literacy and understanding of social justice.

Supplementing the funnel strategy, also informed by Real (1996), is the assumption that people can have a ritual relationship with media as a ritual "denotes activity that has a pattern, is simultaneous with other concerns, and is continuous" (45). Rituals can be annual by watching the televised Super Bowl or daily with social media. Often, people can characterize these rituals as negative as people are "addicted to video games," which has led to the inclusion of "Internet Gaming Disorder" in the DSM-5, recommending conditions for further study. However, a positive force of rituals could be family home movie night or going to the movie theater to see the new release of a film. It was not coincidental that *Incredibles 2* was released on Father's Day weekend as it provided a family activity. This process of creating rituals of joint viewing, while embracing the strategy of funneling questions to create conversation, can make the engagement of media an enjoyable and positive experience between a parent and child. The impact of such engagement has the potential to help children overcome some possible negative effects of a saturated media environment by modeling healthy critical thought about media consumption. For a child, this process of reflecting on the deeper meanings and representations embedded in the media is empowering. First, it turns the unedifying act of passive media consumption into an educational opportunity. Second, it provides them with the intellectual tools to analyze the media they consume when their parents are not around.

Of particular focus for this analysis are representations of masculinity and fatherhood within the context of superhero mediated texts. Hegemonic masculinity can be understood as the "culturally idealized form of masculine character" (Connell 1990, 83). Trujillo (1991) noted five distinguishing features of hegemonic masculinity as "(1) physical force and control, (2) occupational achievement, (3) familial patriarchy, (4) frontiersmanship, and (5) heterosexuality" (291). Examining superheroes in the media reveals, according to Coyne et al. (2014), "that they portray strong gender stereotypes for males" as they "are generally portrayed as strong, assertive, aggressive, fast, powerful, leaders, and as portraying a muscular ideal body type" (418). Analyzing superheroes (male or female) in children cartoons noted a trend insofar as "superheroics" being defined in traditional masculine terms (Baker and Raney 2007, 25). Even parodies of superhero films, which might be expected to question the dominance of hegemonic masculinity, have been noted to "bolster our cultural devotion to a certain type of tough, violent and resourceful masculinity" (Brown 2016, 147). Thus, superhero mediated texts represent a space in our cultural media landscape for children and adults to unpack the meaning of gender.

As noted above, familial patriarchy is connected to masculinity and can be characterized as being the head of the household and breadwinner. Fatherhood is one part of masculinity and research has begun to explore the role of fatherhood in superhero films. Fathers (and father figures) play a central role in many superhero films. As plot and character development devices, fathers motivate superhero protagonists in such ways as playing role models to look up to, evil figures to despise, or someone whose "love must be earned through good deeds and masculine individualism" (Kvaran 2017, 223). According to Kvaran (2017), in superhero films such as *The Dark Knight* (2008) where the father figure is not present in the film, "father figures" such as Alfred "exist to instill in their screen prodigy masculine values and life lessons" (223). Furthermore, many superheroes work to overcome their tragic father-son relationships in these films while any relationship with their mother is absent (Kvaran 2017, 225). Many superheroes in the Marvel Cinematic Universe (MCU), where *Ant-Man* is located, have origin stories motivated by father-hero relationships. For example, Tony Stark in *Iron Man* takes over his father's company after his father's death. His character development is simultaneously motivated and funded by this lost attachment. Likewise, T'Challa inherits the responsibility of being the *Black Panther* from his father and becomes King of Wakanda after T'Chaka dies in a bombing while giving a speech at the United Nations.

Superheroes have begun to be placed within a nuclear family setting as seen by the first *Incredibles* film, which allows gender roles and fatherhood to be further explored. Gillam and Wooden (2008) note that Pixar, and Mr. Incredible in the first film, promotes a new model of masculinity in which Mr. Incredible is shown suffering "from the emotional isolation of the alpha male," but in the process of working to heal his masculinity "must admit his emotional dependence on his wife and children" (4–6). In contrast to past film depictions of male protagonists in action films who fought for their wives and children, Mr. Incredible "faces the need to fight along with them because in *The Incredibles* only the superhero family can find success through reciprocal cooperation and by 'working together'" (Meinel 2014, 188–189). While Gillman and Wooden (2008) do not focus specifically on fatherhood, they do argue that "Pixar consistently promotes a new model of masculinity, one that matures into acceptance of its more traditionally 'feminine' aspects" (4). Even with this potentially new depiction of masculinity, Wooden and Gillam (2014) also note when analyzing the bodies of men in Pixar films that Mr. Incredible demonstrates that "bigger, stronger, and more athletic men and boys are invariably understood as superior to smaller, more delicate or intellectual ones" (32). While there is a diversification of Mr. Incredible as a superhero in the first film, normative views, in terms of family values and masculinity, are upheld as the family still ends up under the leadership of the strong, white male (Jenkins 2013, 214). With the release of *Incredibles 2* (2018), more exploration is needed to unpack the image of father and masculinity in the *Incredibles* film series. Following is an analysis of the *Ant-Man* series and the *Incredible* series, not only critically adding to scant critique of masculinity and fatherhood in superhero films, but also applying our funneling method to help parents and children better engage the media they consume.

The Incredibles *and* Ant-Man: *How to Apply the Funneling Strategy*

This section applies the funneling strategy with the goal of pulling out particular themes of gender and race implicated in each film series' representations of superhero fatherhood. Corresponding with the respective MPAA ratings (PG and PG-13), it is our opinion that conversations about *The Incredibles* and its sequel *The Incredibles 2* are best for young children interested in computer generated films while conversations about *Ant-Man* and its sequel *Ant-Man and the Wasp* are more suitable for older children. However, there is also productive potential in comparing and contrasting the representations in each film to highlight the various implications of understanding fatherhood masculinity.

Starting at the first layer of the funnel are basic plot questions. What is *The Incredibles* about? It is a film series about a superhero family struggling to define itself after the use of superpowers in public is banned. Stripped of the benefit of their powers, the Parr family is representative of an American middle-class heteronormative nuclear family stuck in traditional gender roles. Who are the main characters? Bob Parr (Mr. Incredible) works a tedious job as an insurance adjuster while his wife Helen is a caretaker to their three children: Violet, Dash, and Jack-Jack. What is different between the original and the sequel? The first film centers on Bob's desire to regain purpose by returning to super-heroism no matter the cost to his family. In attempting to invert the gendered dynamic, the sequel sends Helen out of the home as her former super-self Elastigirl while Bob stays home with the kids. What ties the original and sequel together? Both films are primarily about Bob's adjustment to fatherhood and longing for his superhero glory days. When Helen gets to play superhero, Bob becomes a stay-at-home dad who continually fails to maintain household order and stability but lies to his wife to conceal his own incompetence.

What is the *Ant-Man* series about? The eponymously titled film series is a redemption story for two fathers struggling with the loss of their family. Who are the main characters? Hank Pym (the original Ant-Man) is a genius scientist struggling with the loss of his sidekick and wife, Janet van Dyne. In addition to the paternalistic role Hank plays in the life of his daughter Hope, he is a failed mentor for the primary antagonist of the first film, Darren Cross (Yellowjacket). Fearing the loss of his daughter to the same fate of his wife, Hank rebuffs Hope's repeated requests to take on the responsibility of Ant-Man, opting instead to give the suit to a recently released convict, Scott Lang, with whom he has no prior relationship. Scott struggles in his post-incarcerated life to regain the trust of his ex-wife and maintain the love and adoration of his young daughter Cassie.

Moving into the second layer, we begin to narrow the conversation to understand motivations, values, and beliefs embedded in each film. What motivates Mr. Incredible? Bob Parr is a vain patriarchal father whose self-worth is overdetermined by superhero careerism. The character arc of Bob Parr begins with him holding onto past glories often at the expense of his family and ends with him finally settling into the role of the father. In the aftermath of the public backlash against supers (one that Mr. Incredible played an integral part in precipitating), Bob Parr goes to work as an insurance adjuster. His mundane career represents the rarely super, often banal, and occasionally ignoble work of those who play the breadwinner role in the American middle class. At this stage, Bob's primary motivation is securing a paycheck for his family and every so often sticking it to his employer by helping them pierce the bureaucracy of an insurance company.

What challenges does Bob face? His new life physically and psychologically diminishes Bob. After the supers ban, he exhibits symptoms of depression such as weight gain, a somber demeanor, and an irritable disposition. How does Bob's circumstances reflect real life? When folks lose a part of themselves it is understandable they might attempt to recover from that loss through dramatic actions. A father who has lost a career, a spouse/co-parent, or abstractly their sense of purpose may be prone to make life-altering decisions with wide-ranging and unforeseen effects on their family. How does Bob react to the challenges he faces? He takes to sneaking out with Lucius Best (Frozone) to monitor police radio calls and taking secret superhero jobs without his wife's knowledge. How might Bob's behavior be interpreted? These behaviors make sense in the context of a fatherly mid-life crisis trope. Instead of buying a motorcycle or running off with the receptionist, Bob longs for the glory days of being Mr. Incredible. He desires a return to his youth when he could narcissistically bask in the light of the public's adoration for aggressively taking down criminals.

What motivates Hank Pym as a father? In contrast to Mr. Incredible, the two generations of Ant-Man share a desire for redemption after losing their families. Hank Pym is a paternalistic father who is motivated to prevent the spread of his shrinking technology because he lost his wife to the subatomic realm. Emotionally estranged from his daughter, Hank's most prominent act of fatherhood is to play the overprotective dad and rebuff Hope's repeated requests to use the Ant-Man suit to stymie Daren Cross' plans to perfect shrinking technology. Despite Hope being more qualified than Scott Lang, Hank rationalizes his paternalistic behavior as a father saving his daughter from the same fate as her mother. Beyond his biological daughter, Hank's mentor relationship with Darren Cross is a failed surrogate fatherhood that drives the plot of the first movie. Cross is the former protégé of Hank who feels betrayed by his mentor's refusal to share the secrets of Hank's technology with him. Darren's near pathological need to surpass a mentor he believes let him down replicates the "sins of our fathers" trope of a son driven to succeed at any cost because of his father's neglect. A type of traditional fatherhood values is exhibited by Hank's relationship to Hope, Scott, and Darren. He is protective, yet emotionally distant, with his daughter while being neglectful and commandeering with his (not actual) sons.

What motivates Scott Lang as a father? He is a divorced convict motivated by the need to salvage his relationship with his daughter Cassie and ex-wife Peggy Rae. Playing into the archetypical divorced father narrative, Scott has no custodial rights, struggles to make an honest living, and continually meets the negative expectations of his ex-wife and her new husband, Jim Paxton. What does the relationship between Scott and Jim convey about fatherhood? Jim is a perfect, even if predictable, fatherly foil to Scott that drives the plot in a way that laudably avoids the low-hanging fruit of step-dad stereotypes and myths. Despite opposing career choices, the comparison between Jim and Scott reveals they are both good men who make hard and occasionally compromising choices to support their family. There is a narrative equivocation in the treatment of these characters as occupying the same moral ground even though one works within the law to bring down criminals and the other criminally enforces the law through vigilantism. It reflects moral consequentialist values in the tacit acceptance that the intentions and outcomes of one's behavior matter more than the means one uses to get there, which is likely not what most parents' preferred value statement is to their children.

What values are reflected in Bob's parenting? At home, he is a portrayed as a distant husband and neglectful father. For example, he barely pays attention when Helen is trying to tell him about their son Dash's visit to the principal's office for putting a tack on his teacher's chair. Once Bob catches onto the conversation, he undermines Helen's parenting by showing approving interest in the progression of Dash's power instead of reinforcing the message that Dash should not be using his powers in public. How does the sequel reflect these same values? Bob's neglect makes the plot of the second movie possible. Reversing roles, Helen returns to her superhero career to help re-establish credibility for all supers in the court of public opinion. Meanwhile, Bob is left home to take care of the kids. Following the well-tread path of many men-as-caretaker films such as *Three Men and a Baby* (1987), *Mrs. Doubtfire* (1993), and *Daddy Day Care* (2003), *The Incredibles 2* (2018) plays on a common public perception that fathers are generally ill-equipped caretakers. Despite being a father of three, Bob Parr has never learned how to manage his children when his wife is not around. The kids are fighting, the house is in chaos, and the baby is revealing new uncontrolled powers every day. Instead of asking for help, he lies to Helen about how he is adjusting to his new role.

Reaching the third layer of the funnel means turning questions toward critique to understand the implications some representations have on real life. What is the societal impact of Mr. Incredible's parental values? One may easily mistake the plotline of *The Incredibles 2* as a refreshing reflection on the struggles that stay-at-home parents and specifically dads go through in being the primary caregiver of the children. This perspective misses that the narrative relies on the tired trope of the bumbling, incompetent father. Such representations of inept stay-at-home fathers feed patriarchal social values that enable home-confining domestication narratives about mothers (Evans 2015). Essentialist and sexist framings of parenthood can overburden working mothers with unfair expectations and devalue the child-rearing contributions of fathers (Schmitz 2016). The consequences of such logic implicate issues such as custody determinations, family leave policies, and wage discrimination.

What does the relationship between Hank and Scott reveal about fatherhood and masculinity? Hank Pym manipulates Scott into becoming Ant-Man by appealing to his desire to redeem himself and become a hero to his daughter. He infers that Scott has not yet earned Cassie's adoration and claims that becoming Ant-Man would turn Scott Lang into a hero. Hank's success at convincing Scott underscores the difficulty that released convicts have in re-entering society and re-integrating into their families (Naser and La Vigne 2006; Roman and Link 2017). What is a father if not a hero to his daughter? Saving the world is not enough of a motivation for him. Instead, it is the risk of losing his daughter's love and approval that pushes him to follow through with Hank's request. What makes a good father or a good parent? Would Cassie's opinion of Scott diminish if he just merely spent more time with her instead of risking his life and freedom by engaging in vigilante superheroism? The motivations of parenthood are multifaceted, but movies like *Ant-Man* and *The Incredibles* distill our collective beliefs about being parents into relatable plotlines. Active media consumption can help children break apart these narratives and gain a deeper understanding of character motivation as well as the value-statements embedded in their behaviors.

A parent choosing to initiate a conversation about gender roles may ask questions such as which characters are caregivers and why? The plotline of *The Incredibles 2* is made possible by the frequent association of women as the primary caregivers saddled with domestic responsibilities. Without the assumed association of mothering with caregiving, the narrative arc of Mr. Incredible as an inept dad would fail. The broader public falls in line with this essentialist viewpoint, a fact underscored by a Pew Research Center study that found over half of Americans believe moms do a better job of caring for a new baby than dads (Livingston and Bialik 2018). Only 1 percent of respondents felt that dads do a better job of caring for a new baby than moms. Gendered beliefs about caregiving do not arise in a vacuum; they are the result of a patriarchal society where the vast majority of full-time caregivers are still mothers (Lee and Lee 2016, 47). *The Incredibles* and *The Incredibles 2* rely on and reinforce stereotypes about caregiving combined with patriarchal views of the family. Even their powers invoke gendered caricatures of their familial roles: a strong father (Mr. Incredible), flexible mother (Elastigirl), invisible daughter (Violet), speedy son (Dash), and a baby with unknown potential (Jack-Jack).

Segueing into a discussion of sexuality, a parent may ask questions about representations of relationships in superhero films. There is a pervasive heteronormativity in superhero films. Sexual relationships, if presented at all, are constructed to be unambiguously heterosexual in stark contrast with the sexual ambiguity of the comic book origins of the characters (Lendrum 2004, 70). Although there is increasing representation of diverse sexualities in comic books, their analog big screen productions rarely feature LGBTQ characters, and when they do, it is as supporting cast rather than superhero protagonists (Shyminsky 2011, 298). Both *The Incredibles* series and the *Ant-Man* series offer straight protagonists with plotlines that depend on heteronormative assumptions. Stripped of their powers, the Parrs are an exceedingly average heterosexual nuclear family. Although it is a children's movie and does not contain overt sexual imagery, the existence of kids normalizes an assumption of the proper reproductive arrangement of heterosexuality. Other relationships in the films follow suit: Lucius Best has a wife, Violet Parr is interested in boys, and Bob is led astray by Mirage, who is the right-hand woman to the super-villain Syndrome. The narrative coherence of *Ant-Man* is dependent on the brokenness of both Hank and Scott's heterosexual nuclear families. The presumed loss of Hope's mother, Janet van Dyne, is a grounding element of the first film and the thrust of the plot in the second. Additionally, Hope is the object of Scott's affection, a plot element of both the overprotective father and the mentor's daughter. The absence of alternative sexual identities in these films is not abnormal. It is symptomatic of a society still struggling to accept and include non-heteronormative familial arrangements (Carroll 2018, 105; Feil 2014, 97).

In line with the majority of iconic superhero cinematic portrayals that have normalized whiteness, all of the main characters in *The Incredibles* and *Ant-Man* are white (Tyree and Jacobs 2014, 2). People of color are constrained to playing sidekicks and supporting cast. Frozone, Luis, and Dave play into problematic stereotypes about minorities. Frozone is Mr. Incredible's loud and cool (literally because his power is freezing things) black friend. His role is to support the white superhero family, even when that lands him in conflict with his wife. Luis and Dave are career criminals who talk Scott into returning to a life of illicit behavior, a plot element that reinforces the status-quo framings of white criminality. Black and brown criminality is overrepresented and often tied to descriptions of monstrosity and myths of predisposition. In contrast, white criminality is often "constructed as cerebral, sophisticated or as goodness gone awry" (Higgins and Swartz 2018, 98). It is not enough to merely diversify a cast to satisfy a superficial level of multiculturalism by including non-white characters without regard to the roles they play. Substantive representation of ethnically diverse protagonists in superhero films matters, and parents can point out the disparity between portrayals of white folks and people of color in the media their children consume.

In *Ant-Man* there is an opportunity to talk with children about the stereotypes that surround families affected by mass incarceration. Cassie remains in the custody of her mother even after Scott Lang's release from prison. Scott attempting to redeem himself in the eyes of his daughter and ex-wife is a significant portion of the subplot. This arrangement of mothers holding onto custody during a father's incarceration is similarly reflective of reality. An estimated 90 percent of children with incarcerated fathers remain with their mothers, but only 25 percent of children with incarcerated mothers remain with their fathers (National Resource Center on Children & Families of the Incarcerated 2014). This statistic highlights the persistent gender gap in child rearing responsibilities. Additionally, a parent could ask how a child would feel if they were in Cassie's position to encourage them to empathize with children of incarcerated adults or, if applicable, to work through their own experiences of being a child with an incarcerated parent. How has Cassie's relationship with her father changed post-incarceration? What should Scott do to demonstrate his commitment to his family after release from prison? An estimated five million children have experienced the incarceration of a residential parent at some point in their lives (Laub and Haskins 2018). For those lucky enough to avoid exposure to such misfortune, even imperfect representations of incarcerated parents attempting to reconnect with their children can become a vehicle for understanding both their privilege and the societal problem mass incarceration poses for families.

Conclusion: Funneling Strategy Implications and Takeaways

Application of the three-layer funnel process was applied to *The Incredibles* and *Ant Man* series as they provide compelling portrayals of fatherhood in superhero films. Attending to the raced and gendered performances of superheroes can aid children in understanding complex systems of white supremacy and patriarchy. These issues should not be abstracted from their lives; instead, it is important to bring into focus how critical social issues are first shaped in the home. The funneling process is a strategy for parents to help children critically reflect on the media they consume. The depth of questions can vary and develop over time and with respect to the age of the child. Children could be reluctant when first introducing this process so expanding the ritual of media consumption to include a meal or dessert after a film provides a space to discuss. The car ride home from attending the film or any car ride is also an opportunity to begin engagement as children are a captive audience. Also, children may be quiet or just say "I don't know" so beginning to frame questions as either a thumbs up or thumbs down can begin the funneling process. Furthermore, the three-part process, while described as a conversation, can also be adapted as a written journaling process whereby the child can write a response to the funnel questions to be discussed at a later time.

How parents relate to the world, toward each other, and toward their children influences how their children perceive issues of race and gender, along with other critical issues. Teaching children to be critical of the stereotypes and ideologies depicted in the plots of their favorite films will help them to reflect on their own experiences, beliefs, and behaviors. Funneling is an alternative to censorship strategies that prevent children from building a critical toolbox for understanding and processing their media saturated environment. Research notes that children ages two to 11 see an average of 25,600 ads a year and advertising is just one mediated text they encounter (Moses 2014). Censorship is unrealistic as a strategy because parents cannot always control the media their children consume. Additionally, censorship can cause a boomerang effect where children might seek media made taboo by their parents. Learning how to analyze a film is a portable skillset that positively implicates the development of critical thinking in many other situations throughout a person's life.

Fatherhood is a relatable and powerful object of analysis for children. A child's view of their own father may range from archetypical disciplinarians to neglectful absentee parents and everything in between, which makes the representations of different kinds of fathers in media valuable interlocutors for children to make sense of their own unique experiences (Smith 2008, 393). The figure of the super-dad metaphorically represents the adoration some children feel for their father, often seeing them as a hero. However, the figure of the super-dad can also be a fantastical escape from less than desirable patriarchal, neglectful, or missing fathers in a child's life. It is important for children to observe the imperfectness of super-dads in balancing both heroism and fatherhood. Bob Parr, Hank Pym, and Scott Lang are fallible characters who face moral quandaries and make ethically contestable decisions just like all fathers do.

By funneling a conversation about the masculinity, fatherhood, and superhero themes in *The Incredibles* and *Ant-Man* movies, a parent can help a child better process and actively participate in the media they consume. Talking about problematic gender and racial stereotypes with your children can potentially ameliorate some of the worst parts of patriarchy by inculcating critical thinking skills at a young age. Even if a parent does not agree with the specific criticisms outlined in this essay, the funneling strategy promotes media literacy and encourages children to productively challenge the media representations they are inundated with in their everyday lives.

First layer of the funnel: Content

1) What is the film about?
2) Where does the film take place?
3) When does the film take place?
4) What is the historical context of the film?
5) Who are the main characters?
6) Who are the supporting characters?
7) Who are your favorite characters? Why?
8) What narrative elements surprised you?
9) When does the film climax? How do you know?

Second layer of the funnel: Value

1) What value and/or belief systems are represented? How so?
2) When do value and/or belief systems come into conflict?
3) What values do the characters hold and represent?
4) Why do characters behave the way they do?
5) What characters are morally good?
6) What characters are morally evil?

Third layer of the funnel: Critique

1) Who is represented in the film?
2) What stereotypes are inculcated by the film?
3) How does the film deal with issues of race, gender, sexuality, class, ableism, etc.?

WORKS CITED

Austin, Erica Weintraub, Stacey Hust, and Michelle Kistler. 2009. "Powerful Media Tools: Arming Parents with Strategies to Affect Children's Interactions with Commercial Interests." In *Parents and Children Communicating with Society: Managing Relationships Outside of Home*, edited by Thomas J. Socha and Glen H. Stamp, 215–240. New York: Routledge.

Bahr, Lindsey. 2018. "*Incredibles 2* Crushes Animation Record with $180 Million." *AP News*, June 18 2018. https://apnews.com/44c47c96c8f74cedbb101201d8924b37/%27Incredibles-2%27-crushes-animation-record-with-$180-million.

Baker, Kaysee, and Arthur A. Raney. 2007. "Equally Super?: Gender-role Stereotyping of Superheroes in Children's Animated Programs." *Mass Communication & Society* 10(1): 25–41.

Bauer, Karen L., and Ernest Dettore. 1997. "Superhero Play: What's a Teacher to Do?" *Early Childhood Education Journal* 25(1): 17–21.

Brown, Jeffrey A. 2016. "The Superhero Film Parody and Hegemonic Masculinity." *Quarterly Review of Film and Video* 33(2): 131–150.

Carroll, Megan. 2018. "Gay Fathers on the Margins: Race, Class, Martial Status, and Pathway to Parenthood." *Family Relations* 67(1): 104–117.

Connell, Raewyn W. 1990. "An Iron Man: The Body and Some Contradictions of Hegemonic Masculinity." In *Sport, Men, and the Gender Order: Critical Feminist Perspectives,* edited by Michael M. Messner and Don F. Sabo, 83–95. Champaign, IL: Human Kinetics.

Coyne, Sarah M. et al. 2014. "It's a Bird! It's a Plane! It's a Gender Stereotype!: Longitudinal Associations Between Superhero Viewing and Gender Stereotyped Play." *Sex Roles* 70: 416–430.

Evans, John Robert. 2015. "Defining Dad: Media Depiction of the Modern Father in Print Advertising." Master's thesis, Louisiana State University. https://digitalcommons.lsu.edu/gradschool_theses/736.

Feil, Ken. 2014. "From Batman to I Love You, Man: Queer Taste, Vulgarity, and the Bromance as Sensibility and Film Genre." In *Reading the Bromance*, edited by Michael DeAngelis, 93–106. Detroit: Wayne State University Press.

Fixmer-Oraiz, Natalie, and Julia T. Wood. 2019. *Gendered Lives* 13th edition. Boston: Cengage.

Gillam, Ken, and Shannon R. Wooden. 2008. "Post-princess Models of Gender: The New Man in Disney/Pixar." *Journal of Popular Film and Television* 36(1): 2–8.

Hall, Stuart. 1980. "Encoding/Decoding." In *Culture, Media, Language*, edited by Stuart Hall, Dorothy Hobson, Andrew Love, and Paul Willis, 128–138. London: Hutchinson.

Higgins, Ethan M., and Kristin Swartz. 2018. "The Knowing of Monstrosities: Necropower, Spectacular Punishment and Denial." *Critical Criminology* 26(1): 91–106.

Hochwald, Lambeth. 2018. "Incredibles." *Parade*, June 3, 2018.

The Hollywood Reporter Staff. 2016. "Kids' Choice Awards: Adele, Justin Bieber, Star Wars Among Nominees." *Hollywood Reporter*, February 18, 2016. https://www.hollywoodreporter.com/lists/2016-kids-choice-award-nominees-867404/item/favorite-tv-show-2016-kids-867415.

Hughes, Mark. 2018. "*Ant-Man and the Wasp* Will Top $600 Million Box Office." *Forbes*, July 24, 2018. https://www.forbes.com/sites/markhughes/2018/07/24/ant-man-and-the-wasp-will-top-600-million-box-office/#419b7f55908a.

Jenkins, Claire. 2013. "Splitting the Nuclear Family?: The Superhero Family in *The Incredibles* and *Sky High*." In *Ages of Heroes, Eras of Man: Superheroes and the American Experience*, edited by Julian C. Chambliss, William Svitavsky, and Thomas Donaldson, 214–228. Newcastle, UK: Newcastle Cambridge Scholars.

Kvaran, Kara A. 2017. "Super Daddy Issues: Parental Figures, Masculinity, and Superhero Films." *The Journal of Popular Culture* 50(2): 218–238.

Laub, John H, and Ron Haskins. 2018. "Helping Children with Parents in Prison and Children in Foster Care." *Policy Brief, Princeton: The Future of Children*. https://futureofchildren.princeton.edu/sites/futureofchildren/files/media/foc-policy_brief_spring_2018__0.pdf.

Lee, Joyce Y., and Shawna J. Lee. 2016. "Caring Is Masculine: Stay-at-Home Fathers and Masculine Identity." *Psychology of Men & Masculinity* 19(1): 47–58.

Lendrum, Rob. 2004. "Queering Super-Manhood: The Gay Superhero in Contemporary Mainstream Comic Books." *Journal for the Arts, Sciences, and Technology* 2(2): 69–73.

Livingston, Gretchen, and Kristen Bialik. 2018. "7 Facts about U.S. Moms." *Pew Research Center*. May 10, 2018. http://www.pewresearch.org/fact-tank/2018/05/10/facts-about-u-s-mothers/.

Meinel, Dietmar. 2014. "'And when Everyone is Super […] no one will be': The Limits of American Exceptionalism in *The Incredibles*." *European Journal of American Culture* 33(3): 181–194.

Mendelson, Scott. 2015. "Box Office: *Ant Man* Tops $500 Million Worldwide. Can Marvel Be Saved?" *Forbes*, October 29, 2015. https://www.forbes.com/sites/scottmendelson/2015/10/29/box-office-ant-man-tops-500-million-worldwide-can-marvel-be-saved/#5ab13b2a6c7e.

Mendelson, Scott. 2018. "Box Office: *Ant-Man and the Wasp* Nabs Front-Loaded $76M Debut." *Forbes*, July 8, 2018. https://www.forbes.com/sites/scottmendelson/2018/07/08/box-office-ant-man-and-the-wasp-nabs-smallest-mcu-marvel-paul-rudd-evangeline-lilly/#2d212a0043ba.

Moses, Lucia. 2014. "A Look at Kids' Exposure to Ads." *Ad Week*, March 11, 2014. https://www.adweek.com/digital/look-kids-exposure-ads-156191/.

Naser, Rebecca L. and Nancy La Vigne. 2006. "Family Support in the Prisoner Reentry Process." *Journal of Offender Rehabilitation* 43(1): 93–106.

Nathanson, Amy I. 2001. "Mediation of Children's Television Viewing: Working Toward Conceptual Clarity and Common Understanding." In *Communication Yearbook* Vol. 25, edited by William Gudykunst, 115–151. Mahwah, NJ: Lawrence Erlbaum.

National Resource Center on Children & Families of the Incarcerated. 2014. "Children and Families of the Incarcerated Fact Sheet." Camden, NJ: Rutgers University. https://nrccfi.camden.rutgers.edu/files/nrccfi-fact-sheet-2014.pdf.

Real, Michael. 1996. *Exploring Media Culture: A Guide*. Thousand Oaks, CA: Sage.

Roman, Caterina G., and Nathan W. Link. 2017. "Community Reintegration Among Prisoners with Child Support Obligations: An Examination of Debt, Needs, and Service Receipt." *Criminal Justice Policy Review* 28(9): 896–917.

Schmitz, Rachel M. 2016. "Constructing Men as Fathers: A Content Analysis of Formulations of Fatherhood in Parenting Magazines." *Journal of Men's Studies* 24(1): 3–23.

Shyminsky, Neil. 2011. "'Gay Sidekicks' Queer Anxiety and the Narrative Straightening of the Superhero." *Men and Masculinities* 14(3): 288–308.

Smith, Debra C. 2008. "Critiquing Reality-Based Televisual Black Fatherhood: A Critical Analysis of *Run's House* and *Snoop Dogg's Father Hood*." *Critical Studies in Media Communication* 25(4): 393–412.

Trujillo, Nick. 1991. "Hegemonic Masculinity on the Mound: Media Representations of Nolan Ryan and American Sports Culture." *Critics Studies in Mass Communication* 8(3): 290–308.

Tyree, Tia C. M., and Liezille J. Jacobs. 2014. "Can You Save Me? Black Male Superheroes in Film." *Spectrum: A Journal on Black Men* 3(1): 1–24.

Wooden, Shannon R. and K. Gillam. 2014. *Pixar's Boy Stories: Masculinity in a Postmodern Age*. Lanham, MD: Rowman & Littlefield.

Social Media and the Activist Child

MIKE CATELLO

Nikolas Cruz killed 17 high schoolers at Marjory Stoneman Douglas High School in Parkland, Florida, on Valentine's Day 2018. Fourteen others were shot and survived (Chuck, Johnson, and Siemaszko 2018). Marjory Stoneman Douglas students David Hogg and Emma González led gun control campaigns and in doing so both became national household names. As newspapers, television, and radio descended on Parkland, the shootings' survivors turned to social media to express outrage, rally support, and publicize demonstrations and speeches. Brendan Duff, a graduate of the school, returned from college to manage the movement's digital operations. Duff told NPR, "People all over the country want to help. Social media is honestly the best way to reach not only everyone in this country I think, but definitely this generation" (Mann 2018). Teenagers were commanding a new movement.

Duff's assessment proves true for much contemporary youth activism. The Parkland survivors are among a generation of "digital natives," post-millennial young people born into Internet and social media technologies such as chat, video, and messaging applications like Facebook, Instagram, Snapchat, YouTube, and Twitter. Social media has transformed how young people interact with a "hyper-connected world" (Cigelske 2015, 14). This generation uses social media for entertainment, communication, and information. Young activists, like the Parkland students, use social media to support causes and protest injustices.

Activism channeled through social media is often called "hashtag activism." #OccupyWallStreet in 2011 was one of the first movements to employ social media (Hill 2014). Eugene Scott (2018) from the *Washington Post* observes that social media activists are often motivated by the same injustices and oppressions former generations were. They just use different methods. Tim Cigelske (2018) concedes that the tools of activism in the past sometimes meant imprisonment, physical abuse, or death, while "today's activists, [...] work for justice behind the safety of screens," yet he qualifies that these are just the tools available to young activists (14). Young people have realized that social media is often the best and sometimes only way to deliver a message or instigate change in what a young person may describe as a disinterested adult world.

Because of the schism between a young person's vision and the adult's complacency, social media activism exposes the technological divide between digital natives and "digital immigrants," their parents. Social media penetrates young people's lives in ways traditional media does not. Radio and television messages can be controlled by parents. Parents often answer telephone calls on landlines to the home, and parents can overhear phone conversations. Pre-Internet activists had to hit the streets, which meant leaving one's home. They could be physically injured, caught on camera, and even jailed. Their identities could be exposed in a newspaper or on television. Virtual activism, conversely, affords young people the opportunity to participate from a cell phone or computer. Young people—explorative, creative, opinionated, and curious—are apt to be attracted to the vitality of social media activism, even if on the fringes. Parents, though, may not know their child is an activist. Teens, often short-sighted, must understand the implications of their online activism, and while maybe counterintuitive, children want and expect their parents to be involved (Taylor 2013). Parents can help their child pursue causes in a healthy way by discussing their child's online activism with them and then partnering with their child to cultivate their activism. Being an involved parent benefits the child, the parent, and the child's social media activism.

Before starting a conversation with their child, parents should have a working definition of activist, appreciate why young people are drawn to activism, and then understand how activists exploit social media. Michelle Passon, winner of the Jewish Community Relation Council's 2012 Activist Award, asserts that "the core of activism is caring for and nurturing family and […] extended family through […] community" (Henoch n.d.). Brian Martin (2007) defines activism more specifically as an "action on behalf of a cause, action that goes beyond what is conventional or routine" (19–27). Activism includes picketing, speeches, marches, ignoring cultural customs, sit-ins, fasting, and even violence (Martin 2007, 19–27). Activism is not inherently good or bad nor does it sit neatly in left or right politics (Martin 2007, 19–27).

Volunteerism is sometimes confused with activism. While one may volunteer for a charity or even an activist organization, volunteering and activism are different as activists have larger ideals and are seeking societal changes by working on a particular cause (Taib n.d., 2). Not all activists play the same role in an organization or movement. Some activists provide direct action, while others perform supportive and administrative tasks like answering emails or writing content. Mohamed Imran Mohamed Taib (n.d.) identifies two characteristics of all activists. First, activists have an interest in people and advocate "for those who suffer as a result of social processes" (Taib n.d., 4). Secondly, activists have a "sense of historical mission" by acknowledging the past's impact on present conditions and the belief that present action can alter the future (Taib n.d., 3). Martin (2007) submits that activists challenge existing policy for the betterment of society and do not seek power themselves (19–27). Activists commonly join or form groups that often become part of broader social movements (Martin 2007, 19–27).

Young people are sometimes provoked to activism after experiencing a horrific event, like the Parkland shootings. Others are impacted directly or indirectly by oppression and marginalization. Some are inspired simply to act for the general betterment of society. In its 2014 *Conference Report and Policy Recommendations*, the Columbia Global Policy Initiative in collaboration with The Office of the United Nations Secretary General's Envoy on Youth explains that young people are "less likely to be involved in governance and decision-making processes" (Offerdahl, Evangelides, and Powers 2014, 6). Additionally, "youth are also likely to face marginalization due to their membership in excluded demographic groups, including: women, indigenous, disabled, LGBTQI, refugee, ethnic minority, migrant, and economically impoverished" (Offerdahl, Evangelides, and Powers 2014, 6). Such marginalization, the report concludes, degrades their human rights (Offerdahl, Evangelides, and Powers 2014, 6). Consequently, young people often seek safety in social activist organizations because young people see adults and parents as indifferent to their needs (Akiva et al 2017, 20). Rebecca de Schweinitz, author of *If We Could Change the World: Young People and America's Long Struggle for Racial Equality*, opines that apathy from adults and the government provoked young people's 2018 anti-gun and gun violence demonstrations (UNC Press Blog 2018). A student interviewed by NPR after the Parkland shootings confirms de Schweinitz's observation: "Our kids are dying and no one is doing anything about it" (Mann 2018). National Walk Out Day on March 24, 2018, when students from more than 2800 schools advocated for harsher gun control legislation, was the collective youth answer to decades of adults failing to take action.

The Parkland students employed many of the same methods of activism as their predecessors: speeches, protests, demonstrations, and political demands to change laws. The student activists' application of social media, though, illustrates the value Internet technology has for today's young activists. As of February 2018 Emma Gonzalez had more than 300,000 Twitter followers and Cameron Kasky, David Hogg, and Sarah Chadwick each had over 100,000 (Newcomb 2018). Social media has advantages traditional activist methods do not, and young activists utilize social media in ingenious ways—all from their phones or computers and often without their parents' knowledge or consent.

Young people can directly influence the media and manage the message through social media. Writers, editors, and publishers of media content shape stories. They set a story's context and determine which and how quotations are used. Media often has political angles that sway a story's presentation. Social media activists, though, cut through the established news hierarchy and upturn the power structure (Merchant 2016). The activist is the author and editor of their own message and can respond directly to those considered to be in authority. Dinesh D'Souza, political commentator and writer, suggested sarcastically after Florida lawmakers voted down a bill that banned assault weapons that this was the "worst news [for the Parkland students] since their parents told them to get summer jobs" (Newcomb 2018). Sarah Chadwick, a Parkland student activist, retorted on Twitter, "Actually for me the worst news I got was that 17 people died in my school" (Newcomb 2018). D'Souza's comment was not insulated from Chadwick's counter-argument by his prestige or editorial boards. Chadwick injected her rejoinder directly into his Twitter feed, as if she confronted D'Souza at his home or office. Her sharp reaction was personal and unaltered. Generally, such an immediate response to a member of the intellectual elite is not possible through conventional media.

Also, social media activists share images and video that the mainstream media overlooks or that government officials suppress. New York University Professor Nicholas Mirzoeff calls this "visual activism" (Funnel 2018). According to Mirzoeff visual activism works because it "catalyses real life social activism through social media" (Funnel 2018). Leading up to the Arab Spring Egyptian activists uploaded images to Facebook and Twitter of citizens being beaten by government authorities. A Facebook page, "We Are All Khaled Said," was created after Said was murdered by Egyptian police in 2010 following Said's posting of a video online exposing police corruption. The official autopsy report concluded that Said choked to death on drugs, but a viral video of his beaten face on the Internet contradicted the report. The Facebook page attracted over 800,000 members "as Egyptians increasingly used social networking platforms to produce and consume political content, organize protests, stay connected, and spread word to others about the abuses of the Mubarak regime" (Browning 2013, 65). In America, Mirzoeff claims Black Lives Matter's (BLM) use "of images of black oppression to continually and systematically confront US authorities, […] draws on the successful experience of the civil rights movement of the 1960s" (Funnel 2018). This kind of imagery punctuates incidents or conditions, often igniting support from the general public.

Marginalized youth like transgender and women find kinship and a voice through social media. Eli Erlick, a transgender activist, grew up in rural California in a town hostile to transgenderism. This left her isolated and bullied by classmates. She started Trans Student Educational Resources (TSER), an online resource for transgendered young people (Erlick 2018, 73). Erlick (2018) decided early that TSER outreach would be through social media and the Internet because, according to Erlick, these "are frequently the only options these youth have for connecting with the community" (74). Eve Shapiro (2004) corroborates Erlick's sentiments. Shapiro (2004) explains that the medical community typically advises trans children to lie low after initially going trans. The online community, however, encourages recent trans to "self-determine critically rather than remain reliant on the cisgender medical constructions of transness" (Shapiro 2004, 170).

Women activists have used social media to expose sexual assault and demand rights and freedom. Three hundred people joined a Walk a Mile organized by Karen Eliofor and Abigail Smith to protest sexual assault on their small Catholic Saint Anselm College campus in New Hampshire (Cigelske 2015, 17). Steven DiSalvo, the university's president, reflected about the students' strategy: "They realized they could use social media and be as effective or more effective in reaching people their age and have this incredible call to action[. ...] I don't think this would happen at the scale it did if they hadn't used social media to advance their cause" (Cigelske 2015, 17). At Joseph-François Perrault High School in Quebec, teen girls started a Facebook group called Les Carrés Jaunes to protest what they call a "restrictive and sexist" school dress code. They appended yellow squares to their clothes. Their goal is to attain the right to forego bras. A student who started the group told *Yahoo Lifestyle*, "We launched the movement to fight the culture of rape and hypersexualization. We want the equality of men and women both in our treatment and how the world views our bodies" (Solé 2018). These examples illustrate the wide range of activism executed by young people through social media. Parents, though, may be unaware of their child's online activism because parents know little about their child's online interests generally.

According to a study by McAfee, the Internet security company, 25 percent of parents cannot keep up with their child's online life, and 70 percent of teens withhold most of their online activity from their parents (Field 2016, 158). Lacking technical confidence and competency, parents are less willing to intervene (Taylor 2013). Jim Taylor (2012) in *Psychology Today* argues that with social media and other innovations such as viral marketing and the pervasiveness of smart phones, "popular culture is now an almost inescapable presence in your children's lives, enabling it to influence [children] more often, more directly, and more powerfully than at any time in the past." Cell phones and other devices distract both children and their parents from "engaging in positive, nurturing conversations" (Byrum 2015). The technological divide can unsettle the family structure, affecting children especially, if parents are uninvolved.

Taylor (2013) outlines four negative outcomes of this new family dynamic. First, families cannot build strong or enduring relationships. Secondly, children do not trust or feel as much love from their parents. Thirdly, because there is less sharing, parents know less about what their children are doing and therefore have less influence on them. Lastly, the parent's model of emotional and mental health, which transfers positive values to the child, is weakened. The World Economic Forum validates Taylor's conclusions. The Forum maintains that technology has "the power to disrupt personal relationships[, …] deliver uninvited content[, … and impact] the well-being of children and the strength and social cohesion of families" (Byrum 2015). Lower-income families exhibit a greater rift between parents and children because parents in these families tend not to have the same digital literacy as those from higher-income families (Byrum 2015). In addition to instability within the family dynamic, parents need to consider the external dangers that confront online activists, largely without the activist's knowledge.

A young person may feel insulated within the confines of a social media platform, and children, enmeshed in the energy of their opinions and online activism, often act without self-censorship or restraint. This can get them into trouble. Social media activists attract attention from government officials and police. State authorities, including those in the United States, deploy surveillance programs against social media and take action against anyone authorities believe may be a "threat to the state," however that is defined. Social Media Monitoring Software (SMMS) such as XI Social Discovery, Geofeedia, Dataminr, Dunami, and SocioSpyder interfaces with social media platforms and is used by corporations, politicians, the military, the government, and law enforcement (McCullough 2016). The software allows users to search for specific hashtags like #BlackLivesMatter and #PoliceBrutality.

Geofeedia has been used widely by law enforcement to monitor protestors. A 2016 American Civil Liberties Union (ACLU) report shows that Facebook, Twitter, and Instagram provided user data to Geofeedia, which then marketed the data to police. A Geofeedia email promoted that its product "covered Ferguson/Mike Brown nationally with great success" (Powers 2016). Nicole Ozer (2016), the Technology and Civil Liberties Director of the California ACLU, reported that San Jose Police used Geofeedia to monitor South Asian, Muslim, and Sikh protestors. Also, Geofeedia assisted Baltimore police after the Freddie Gray killing and jury acquittal. After gathering images of protestors from their social media profiles, Geofeedia ran the images through their facial recognition database and provided the protestors' identities to police (Powers 2016).

Geofeedia does not have a monopoly on the SMMS market. Kimberly McCullough (2016), the Legislative Director of the ACLU of Oregon, reported that the Oregon Department of Justice used a product called Digital Stakeout "to surveil people who used over 30 hashtags on social media, including

#BlackLivesMatter and #FuckThePolice." In 2016 the ACLU reported that another product, MediaSonar, monitored #BlackLivesMatter, #DontShoot, #ImUnarmed, #PoliceBrutality, #ItsTimeForChange (Powers 2016).

Monitoring often results in arrests. Human Rights Watch (2018) chronicles the arrest of Abdallahi Salem Ould Yali by Mauritanian authorities on January 24, 2018. Abdallahi Salem Ould Yali used social media to urge the Haratines, a group descended from slaves that comprises more than one-third of the Mauritanian population, "to resist discrimination and demand their rights." Under cybercrime and counterterrorism laws, authorities accused Abdallahi Salem Ould Yali of "incitement to racial hatred and violence" (Human Rights Watch 2018). Egyptian activist, Amal Fathy, was arrested for posting a video online accusing her government of "failing to protect women against sexual harassment" (Cullinane 2018). An Egyptian official justified her arrest: "she is accused and wanted for arrest in relation to complaints accusing her of insulting the Egyptian state, by publishing a posting that contained swearing and defamation against Egypt" (Cullinane 2018). IFEX (2018), the Global Network Defending and Promoting Free Expression, reported that authorities in Burkina Faso, a West African nation, arrested Naim Toure in June 2018, accusing him of "inciting the armed forces to revolt" after he condemned the country's security forces. In the United States, Robert Peralta, a San Francisco activist, responded to a Facebook post from another activist who was recounting his beating by police. Peralta posted, "Wow, brother they wanna hit our general. It's time to strike back. Let's burn this motherfucker's house down" (Levin 2017). Police issued an arrest warrant, and Peralta was subsequently detained (Levin 2017).

The Arab Spring saw the greatest concerted effort across the Middle East to suppress online revolutionary voices. Threatened by dissidents' use of social media, governments used technology, often created by Western nations, to stifle opposition and "unplug democracy" (Browning 2013, 76). Following the success of the We Are All Khaled Said Facebook page and the use of Twitter to organize protests, Hosni Mubarak's government blocked access to Facebook, Twitter, among other social media platforms on January 25, 2011 (Browning 2013, 69). This reduced Internet traffic from Egypt by 90 percent (Ritchel 2011). The Assad regime took a similar course of action to quash anti-government communication in Syria (Browning 2013, 79). Knowing that they have a responsibility to maintain the family unit and protect their children, concerned and often well-intentioned parents sometimes use similar surveillance tactics against their children.

According to a Pew Research Center's 2016 study, 39 percent of parents use "controls for blocking, filtering or monitoring their teen's online activities" (Anderson 2016). The same study reveals that 48 percent of parents know their child's email account password, 43 percent know their child's cell phone password, and 35 percent know the password of one of their child's social media accounts (Anderson 2016). Nick Wingfield (2016) in *The New York Times* admits that monitoring and tracking is the natural result of social and cultural changes where so much of a child's life is spent using technology. Most people disapprove of governmental and corporate spying, but when they "are presented with the tools and opportunity to play Big Brother with others in their family, it's tough for some to resist" (Wingfield 2016). These methods, though, can backfire.

The human perception of privacy begins early in development. Jason Nolan, Associate Professor and Director of Responsive Ecologies Lab and Experimental Design and Generative Environments Lab, explains that "children as young as 18 months are aware they are being watched and require privacy and autonomy" (Bisby 2018). Danah Boyd observes that as a person matures the parental "watching" may feel more like stalking "because the sharing of information isn't a mutual sign of respect but a process of surveillance" (Wingfield 2016). Consequently, children may never learn to value privacy if their privacy is not respected (Bisby 2018). Many child psychologists and media experts contend that a "lack of privacy can undermine trust, promote secrecy and hinder [a child's] ability to assess risk and develop independence" (Bisby 2018). Boyd offers examples of teens sharing passwords with their boyfriends or girlfriends, which can be dangerous in unhealthy relationships (Wingfield 2016). Nolan predicts that as businesses, government, and parents participate in surveillance, "we are faced with a generation who will be less independent in their thinking, relying on the external authority of governments and corporations, and more easily manipulated by public opinion" (Bisby 2018). Parents should not resort to clandestine methods but instead rely on traditional approaches that parents have always practiced with their children.

Parents of social media activists, specifically, should start simply by talking to their child and focusing on family and values, or what Elissa Strauss (2018) qualifies as "lead[ing] with values rather than issues." Because teen activism is often emotional, Alexandra Styron, a teacher at Hunters College and who has written about activism, recommends that parents start a discussion by saying, "Instead of imposing a sense of anger or activism, let's talk about what we care about as a family" (Strauss 2018). Only then, Styron concludes, should parents talk to their children about "what can we do to make the world a better place" (Strauss 2018). This strategy serves the parent and the child. First, it affords the digital immigrant an opening to learning about their child's online activism. Secondly, young activists often only understand societal problems abstractly. By contextualizing digital activism within family values, the young activist's online passion is connected with their core values, something more concrete and familiar. The child's online identity, then, is more likely to be authentic and their online activism to be genuine.

Having a centered identity fortifies the child against social media's tendency to foster identity and personality confusion. Some studies indicate social media adversely impacts identity creation by forming a "fragmented self-image from the struggle with which teenagers are faced to integrate the varied online experiences of self-exploration into a cohesive picture of self" (Patrikakou 2016, 13). Each social media platform is like a unique culture, containing its own ethos, linguistic, and behavioral conventions. A person may adapt their personality to the expectations of the social media platform: how they represent themselves through language, videos, pictures, and the opinions they express. Tim Rayner (2012a), Honorary Research Associate in Philosophy at the University of Sydney, cautions that "we must guard against the danger that our tweets, posts, and shares become mere performances, a play or masks that is disconnected from our authentic self." By using social media to express their authentic selves, or what Rayner (2012b) calls their "inner awesome," young activists are more likely to contribute meaningfully rather than through ephemeral "likes" because the activism is not a means to popularity. Now, the young activist is ready to act.

Many activists maintain that online activism can be effective only if it is paired with conventional activism. Paula White (2017) implores parents to help their teens shift from the online space to the "streets" by coming up with a plan "for translating emotion into action." Caroline Paul (2018) advises parents to not just talk to their children but also "teach kids how to respond, with tactics that range from volunteering and raising money to boycotting and marching." White and Samantha McGarry recommend starting locally through volunteer work and moving onto other forms of activism. For example, a young person can volunteer to tutor younger children in reading, then meet with a school official to discuss the school district's reading programs, and eventually propose budgetary changes to the school board (White 2017). Lastly, parents can help their children find mentors and join positive activist organizations.

While young people escape to social media, in part, to separate from their parents and develop as individuals, social media activism is serious business. Children need their space away from their parents, but parents must recognize when their child may be participating in activism and become involved. Parents will regain intimacy with their child, and their child, in turn, will trust and confide in their parents. Consequently, children will feel safer and more confident in their online experience. Not only will the child's online interactions be more prudent, but their social activist choices will be healthier and more closely tied to the child's values. Social activism profits because it has authentic participation. Parents should be proud of their socially engaged and technologically proficient child. Parents just need to keep pace.

Works Cited

Akiva, Thomas et al. 2017. "Reasons Youth Engage in Activism Programs: Social Justice or Sanctuary." *Journal of Applied Psychology* 53: 20–30.

Anderson, Monica. 2016. "Parents, Teens and Digital Monitoring." *Pew Research Center*, January 7, 2016. http://www.pewinternet.org/2016/01/07/parents-teens-and-digital-monitoring/.

Bisby, Adam. 2018. "When Does Protecting Your Child Become an Invasion of Privacy?" *The Global Mail*, May 11, 2018. https://www.theglobeandmail.com/life/parenting/when-does-protecting-your-child-become-invasion-of-privacy/article17041213/.

Browning, John G. 2013. "Democracy Unplugged: Social Media, Regime Change, and Governmental Response in the Arab Spring." *Michigan State International Law Review* 21(1): 63–86.

Byrum, Greta. 2015. "Has Technology Changed America's Families?" *World Economic Forum*, May 1, 2015. https://www.weforum.org/agenda/2015/05/how-has-technology-changed-americas-families/.

Chuck, Elizabeth, Alex Jonson, and Corky Siemaszko. 2018. "17 Killed in Mass Shooting at High School in Parkland, Florida." *NBC News*, February 15, 2018. https://www.nbcnews.com/news/us-news/police-respond-shooting-parkland-florida-high-school-n848101.

Cigelske, Tim. 2015. "Instant Activism." *U.S. Catholic* 80(9): 12–17.

Cullinane, Susannah. 2018. "Egyptian Activist Detained Over Social Media Video Post Criticizing Government." *CNN*, May 11, 2018. https://www.cnn.com/2018/05/11/middleeast/egypt-amal-fathy-activist-detained/index.html.

Dino. 2018. "Rebecca de Schweinitz: Youth Activism, Yesterday and Today." *UNC Press Blog*, February 23, 2018. https://uncpressblog.com/2018/02/23/rebecca-de-schweinitz-youth-activism-yesterday-and-today/Erlick, Eli. 2018. "Trans Youth Activism on the Internet." *A Journal of Women Studies* 39(1): 73–92.

Field, Genevieve. n.d. "Parenting Against the Internet: What Are Our Kids Doing Online, and How Can We Protect Them from Danger?" *Real Simple*. https://www.realsimple.com/work-life/technology/safety-family/internet-safety-for-kids.

Funnell, Anthony. 2017. "From Slacktivism to 'Feel-Good' Protests, Activism Is Broken: Here's How to Fix It." *ABC News*, October 25, 2017. https://www.abc.net.au/news/2017–10–25/activism-is-broken-heres-how-we-fix-it/9077372.

Henoch, Vivian. 2012. "What It Means to Be a Social Activist." *My Jewish Detroit*, September 1, 2018. http://myjewishdetroit.org/2012/05/what-it-means-to-be-a-social-activist/.

Hill, Alex. 2014. "Hashtag Activism: Is It #Effective?" *Law Street*, June 19, 2014. https://lawstreetmedia.com/issues/technology/hashtag-activism-effective/.

Human Rights Watch. 2018. "Mauritania: Activist Arrested for Social Media Posts." February 10, 2018. https://www.hrw.org/news/2018/02/10/mauritania-activist-arrested-social-media-posts.

Levin, Sam. 2017. "Jailed for a Facebook Post: How US Police Target Critics with Arrest and Prosecution." *The Guardian*, May 18, 2018. https://www.theguardian.com/us-news/2017/may/18/facebook-comments-arrest-prosecution.

Mann, Brian. 2018. "Students Who Lived Through Florida Shooting Turn Rage into Activism." *NPR*, https://www.npr.org/2018/02/18/586958556/student-activists-who-lived-through-florida-shooting-plan-march-on-washington.

Martin, Brian. 2007. "Activism, Social and Political." In *Encyclopedia of Activism and Social Justice,* edited by Gary Anderson and Kathryn G. Herr, 19–27. Thousand Oaks, CA : Sage.

McCollough, Kimberly. 2016. "#BlackLivesMatter Tracked by Oregon DOJ with Social Media Monitoring Software." *ACLU of Oregon*, May 4, 2016. https://www.aclu-or.org/en/news/blacklivesmatter-tracked-oregon-doj-social-media-monitoring-software.

McGarry, Samantha. n.d. "How to Raise an Activist Kid: 7 Things Parents Can Do." https://grownandflown.com/raise-activist-kid-7-things/.

Media Foundation for West Africa. 2018. "Burkina Faso Authorities Arrest Activist for Critical Social Media Posting." June 22, 2018. https://www.ifex.org/burkina_faso/2018/06/23/activist-arrested/.

Merchant, Aashka. 2016. "Youth Activists: A Force to Be Reckoned With." *Huffington Post*, February 29, 2016. https://www.huffingtonpost.com/the-youth-assembly-at-the-united-nations/youth-activists-a-force-t_b_9348276.html.

Morozov, Evgeny. 2012. *The Net Delusion: The Dark Side of Internet Freedom.* Philadelphia: Perseus Books Group.

Newcomb, Melissa. 2018. "How Parkland's Social Media-Savvy Teens Took Back the Internet—and the Gun Control Debate." *NBC News*, February 22, 2018. https://www.nbcnews.com/tech/tech-news/how-parkland-students-are-using-social-media-keep-gun-control-n850251.

Offerdahl, Kate, Alicia Evangelides, and Maggie Powers. 2014. "Overcoming Youth Marginalization: Conference Report and Policy Recommendation." *United Nations.* http://www.un.org/youthenvoy/wp-content/uploads/2014/10/Columbia-Youth-Report-FINAL_26-July-2014.pdf.

Ozer, Nicole. 2016. "Police Use of Social Media Surveillance Software Is Escalating, and Activists Are in the Digital Crosshairs." *ACLU*, September 22, 2016. https://www.aclu.org/blog/privacy-technology/surveillance-technologies/police-use-social-media-surveillance-software.

Patrikakou, Eva A. 2016. "Parent Involvement, Technology, and Media: Now What?" *School Community Journal* 26(2): 9–24.

Paul, Caroline. 2018. "Activism Isn't Just for Adults and Teens. We Need to Teach Younger Kids to Be Activists, Too." *TED.* https://ideas.ted.com/activism-isnt-just-for-adults-and-teens-we-need-to-teach-younger-kids-to-be-activists-too/.

Powers, Benjamin. 2016. "How Police Used Social Media to Track and Target Activists of Color." *Complex*, November 17, 2016. https://www.complex.com/life/2016/11/police-surveillance-activists-people-of-color.

Rayner, Tim. 2012a. "Foucault and Social Media: I Tweet, Therefore I Become." *Philosophy for Change*, July 4, 2012. https://philosophyforchange.wordpress.com/2012/07/04/foucault-and-social-media-i-tweet-therefore-i-become/.

Rayner, Tim. 2012b. "Foucault and Social Media: The Call of the Crowd." *Philosophy for Change*, July 26, 2012. https://philosophyforchange.wordpress.com/2012/07/26/foucault-and-social-media-the-call-of-the-crowd/.

Richtel, Matt. 2011. "Egypt Cuts Off Most Internet and Cell Service." *New York Times*, January 28, 2011. https://www.nytimes.com/2011/01/29/technology/internet/29cutoff.html.

Scott, Eugene. 2018. "#NationalWalkoutDay Protesters Continued a Long History of Youth Activism." *Washington Post*, March 15, 2018. https://www.washingtonpost.com/news/the-fix/wp/2018/03/15/nationalwalkoutday-activists-continued-a-long-history-of-youth-activism/?utm_term=.6867780a792e.

Shaprio, Eve. 2004. "'Trans'cending Barriers: Transgender Organizing on the Internet." *Journal of Gay & Lesbian Social Services* 16(3–4): 165–179.

Solé, Elise. 2018. "Teens Protest School Dress Code for the Right to Go Braless." *Yahoo Lifestyle*, April 10, 2018. https://www.google.com/amp/s/www.yahoo.com/amphtml/lifestyle/teens-protest-school-dress-code-right-go-braless-013339549.html.

Strauss, Elissa. 2018. "Should Children Be Activists?" *CNN*, October 18, 2018. https://www.cnn.com/2018/10/18/health/child-activism-parenting-strauss/index.html.

Taib, Mohamed Imran Mohamed. n.d. "(de)Meaning of Social Activism." *The Reading Group.* http://www.thereadinggroup.sg/articles.htm#articles01.

Taylor, Jim. 2012. "Parenting: Who Is More Powerful: Technology or Parents?" *Psychology Today*, August 9, 2012. https://www.psychologytoday.com/us/blog/the-power-prime/201208/parenting-who-is-more-powerful-technology-or-parents.

Taylor, Jim. 2013. "Is Technology Creating a Family Divide?" *Psychology Today*, March 13, 2018. https://www.psychologytoday.com/us/blog/the-power-prime/201303/is-technology-creating-family-divide.

White, Paula. 2017. "Children & Activism in 2017: Parents Help Kids Do It Right." *Psychology Today*, January 23, 2017. https://www.psychologytoday.com/us/blog/shape-parenting/201701/children-activism-in-2017-parents-help-kids-do-it-right.

Wingfield, Nick. 2016. "Should You Spy on Your Kids?" *The New York Times*, November 9, 2016. https://www.nytimes.com/2016/11/10/style/family-digital-surveillance-tracking-smartphones.html.

Part Two

Curious George Explores the Diaspora

Postcolonial Children's Literary Criticism

Rae Lynn Schwartz-DuPre

In 2016, Curious George fans around the globe celebrated the 75th anniversary of their curious monkey and paid tribute to the myriad ways he has entered their hearts and enriched their lives (Dirda 2016). Classrooms for children of all ages lauded the broad circulation and celebrated the *Curious George* books. For instance, as early as 1953, the New York Public Library Superintendent of Children's Work reported that "all of the Curious George books have proved 'naturals' for the most handicapped (mentally and physically) of the deaf children" (Ross 1953). John A. Miller (1971), vice president of Teaching Resources Films, wrote to the authors, Margret and H.A. Reys, recommending that Curious George stories be made into educational films because the books offered "innovative concepts," making them "unusually attractive and entirely practical in the classroom." In short, from the original in 1941, to its current iteration, the *Curious George* series has been both popular and widely read in U.S. classrooms, homes, and libraries.

This essay makes the case that the *Curious George* book series, both past and present, fits neatly into the genre of colonial literature and accordingly benefits from a postcolonial (re)reading. One of the recurring elements of a colonial genre is a subset of books highlighting a hero/adventure novel (Shaddock 1997). This approach is especially relevant to the *Curious George* series because both the Man in the Yellow Hat and George play the role of adventurer. The Man in the Yellow Hat has clear imperial overtones beginning with his journey to the Africa continent where he captures a brown animal. George also engages in a host of adventures that, no matter how disastrous, always position him as heroic. Using *Curious George* as an example, this essay makes the case that postcolonial children's literature offers a significant theoretical lens for academics, educators, parents, and children to make sense of the cultural icons children hold dear. The first *Curious George* (1941) story can be read as a slavery narrative. In its more contemporary form, *Curious George*

86

can be read as a diasporic tale in which the central figure performs his desire to return to his jungle home and place of capture.

Few children's series parallel the scope and sales of the *Curious George* series. Despite its longevity and fame, just a handful of children's literary critics have focused on this series. The lack of critical attention is surprising, given that *Curious George* provides such a rich example, especially considering the enormous influence of this beloved cultural icon of children's literature. Teachers have used George as an important pedagogical tool for U.S. children learning about their national culture. While the cultural iconicity of Curious George has changed across time, space, and medium, the book series has remained relatively stable—the curious African monkey is left alone in the United States to experience successive adventures.

My proposed strategy of (re)reading does not promote censorship or banishment; rather, its process should embolden educators, parents, and most importantly children to read with a critical sensibility aimed at discerning how U.S. audiences are socialized and habituated to participate benevolently with colonialism. Reading texts through a postcolonial lens demands that readers make sense of these texts as integral in the fabric of ideologies. By considering a literary series with such extensive readership and longevity through a critical lens, readers can learn about how the beliefs, values, and practices of American culture are manufactured and produced. Communication scholar Clare Bradford (2007) maintains that readers should begin to understand how texts positions audiences to embrace imperialism, especially ones that situate young readers "as citizens of nations marked by the violence of colonialism" (225). Instead of defending *Curious George* as dismissive nostalgia or a sign-of-the-times refutation, I read *Curious George* as a colonial book starring George, a cultural icon who, since 1941, has played an important role in training children about the customs and conventions of U.S. citizenship and colonialism.

My intention is not to correct a wrong or re-imagine a history and replace it with a more accurate account of events. Instead, I acknowledge that no text is innocent or free from ideology. Using postcolonial children's literary criticism creates a valuable lens through which to understand how a cultural icon, such as *Curious George*, performs through traces of the past while simultaneously ignoring the narrative's historical violence. By unpacking how *Curious George* nurtures imperialistic narratives, I am not foreclosing other possible readings, nor do I aim to uncover any intentional colonizing practices by the Reys. Instead, I follow a critical rhetorical model that rejects intentionality, as articulated here by John Sloop (2004):

> Critical rhetoric places its focus on *doxastic* rather than *epistemic* knowledge. That is, rather than being concerned with knowledge of the essence of objects [...] or philosophical discussions about meanings, critical rhetoric is concerned with public argument and public understandings about these objects [18].

Rather than the intention, critical rhetoric practices direct scholars to help explain how texts can position audiences. Accordingly, I understand a postcolonial rhetorical (re)reading of George as a means to analyze and evaluate contemporary knowledge construction. My goal is not to uncover George's "real" story. Instead, I read it with the desire to understand the ways in which cultural icons come to constitute rhetorically neutral yet nostalgic representations of the United States.

Naturally, not all children's narratives come to constitute benign colonial mentalities. However, I contend that books such as *Curious George* should have a principal place in the canon of colonial children's literature. The series' permanency and broad circulation have done a great deal to teach children how to ignore the colonial narratives of slavery and diasporic identities that underwrite the collection by focusing instead on the wild adventures of a curious monkey. A (re)reading of the series can bring into focus the assumption that cultural icons can teach young children and adults to participate in contemporary colonialism. Postcolonial theory is especially insightful when considering texts such as *Curious George* because they can clarify for children, and the adults in their life, how colonizing forces operate within literature (McGills and Khorana 1997, 8). Postcolonial scholars call for (re)reading children's literature, especially those texts that protect and promote the colonial enterprise. As soon as young children begin listening to stories, they are likely to engage books that secure the imperial mentality and perpetuate colonial ideologies. Don Randall (2010) explains that it is not surprising that "modern literature for children does much to shape and specify the child's being, doing, and becoming. In many texts […] children readers are called upon to learn and adopt certain sociocultural ideals and aspirations" (30). Put simply, I argue that children's literature in general, and *Curious George* specifically interpolates children to understand what it means to be a successful citizen.

A Brief History of Postcolonial Children's Literary Criticism

Children's books can play a significant role in interpolating young potential citizens about the world in which they live. Critical scholars of children's literature encourage adults to continue to ask hard questions that undergird a reflexive reading: who is represented and how, who is absent, and what are the implications of their absence? Children's literature provides a significant, informative way that young people learn who they are and what roles they play, or are expected to play, in their culture (Perrot 1997). The ideology of the American Dream dominates most U.S.-produced children's literature, and this literature all too often negatively represents characters through inequitable narratives of class, race, sexuality, and gender. If books are to give children a means to understand the world in which they actually live then children need to become aware at a young age of the notion of social location by "uncovering systems of meaning that perpetuate social inequities" (Botelho and Rudman 2009, xv). Children's books create the conditions of possibility for producing socially-conscious citizens. Given the importance of children's literature, scholars, teachers, and parents should not only attend to popular books, but also should direct their attention to a series that spans generations.

Just as educational policy and customs upheld the racism of the era, so too did children's literature. Scholars have documented the depiction of African Americans in children's literature back to the 1850s (Williams and Carver 1995). In response to the profound racist depictions in children's books, W.E.B. DuBois and A.G. Dill started a monthly magazine in 1919 entitled *The Brownies Book*, designed for Black children to read about themselves and their culture (Ashmore 2002, 44). Racism against African Americans in children's literature thrived during the 1920s and 1930s, and continues to remain a problem to this day (Ashmore 2010; Mickenberg 2005). In the 1940s, the decade in which *Curious George* was first published, overt racism was prevalent in children's books. In 1949, African American parents appealed to education boards to discontinue the use of overtly racist books, such as *Black Sambo*, though literary critics did not recognize the problem.

It was not until the 1980s that children's literary criticism as a mode of resistance became popular within the academy, in part thanks to the resurgence of postmodern literary criticism (Jones 2006). Since then, multicultural children's literature has spent decades advocating for more diverse representations of race and ethnicity (Mickenberg 2005). While some children's books depicted positive representations of race and gender, most narratives continued to reaffirm the existing racist, sexist, and imperial social order. Much of the familiar children's literature of the 20th century implicitly supports the individualist values of capitalism in the United States, as well as traditional gender roles, white racial hegemony, and middle-class norms. Some "is strikingly racist" (Mickenberg 2005, 7). Even when presented with alternatives, the general community often fails to read more progressive books. Postcolonial literary critics are an important exception.

Postcolonial theory emerged not only by offering critiques of believed-to-be great canons of literature, but also by emphasizing intersectional identities and matrices of oppression to offer a vital foundation for (re)reading children's literature. Postcolonial literary critics "consider how texts inscribe the shifting relations of power […] and resist universalizing interpretations, preferring to focus on the local and the particular" (Bradford 2007, 8). Postcolonial readings offer constitutive criticism that strives to make sense of how the cultural production of texts participate in the politics of colonialism. In short, they are interested in how "children's texts represent the experience of colonization in the past and its effects in the present" (Bradford 2007, 8–9). Postcolonial literary readings consider the construction of cultural identity; in doing so, "they seek the acceptance of the Other" (12).

One of the originators of postcolonial studies, Edward Said (1978), famously defines colonial discourse as "a text purporting to contain knowledge about something actual[. … S]uch texts can *create* not only knowledge but also the very reality they appear to describe" (94). His scholarship is useful for unpacking the ways in which literature produces a trajectory of realities that readers come to believe without suspicion. Said (1993) argues that stories "are at the heart of what explorers and novelists say about strange regions of the world," as well as a tool that colonized peoples use to assert their identity and resist occupation (xii). The battle over imperialism, he maintains, is determined by the narrative. Importantly, he admonishes scholars who maintain neutrality and suggests that not to "look at the connections between cultural texts and imperialism is therefore to take a position" that supports and bolters the dominant power (Said 1993, 8). In short, to let the narrative stand unchanged and unexamined is to be complicit in a powerful constitutive act that supports the status quo.

Perry Nodelman (1992) gained public attention for applying Said's work to the narratives of children's literature. Arguing that children's literature is a site worthy of postcolonial attention, Nodelman (1992) argued that adults use books to restore their lost childhood and return to their image of ideal childhood. Nodelman (1992) encourages adults to ask of children's literature, and scholars writing about children's literature, "what does it do" (34)? This notion of doing avoids a consideration of authorial intention and instead directs attention to the ways in which children identify with literature.

Postcolonial children's literary criticism is committed to discerning how books constitute people as subjects who participate within and frequently extend colonial discourses. For example, some scholars are more concerned with place: colonized, decolonized, or colonizing (Bradford 2007; Cadden 1997). This position is crucial to a reading of *Curious George* because George's new "home," in the United States with the Man in the Yellow Hat, and his previous home, the African jungle, both influence his hybrid identity as a diasporic subject. Postcolonial theorists are also interested in possibilities of resistance. To this end, *Curious George* books offer a partially resistant perspective because George's affection for the jungle and other animals signal his refusal to fully assimilate into U.S. culture. *Curious George* is a particularly interesting series to consider in this regard; while the overall narrative of slavery and captivity is oppressive, George's adventures often pose as acts of resistance.

Despite the popularity of *Curious George*, only four notable academic critics, June Cummins (1997), Joseph Zorando (2001), Daniel Greenstone (2005), and Ann Mulloy Ashmore (2002, 2010, 2012) address this icon through critiques. All of them draw heavily on the original seven books, often known as the "original" collection, and their arguments do not significantly attend to books published after 1966. My intervention extends and significantly develops the arguments advanced by previous scholars by proposing that *Curious George's* colonial history was not a sign of the times; instead, the colonialist component of the series reflects a current and evolving element within the canon of children's literature.

Literary critic June Cummins (1997) offers audiences the first and most comprehensive critique of the first seven books. She details the parallel between North America's cultural ambivalence towards slavery and the original *Curious George* book. She judiciously argues that the first book

> recalls the accounts of capture and enslavement undergone by Africans during the era of the slave trade. George's association with slaves allows us to position him as a colonial subject, and his relationship with his captor, the Man in the Yellow Hat, brings to mind parallel relationships, notably of slaves to masters and children to parents. Viewing George from a postcolonial perspective allows us to see how the book series reflects American cultural ambivalence towards its own colonial history [Cummins 1997, 69].

Cummins (1997) explains how the original seven *Curious George* books adhere to a parallel narrative structure: George creates mischief because he lacks discipline, obedience, maturity, and civility; he saves the day in some way and receives praise; he then learns a lesson and assimilates to convention.

Cummins (1997) considers the interaction between imperialism and civilizing practices of citizenship in the original *Curious George* books. Readers must "view how the books make use of those blurry comparisons to assuage American ambivalence" to our colonial past (Cummins 1997, 72). Her connections explore the ways that cultural texts reify colonialism by teaching children and educators to ignore and/or rationalize the oppressive acts of its country's past and present. Cummins (1997) identifies four ways in which the *Curious George* original series performs a sanitized and ambivalent slave narrative. First, the Man in the Yellow Hat tricks George into leaving the African jungle by enticing George with objects belonging to the white man—"many captivity narratives recount similar trickery" (Cummins 1997, 72). Next, the Man with the Yellow Hat captures George and forces him into new circumstances that position George between horror and wonder. Third, just as slaves attempting to escape from bondage were shackled as their ships journeyed through the Middle Passage, so too is George shackled when he jumps overboard. Finally, as was the case with most slaves, George is restrained and imprisoned, first in a jail and then in a zoo. Cummins (1997) acknowledges that the conditions of George's capture were better than those of most slaves. However, George's tale provides a means for readers to interpret slavery as tolerable, if not acceptable. Drawing on Henry Louis Gates, Jr.'s discussion of African American literature, Cummins (1997) proposes that George maintains elements of satire, irony, uncertainty, disruption, and reconciliation, yet fails to communicate them because he lacks the ability to speak (74). She draws parallels between the *Curious George* narratives and slavery by highlighting George's inability to communicate, suggesting that this deficit marks him as an Othered colonial subject. While many children's books anthropomorphically grant animals speech, George is "rendered voiceless precisely at the moment of capture" (Cummins 1997, 74). Using similar strategies, slave traders separated slaves from other members of their language groups. George's "lack of speech is a constant reminder of his lack of power and place" (Cummins 1997, 74).

Like most slaves, George embodies a hybrid colonial subject. Cummins (1997) argues that "[b]ecause he is cute and cuddly, he is partially acceptable" (77). "But his blackness, or animalness, ultimately point[s] to and maintain[s] his difference" (Cummins 1997, 77). Drawing on Homi Bhabha's theory of mimicry, Cummins (1997) suggests that George's desire to mimic undergirds his form of establishing difference or perhaps disavowal (78). While George continuously performs heroic tasks, his hybridity marks him as Other as his mood fluctuates between his longing to return home and his desire to fit in. She cites instances in which George's escape is not literal but takes place in his mind. In these moments, he is yearning for home through images and dreams. Finally, Cummins (1997) points to George's infatuation with African scenery, specifically his tree in the first book.

Daniel Greenstone (2005) offers a similar reading of the first book, describing the Man in the Yellow Hat as a "gun-toting" kidnapper (221). He explains the first volumes in the series as portraying "a protagonist who eagerly, and almost entitled without apprehension, confronts some of the most profound childhood fears imaginable, including physical danger, illness, abandonment and exploitation by adults" (Greenstone 2005, 221). Training children to respect the authority of adults is a lesson that Joseph L. Zornado (2001) echoes. Zornado (2001) maintains that one of the implicit messages of *Curious George* is "that Western culture can fabricate a reality more suited to George's needs than nature itself" (127). George reproduces the paternalist logic that predicates colonialism: if subjects are unable to parent themselves, in the name of the civilizing mission, others should forcibly do so.

Greenstone's (2005) critique focuses on George's desire to return to the jungle. He points out that *George Takes a Job* (1947) begins with George escaping from the zoo, then returning to the Man in the Yellow Hat, from whom he takes a paint brush and "paints a jungle scene with himself climbing a tree"

(Greenstone 2005, 223). The book also illuminates George's former life when the Man in the Yellow Hat takes him to a movie studio and George signs a contract to make a film about his life in the jungle. The narrative essentially asks George to remember and re-live those jungle memories. Greenstone also points to the picture of George's jungle tree over the breakfast table as a reminder of George's capture. Greenstone (2005) suggests that George's adventures become tamed or subordinated in order to teach children to adhere to the larger social aims of society (226).

Ann Mulloy Ashmore, former Reys collection specialist at the de Grummond Children's Library, is likely the most well-published *Curious George* scholar. Ashmore uses her historical knowledge of the Reys to defend what she believes was their anti-racist intentions. The Reys collection, Ashmore (2010) explains, "affords access to information earlier critics lacked [...] clues to their intentions, and [...] their motivations and goals" (358). By highlighting the Reys' mentoring relationship and friendship with Jesse Jackson, Ashmore (2010) attempts to guard the Reys' reputation: "Of particular significance," she claims, "is the impact his [Jackson's] friendship had on the Reys understanding of the consequences of racist attitudes throughout America and within the postwar world of children's publishing" (358). What is remarkable is how a friendship of Reys to a prominent Black public figure is presented as a responsible alibi to defend the books' innocence and lack of complicity with slavery. The logic, patently absurd, is that a positive relation with a person of color must necessarily negate the possibility of racism. This logic rests on a naive and simplistic view of identity that years of critical race theory and postcolonial studies, among other critical theoretical traditions, have long since dismissed.

In divergent spatial and temporal contexts, *Curious George* functions well outside his creator's desires. Whether the Reys had conscious or unconscious beliefs about race when they designed George is of little consequence to the reading of a public perception. Postcolonial scholars such as Spivak (1999; 1988) have demonstrated the value of waging critiques regardless of the authors' best intentions. These practices are instructive here, and support the proposition that regardless of intention, that the *Curious George* books reflect and maintain a colonial narrative. A necessary postcolonial (re)reading can help analyze how children's books participate in the colonizing enterprise by offering powerful Eurocentric biases and patriarchal lessons (McGills and Khorana 1997, 8). Criticism helps people learn. By engaging with adults who ask children questions about the curious, troubling, or resistant aspect of texts, they can enable even the youngest child to have insights that expand beyond their initial encounter with books.

Herbert Kohl's famous book, *Should We Burn Babar* (1995), insightfully explains that "children quickly come to understand that critical sensibility strengthens them. It allows them to stand their ground, to develop opinions […] and understanding rather than being subject to the pressures and seduction of others" (16). The opportunity to expose children to criticism is reason enough not to ban canonical books like *Curious George*, even if they do advance colonialist narratives.

George the Diasporic Monkey

Though Cummins (1997) argues that the original seven books resurrect racist slave narratives, I maintain that George's traumatic removal from the jungle continues to haunt him throughout the *entire* book series. Further, George's refusal to forget his jungle home positions him as a diasporic figure with the potential to resist. I offer a reading of George as a diasporic subject longing to return to his original home in the African jungle. This longing is an essential part of the story that persists through subsequent retellings and recasting. Longing to return to a place, or time that no longer exists as it once was, is a central aspect of diaspora. This reading of George's diasporic identity throws into focus both his captivity and his resistance to his captive condition. Three resounding themes mark George as a diasporic subject. First, his longing to return to his African home and his inability to fit in with U.S. culture spark his desire to be among, and to free, animals. Second, he maintains a preoccupation with the jungle environment in which he lived prior to his abduction, namely the jungle tree he was swinging in prior to capture. Finally, he has a precarious and undefined relationship with the Man in the Yellow Hat, who is not his master, his father, or his owner. Read congruently, George is a diasporic figure.

In the literary series George's diasporic subjectivity emerges through his affinity with and yearning to be with animals. Several *Curious George* books have a plot that centers on George's confinement, eventual escape, and search for some sort of freedom, either for himself or for other animals with whom he seems to share a special kinship. This theme continues from the early books to the present. For example, in *Curious George Rides a Bike,* the Man in the Yellow Hat wants to celebrate the three-year anniversary of the occasion when he took George from the jungle (H. A. Rey 1952, 4). In this early tale, George is actually "stolen" once again, and forced to ride a bike in an animal show. In *Curious George Flies a Kite*, George gravitates toward a neighbor's bunny cage, freeing the rabbits from captivity (H.A. Rey 1958, 16). Later books continue to demonstrate George's commitment to freeing and being with animals, thus underscoring his standing as a diasporic figure.

George's preoccupation with animals extends to more recent books. In *Curious George Visits the Zoo*, he is intent on watching the monkeys in the cage taunt the little children (M. Rey and Shalleck 1985, 19–23). In *Curious George Hide-and-Seek* George only plays with the cat, dog, bunny, and squirrel (H.A. Rey 2008). At the aquarium, George climbs trees to be close to the fish (M. Rey and Shalleck 1984, 6). In *Curious George and the Puppies*, George is so fascinated with the puppies that "he had to pet one," so he opened the cage door slowly and they all escaped (H. A. Rey and M. Rey 1998, 14). In the end, George emerges as a hero for finding the last puppy and is subsequently allowed to take one home. Thus, when George is able to model his control by locating and returning the puppies, he is rewarded with the human characteristic of owning a pet. In other words, he gets positive reinforcement for assimilation.

In the Public Broadcasting Stations' (PBS) television rendition of the books, George becomes allies with the doorman's dachshund, Hundley. PBS' character descriptions consider Hundley and George as allies because they "have to work together" ("Curious George, Character Descriptions"). George's other regular animal friends include: Charkie, the cocker spaniel, who is "happy to get involved with anything George is up to"; Gnocci, the free spirited cat; Compass, the homing pigeon; and Jumpy, the daredevil squirrel who "shares George's love of discovering new things" ("Curious George, Character Descriptions"). If the animal is not caged, George regularly teams up with them. In short, George's simian nature often overcomes him and he continually sympathizes with and works to free other animals. Read alone, each instance of animal camaraderie is part of George's many adventures; together they suggest an alignment with other colonized and displaced groups. Like so many diasporic subjects, George may never really escape or be able to help others in similar situations. Nevertheless, he retains his desire to be with other displaced or caged subjects.

Diasporic conditions presuppose a homeland orientation, suggesting a subject's value, identity, and loyalty towards his land of origin. George's infatuation with the jungle palm tree where he lived prior to his capture is perhaps the most striking element of his diasporic character. As the iconic reminder of George's homeland, the tree is a synecdoche for the jungle in its repeated representations. Maintaining collective memory or myth of the homeland and "regarding the ancestral homeland as the true, ideal home, and the place to which one would (or should) return" is a guiding principle that constitutes diaspora (Brubaker 2005, 5). The iconic image of the jungle tree where he was captured remains the most memorable image of the series. In the initial story, the jungle tree represents George's site of capture (H. A. Rey 1941). In *Curious George Takes a Job*, the monkey takes over for painters on lunch and paints a whole room "into a jungle with palm trees all over the walls and a giraffe and two leopards and a zebra" (H. A. Rey 1947). George even paints himself climbing the iconic tree from which he was swinging when he is first introduced to the readers. Finally, George gets a job as a movie actor in a jungle, featuring his own captor. An image of George's capture is above the Man in the Yellow Hat's breakfast table in *Curious George Rides a Bike* (H. A. Rey 1952). In *Curious George Gets a Medal,* after freeing the pigs from the farm, George jumps into the dinosaur exhibit in the museum to climb the iconic jungle tree (H. A. Rey 1957). In *Curious George Flies a Kite,* George frees bunnies and flies with a friend's kite into a tree and has to be rescued by the Man in the Yellow Hat (H.A. Rey 1958). When George learns the alphabet, the letter "J" features a jaguar looking up at the iconic jungle tree. The caption reads, "Jaguars live in the Jungle. George knew Jaguars. He had lived in the Jungle once" (H. A. Rey 1963). In the last of the original books, *Curious George Goes to the Hospital,* George swallows his past (M. Rey, H.A. Rey, and Children's Hospital Medical Center 1966). During the initial scene, the Man in the Yellow Hat helps George put together a puzzle, featuring an image from the first book where George was tempted by the Man in the Yellow Hat's hat. Watching himself gazing at the scene in his past, George decides to literally shallow his past by eating a piece of the puzzle. George gets sick. Even his consumption of the past does not rid him of its memory.

In the more recent books, George continues to be obsessed with the jungle environment, a memory of the homeland. *Curious George Goes to an Ice Cream Shop* begins with telling the reader, "George and his friend [referring to the Man in Yellow Hat] were cleaning the house" (M. Rey and Shalleck 1989). Near the written text there is an image of George and the Man in the Yellow Hat sweeping a bedroom. Everything in the bedroom was yellow, peachy-brown, and blue except the framed picture image of the jungle tree above George's bed (M. Rey and Shalleck 1989). It is likely that this is George's room because there is a bowl of bananas on the table. As it was in the original 1941 book, the picture is the same—a green and brown depiction of the iconic palm tree. Representations of the jungle emerge as subtle reminders of his past, typically when George is engaged in "civilized" activities in the modern world, such as watching a movie or participating at school. Whether picking out a Christmas tree or fishing, George repeatedly gives in to his instinctive need to swing through trees (Hapka, M. Rey, H.A. Rey, and Young 2006; H.A. Rey 2001). On his birthday, George's animal friends decorate the Man in the Yellow Hat's house with jungle and tree decorations and invite George to play pin-the-tail-on-the-zebra (H. A. Rey and M. Rey 2003). There are many other instances in which his love for animals and the image of his tree helps ease George's loss for his jungle home.

In *Curious George's Dream* (H.A. Rey and M. Rey 1998), George sits down to eat after a disappointing day at the amusement park. He was too small to ride the rides unaccompanied (directing the reader to assume that the Man and the Yellow Hat was not with him), and George's hands were too small to hold the bunnies at the petting zoo. After dinner, the Man in the Yellow Hat surprises George with a movie. Judging from the illustration of the television screen, George is watching a movie resembling *King Kong* (1933): "George was enjoying the movie, but it had been a full day and now he had a full stomach. Soon he could not keep his eyes open" and just as the movie showed the large gorilla holding up a screaming lady next to the iconic palm, George fell asleep (H.A. Rey and M. Rey 1998). The movie imagery is important; it is a scene of familiarity, another primate and the beloved jungle palms. As George sleeps, readers are positioned to watch his anxiety play out in his dream.

George "was back at the petting zoo" (M. Rey and H.A. Rey 1998, 7–10)! "But this time something was different. The petting zoo was very small. In fact everything was small" (M. Rey and H.A. Rey 1998, 10). The illustration shows a big Curious George sleeping and propped up against a tree. "Maybe he was big … then he remembered the bunnies. Why, he was not too small to hold a bunny … he went to the bunny hitch. Now George could hold LOTS of bunnies, and he cuddled them to his face. The bunnies liked George … but the manager of the petting zoo did not. 'Put those bunnies down,' she said. 'You'll scare them. You are too big'" (M. Rey and H.A. Rey 1998, 11–13). Thus, George's size again becomes a problem. Even in his dream he did not fit in. He was still not allowed to be with other animals. In fact, the people at the park became frightened of big George and ran away from him. He "felt awful" and "lonely" (M. Rey and H.A. Rey 1998, 13–15). When the Man in the Yellow Hat appears in the dream, George is at first relieved only to realize he was too big to go with the man. George is disappointed again until he woke up from his dream to realize he was he no longer big.

Arguably, George's fear over his inability to be the right size is a point of connection with diasporic individuals and with some young readers who may feel uneasy about their inability to do what bigger people can do. If it is the former, then George's diasporic memory of home is evidence in numerous books. If the later, then George's dream suggests growing up is much better. One moral is perhaps that readers who are different might never fit in. Unless, of course, they are a tall, white skinned, male explorer who likes yellow hats.

Curious George Says Thank You tells a tale of all the people George can send thank you cards to (H.A. Rey and M. Rey 2012). He gathers tons of paper, envelopes, crayons, and stickers. On the following page, the text reads at the top "the Man in the Yellow Hat walked in to find George covered from head to toe … 'Oh-oh, George! What are you doing?'" (H.A. Rey and M. Rey 2012, 8). The illustration from left to right features a concerned looking man dressed in yellow, a green desk, George covered in stickers, his supplies in front of the desk, and a familiar image above the desk. Framed in yellow, there is the scene from the 1941 book of George and his jungle palm and the yellow hat. The placement of the desk chair suggests the framed picture would not face the Man in the Yellow Hat when he sits at his desk, as a beloved family picture often does. Instead, it faces whomever the Man in the Yellow Hat is talking to across the desk, as a diploma, certificate of accomplishment, or trophy would. The Man in the Yellow Hat agreed to help George with his thank you cards. The man sat in his desk chair and George on the other side of the desk, facing the framed illustration. While the image was not mentioned in the book, it is a subtle inclusion as it is in most books. After delivering all his thank you cards, "George has one more very special thank you card to deliver. He had saved the best for last" (H.A Rey and M. Rey 2012)! On the last page of the book George hands the Man in the Yellow Hat a card." While there is no mention of what the card says, the gesture implies that, though George may love his jungle palm, he is attempting to assimilate. Additional efforts to assimilate can also be read in other *Curious George* books.

In a more recent volume, *Curious George's Big Adventures*, the only human is the Man in the Yellow Hat; all of the other characters are jungle friends (Anderson, Kaufman, Reynolds, H.A. Rey, and M. Rey 2005). George's room is painted to look like the jungle; however, the author only describes the monkey as experiencing adventure after he left his animal friends in Africa (Anderson, Kaufman, Reynolds, H.A. Rey, and M. Rey 2005). In these instances, George presents for readers the conditions for choosing to be happy, situating him neatly into a long history of the cheerful slave trope, popular in U.S. children's literature (Nel 2017, 218). The jungle, the place the Man in the Yellow Hat or narrator describes as George's place of origination, is important to the colonial narrative in which George is "saved" from the wild. The original images may have been representative of the 1940s and 1950s, when jungle pictures were particularly popular in the United States (Foster 1999, 42–43).

Despite tricking George into a burlap bag and taking George from Africa to the United States, and being the only other primary reoccurring character in the series, no scholar devotes much attention to the Man in the Yellow Hat as the quintessential colonial explorer. As George's captor and negligent paternal master, the Man in the Yellow Hat provides George a third constitutive criterion of diaspora—boundary maintenance. According to Brubaker (2005), boundary maintenance involves "a preservation of a distinctive identity vis-a-vis a host society" (6). George's condition never changes; he never gets more skilled in the traditions and habits of the United States and, what's more, he never ages. He never overcomes his hybrid existence when each episodic narrative begins with a new story, independent from the last. The Man in the Yellow Hat never treats him differently. George never learns the language and never grows in body or mind. Static in both time and age,

George finds himself reiterating the same mistakes and engaging in the same assimilative moves.

As is the case of much colonial narratives, the male explorer stands in for the heroic father and master of the land. He is brave enough to traverse new worlds with courage and has the ability to return. While some explorers take an indigenous treasure or woman, the Man in the Yellow Hat takes a monkey and names him George, after the first U.S. president. Characterized by his big-brimmed yellow hat, he is the companion and remiss-caretaker of Curious George. Featured in every book, the Man in the Yellow Hat always appears the same. He is a tall, white man with dark hair and eyes who always wears a bright yellow, *National Geographic*–style, explorer ensemble. If he is not wearing a yellow jacket, the Man in the Yellow Hat's sunny yellow collared shirt is almost always accompanied by a yellow tie or scarf, a belt, a three-quarter length safari-style yellow pants, and brown, antique army-style, calf-length boots.

The Man in the Yellow Hat lives alone until George moves in. His New York doorman-attended apartment, house in the country, convertible car, and frequent visits to Pisghetti's Ristorante (Italian restaurant) suggest that the Man in the Yellow Hat is wealthy. In the book series, he is never working and never with friends or romantically involved. The Man in the Yellow Hat represents an exceptional character. He replicates his role in book after book as the quintessential white hunter/savior of the colonial narrative, who is always present at end of the book to rescue or celebrate George's heroic act. The narrator or other characters refer to the Man in the Yellow Hat as George's "friend," while his role is more of a deadbeat fatherly character, who provides a continued reminder of George's curiously copious diasporic condition. George is never completely his slave, nor entirely his child, and too functional to be a pet. However, echoing other diasporic figures, George seems to care a great deal for the Man in the Yellow Hat, even though the Man in the Yellow Hat is continually absent. Like all good colonizers, the Man in the Yellow Hat returns (with George) to the colonizing country—the United States. As is true for most colonial missions, the mother country "becomes valorized as a place of 'positive values, good climate, harmonious landscape, social discipline and exquisite liberty, beauty, morality and logic'" (Ball 1997, 167).

Sadly, instead of citing the Man in the Yellow Hat's continued absence or negligent role of educator or parent, fans of Margret Rey write numerous letters to her, advising George to do a better job of listening to the Man in the Yellow Hat's instructions. Many children read the Man in the Yellow Hat as George's stand-in for a parental figure. For example, when a second-grade teacher from Lockport, New York, sent a package to Curious George (care of Margret Reys), she included letters from her students documenting "advice from each student telling George how he could keep out of mischief"

(Fletcher 2000). What could have been a moment of rupture was foreclosed when readers learn the writers all asserted that George should do a better job adhering to the rules of his parental figure: "George, ask The Man in the Yellow Hat if you can do stuff before you do it," instructed Ashley Boots (2000). One classmate advised: "George you should wait and ask The Man with the Yellow Hat if you can do something" (Megan 2000). While the children direct their recommendations toward George, critics might question the type of father the Man in the Yellow Hat exemplifies.

The absence of the Man in the Yellow Hat offers a double reading. On one hand, it is not common for colonizers to leave their slaves alone unless they trust that their subjects will not misbehave or run away. On the other hand, if readers position the Man in the Yellow Hat as a loving, or at least responsible father figure, then it is curious why that same audience is willing to accept an absent father. George's situation is explained by the natural conditions of colonialism. George knows nothing of this world, cannot speak the language, and is completely dependent on the Man in the Yellow Hat for food and accommodations. As such, there is no logical reason for George to resist. As is the case with many diasporic subjects, while they long for home, they also long to fit into their current conditions and not to disrupt any benefits of their dependent condition. This state of difference and confusion exemplifies the reasons that, while habitually left alone, George's rebellions are rarely targeted at the Man in the Yellow Hat.

Conclusion

After (re)reading the original series, I expected to find that the endurance and esteem of *Curious George* would yield many critiques. I was concerned when I discovered few criticisms. Not only does the series continue to sell, but it is also more popular today than it ever was. While the original series has received some critical attention, since 1966, 172 books have been published. In more than 75 years, only a handful of scholars have raised concerns about George's abduction. To my knowledge, this essay represents the first in-depth critique of George's continued discomfort and diasporic relationship with his new "home." George's obsession with freeing caged animals, his desire to be among them, his preoccupation with the jungle environment, specifically the palm, and his inquisitive relationship with the Man in the Yellow Hat position audiences to understand why George is not comfortable in his U.S. home. George's diasporic subjectivity can be read in a majority of *Curious George* books. The lack of critique is particularly concerning because *Curious George* is designed for young readers.

When books are introduced to pre-readers, and then reintroduced in classrooms and libraries, children come to understand that those books are written for them as a primary audience. However, too often their lessons are rehearsing the colonial tropes of white imperialism. The narratives do not raise concern about the history of slavery or assimilation. Read in concert with the postcolonial lexicon, *Curious George* narratives should invite a resistive reading that extends beyond the adventures of a cute monkey.

Children's literary narratives form and teach children about their own history, about the people with whom they share their environment, and about their understanding and predispositions of people's values. Children's books impart upon young people what is expected of them, a benign tool teaching them how they are expected to behave. These lessons get multiplied by a book series with high circulation over a long time in which adults share similar stories and perhaps long for the same understandings. Teaching children, early on, critical reading practices is an important way to hedge against harmful lessons imparted by imperial books. (Re)reading popular works, like *Curious George*, with a postcolonial sensibility is crucial to understanding the ways in which racism and colonialism is learned.

Works Cited

Anderson, R.P., Kenneth Kaufman, David Reynolds, H.A. Rey., and Margret Rey. 2005. *Curious George's Big Adventures*. Boston, MA: Houghton Mifflin.

Ashmore, Ann Mulloy. 2012. *All Things Rey*. May 31, 2012, http://allthingsrey.blogspot.com/2012/05/.

Ashmore, Ann Mulloy. 2010. "From Elizabite to Spotty: The Reys, Race and Consciousness Raising." *Children's Literature Association Quarterly* 35(4): 357–372.

Ashmore, Ann Mulloy. 2002. "Reflection on the Black Experience in Children's Literature." *Mississippi Libraries* 66: 44–45.

Ball, John Clement. 1997. "Max's Colonial Fantasy: Rereading Sendak's 'Where the Wild Things Are.'" *ARIEL: A Review of International English Literature* 28(1): 167.

Boots, Ashley. 2000. "Letter from Ashley Boots to 'Curious George.'" In *H.A & Margret Rey Papers*, Box 69, Folder 2. *de Grummond Children's Literature Collection*. The University of Southern Mississippi Libraries.

Botelho, Maria José, and Masha Kabakow Rudman. 2009. *Critical Multicultural Analysis of Children's Literature: Mirrors, Windows, and Doors*. New York: Routledge.

Bradford, Clare. 2007. *Unsettling Narratives: Postcolonial Readings of Children's Literature*. Waterloo, Canada: Wilfrid Laurier University Press.

Brubaker, Rogers. 2005. "The 'Diaspora' Diaspora." *Ethnic and Racial Studies* 28(1): 1–19.

Cadden, Mike. 1997. "Home Is a Matter of Blood, Time, and Genre: Essentialism in Burnett and McKinley." *ARIEL: A Review of International English Literature* 28(1): 53–67.

Cummins, June. 1997. "The Resisting Monkey: 'Curious George,' Slave Captivity Narratives, and the Postcolonial Condition." *ARIEL: A Review of International English Literature* 28(1): 69.

"Curious George: Character Descriptions." n.d. *PBS Kids: For Parents*. http://www.pbs.org/parents/curiousgeorge/program/char_desc.html.

Dirda, Michael. 2016. "Curious George Turns 75: Why the Monkey and the Man in the Yellow Hat Endure." *The Washington Post*, September 6, 2016. https://www.washingtonpost.

com/entertainment/books/curious-george-turns-75-why-the-monkey-and-the-man-in-the-yellow-hat-endure/2016/09/06/e0298f26–6f98–11e6–8365-b19e428a975e_story.html?utm_term=.d9a80b9cbd82.

Fletcher, Lynne A. 2000. "Letter from Lynne A. Fletcher to 'Curious George.'" In *H.A & Margret Rey Papers*, Box 69, Folder 2. *de Grummond Children's Literature Collection*. The University of Southern Mississippi Libraries.

Foster, Gwendolyn Audrey. 1999. *Captive Bodies: Postcolonial Subjectivity in Cinema*. Albany: State University of New York Press.

Greenstone, Daniel. 2005. "Frightened George: How the Pediatric-Educational Complex Ruined the Curious George Series." *Journal of Social History* 39(1): 221–228.

Hapka, Cathy et al. 2006. *Margret & H.A. Rey's Merry Christmas, Curious George*. Boston, MA: Houghton Mifflin.

Jones, Katharine. 2006. "Getting Rid of Children's Literature." *The Lion and the Unicorn* 30(3): 287–315.

Kohl, Herbert R. 1995. *Should We Burn Babar?: Essays on Children's Literature and the Power of Stories*. New York: New Press.

McGills, Roderick, and Meena Khorana. 1997. "Introductory Notes: Postcolonialism, Children and Their Literature." *ARIEL: A Review of International English Literature* 28(1): 7–20.

Megan, Lynne A. 2000. "Letter from Megan to 'Curious George.'" In *H.A & Margret Rey Papers*, Box 69, Folder 2. *de Grummond Children's Literature Collection*. The University of Southern Mississippi Libraries.

Mickenberg, Julia L. 2005. *Learning from the Left: Children's Literature, the Cold War, and Radical Politics in the United States*. Oxford, UK: Oxford University Press.

Miller, John A. 1971. "Letter from John A. Miller to the Rey's." In *H.A & Margret Rey Papers*, Box 93, Folder 2. *de Grummond Children's Literature Collection*, The University of Southern Mississippi Libraries.

Nel, Philip. 2017. *Was the Cat in the Hat Black?: The Hidden Racism of Children's Literature, and the Need for Diverse Books*. Oxford, UK: Oxford University Press.

Nodelman, Perry. 1992. "The Other: Orientalism, Colonialism, and Children's Literature." *Children's Literature Association Quarterly* 17(1): 29–35.

Perrot, Jean. 1997. "Review Article: Children's Literature Comes of Age." *ARIEL: A Review of International English Literature* 28(1): 209–220.

Randall, Don. 2010. "Empire and Children's Literature: Changing Patterns of Cross-Cultural Perspective." *Children's Literature in Education* 41(1): 28–39.

Rey, H. A. 1941. *Curious George*. Boston: Houghton Mifflin Harcourt.

Rey, H. A. 1958. *Curious George Flies a Kite*. Boston: Houghton Mifflin Harcourt.

Rey, H. A. 2005. *Curious George Gets a Medal*. Boston: Houghton Mifflin Harcourt.

Rey, H. A. 2001. *Curious George Goes Fishing*. Boston: Houghton Mifflin Harcourt.

Rey, H. A. 2008. *Curious George Hide-and-Seek*. Boston: Houghton Mifflin Harcourt.

Rey, H. A. 1963. *Curious George Learns the Alphabet*. Boston: Houghton Mifflin Harcourt.

Rey, H. A. 1952. *Curious George Rides a Bike*. Boston: Houghton Mifflin Harcourt.

Rey, H. A. 1947. *Curious George Takes a Job*. Boston: Houghton Mifflin Harcourt.

Rey, H. A., and Margret Rey. 2003. *Curious George and the Birthday Surprise*. Boston: HMH Houghton Mifflin Books for Young Readers.

Rey, H. A., and Margret Rey. 1998. *Curious George and the Puppies*. Boston: Houghton Mifflin Harcourt.

Rey, H. A., and Margret Rey. 2012. *Curious George Says Thank You*. Boston: Houghton Mifflin Harcourt.

Rey, H. A., and Margret Rey. 1998. *Curious George's Dream*. Boston: Houghton Mifflin Harcourt.

Rey, Margret, and Alan J. Shalleck. 1989. *Curious George Goes to an Ice Cream Shop*. Boston: Houghton Mifflin Harcourt.

Rey, Margret, and Alan J. Shalleck. 1984. *Curious George Goes to the Aquarium*. Boston: Houghton Mifflin Harcourt.

Rey, Margret, and Alan J. Shalleck. 1985. *Curious George Visits the Zoo*. Boston: Houghton Mifflin Harcourt.

Rey, Margret, H. A. Rey, and Children's Hospital Medical Center. 1966. *Curious George Goes to the Hospital*. Boston: Houghton Mifflin Harcourt.

Ross, Eulalie Steinmetz. 1953. "Letter from Mrs. Eulalie Steinmetz Ross to H.A. Rey." In *H.A & Margret Rey Papers,* Box 64, Folder 4, *de Grummond Children's Literature Collection*, The University of Southern Mississippi Libraries.

Said, Edward W. 1993. *Culture and Imperialism*. New York: Knopf, 1993.

Said, Edward W. 1978. *Orientalism*. New York: Pantheon Books.

Shaddock, Jennifer. 1997. "Where the Wild Things Are: Sendak's Journey into the Heart of Darkness." *Children's Literature Association Quarterly* 22(2): 155–159.

Sloop, John M. 2004. *Disciplining Gender: Rhetorics of Sex Identity in Contemporary U.S. Culture*. Amherst: University of Massachusetts Press

Spivak, Gayatri Chakravorty. 1988. "Can the Subaltern Speak?" In *Marxism and the Interpretation of Culture*, edited by Cary Nelson, 271–313. Champaign: University of Illinois Press.

Spivak, Gayatri Chakravorty. 1999. *A Critique of Postcolonial Reason: Toward a History of the Vanishing Present*. Cambridge, MA: Harvard University Press.

Williams, Mary Thompson, and Helen Bush Carver. 1995. "African-Americans in Children's Literature—From Stereotype to Positive Representation." In *The All White World of Children's Books and African American Children's Literature*, edited by Osayimwense Oso, 13–31. Trenton, NJ: Africa World Press.

Zornado, Joseph, L. 2001. *Inventing the Child: Culture, Ideology, and the Story of Childhood*. New York: Garland.

Odd Squad Pedagogy

Learning from Children Together as a Team

KEVIN D. KUSWA

Many of us live in tumultuous times and perhaps always have, making the way we raise and teach our children one of the most important individual and societal roles on the list of human responsibilities. Both for a viable future and for a sense of active engagement across generations, the method and practice of teaching we deploy when we teach children and young adults is a factor that must be considered. There is a tome of insight within the field of critical pedagogy across the last half century that argues as much (Freire 1970; Giroux 1999). Some of the most profound contributions are also quite simple: "education has the power to change social inequality" (Coles 2014). To this end, the moral purpose of education should include "nurturing a generation with an educated mistrust of everything that has been indoctrinated before" (Coles 2014). Following this guidance, however, means encouraging a radical cynicism both inside and outside the classroom. Indeed, change in the classroom may be insufficient, for many of these struggles are also at home, on the athletic field, in community groups, or with friends and peers. In all of those settings and more, the media that young adults digest has influence on the expectations, conduct, and education that emerge. There should be little doubt that "the texts, imagery and commodities of popular culture encode constructs of childhood" (Luke 1994). With that in mind, it becomes crucial for parents and educators to emphasize the places where new models and arrangements, even as they act "as powerful public pedagogies in the production of social identities," may also challenge and critique existing norms surrounding "the 'child,' 'family,' 'gender,' and 'race'" (Luke 1994). Aiming to highlight a few such goals for a "youth-centric pedagogy," this discussion will bracket the debate over the exact degree of influence exerted by television programming on children in favor of a more contextualized analysis of one show in particular. Analyzing *Odd Squad* as a starting point will help to provide a platform that positions existing arguments in favor of more autonomy or independence for children alongside a broad sense of diversity, a measured relationship to technology, and a skeptical acceptance of the influence of screen-based culture.

In other words, *Odd Squad* offers some valuable lessons to absorb and model in our construction of a more vibrant and socially responsible future based on how our young people learn, cooperate, and progress. Offering at least one bright spot in a vast heap of television programming, *Odd Squad* bucks a number of trends and presents a unique relationship to technology, race, and gender all within a storyline that is almost exclusively driven and acted out by young people. The cast is made up of more girls than boys, more non-whites than whites, and far more young people than adults. In addition, the way "oddities" in the world are confronted in the show relies on a complex view of technology—a view that admits to flaws that can result from an over-reliance on technological solutions while still embracing the growing power of our gadgets and devices. It is rare to see a show for children that pays more than lip service to multiple levels of diversity, including race, gender, and age. It is also rare to see a show for children build in a skeptical, yet participatory relationship to technology. This progressiveness can be seen in the diversity of the *Odd Squad* actors, the show's unique perspective on crisis and technology, and the underlying message of trust and independence in the plot's reliance on young people. Ultimately, I argue that the *Odd Squad* reveals the radical potential hidden within children's capability to confront problems in the world when unencumbered by adult bureaucracy and control. Does this mean that adults are no longer absolutely indispensable to the lives of children and no longer have a significant everyday role? Of course not—it is simply an argument in favor of trust, a healthy cultivation of independence and problem-solving skills, and space to model autonomous and peer group decision-making without an overly paternal "adult behind the curtain."

Framing an Odd View

Before discussing some of the many provoking episodes of the *Odd Squad*, it makes sense to return briefly to critical pedagogy in the context of media and culture to frame the perspective of "consuming television" for children. I happen to be the proud parent of a five-year-old daughter and nine-year-old son and spend a great deal of time thinking about the media they consume.[1] In fact, I would not have ever encountered *Odd Squad* were it not for my kids. When I see my kids exhibiting troubling behavior, I cannot help but try to link it to various shows or movies they have watched in an attempt to expunge such influences from their lives. Of course there is not a one-to-one correspondence between watching something and acting on it, but it is natural to make those links. At any rate, in the case of the *Odd Squad*, it appeared that the show was having a positive impact on my kids in terms of some of their cooperation skills. Yes, I want to be a thoughtful and multidimensional parent but, if I can find an easy answer—typically one that involves blaming media consumption rather than celebrating it, I will quickly adopt it and convince myself that it is the best response. Maybe some of those responses are helpful, maybe not; but, if it is true that children are partly products of the media they digest, then it should also be true that the street runs both ways. If a given show valorizing pettiness or gratuitous consumerism is appearing in the children's behavior, then a show about cooperation and the value of diversity should also show up in their comportment. The more our children experience and absorb a youth-centric pedagogy that emphasizes the values of diversity, mutual encouragement, and a balanced relationship to technology, the better. Dobrow, Gidney, and Burton (2018) have found that "attitudes toward other-race children were more positive depending on the combination of characters in the television show (Graves, 1975); and children's moral reasoning about social exclusion improved in most cases." Moreover, Graves (1999) confirms that "televised role portrayals and interracial interactions, as sources of vicarious experience, contribute to the development of stereotypes, prejudice, and discrimination among children" (707).

Armed with this information, the notion of a team and a squad (the core of the *Odd Squad*) is crucial to how we motivate young students to learn and cooperate in the most effective ways possible. The ways that children and young adults confront problems and develop solutions also instills different forms of group pedagogy. These pedagogies are instilled as future formulas for responding to obstacles and challenges that will inevitably arise. In other words, when groups of children negotiate with one another and bring their various attributes to the fore, larger methods of how to contribute to group efforts will form that may be more important than the specific details of each situation. When we assist or guide children and young adults to organize and progress independently, when feasible, the results are usually better and the long-term training generates a better platform for future actions (Gordon 2000).

In the same way that media sources offer texts for consumption, these artifacts can also be seen as part of a "curriculum" generated by society for the inculcation of norms and values (Giroux and Simon 1989). This means that particular shows attempting to work against the grain contribute to children's understanding of the world in significant ways as the lines blur between teacher, student, parent, and text. Recent work in this area connects the process of parenting and teaching to the larger sense of cultivating who our students and children are in the world and what that world should and could look like. This compels us to pursue at least two forms of praxis: "First, a pedagogy that enables both students and teachers to develop a critically conscious understanding of their relationship with the world. Second, and intertwined with the first, pedagogy that enables students and teachers to become subjects consciously aware of their context and their condition as a human being" (Shih 2018, 231). The possibilities of achieving such a sense of self-awareness in children are subtle, but so are the ways various norms are ingrained in children's expectations and perceptions. To move away from Hirsch's contention that cultural literacy "is a hegemonic vision produced for and by the white middle class to help maintain the social and economic status quo," there has to be counter-examples of race, class, and gender diversity (Coles 2014). Such counter-hegemonic influences align with Freire's observation that "changing the world into a humanized one is feasible only through true dialogue" (Nouri and Sajjadi 2014, 79).

This dialogue, however, comes from multiple sources, requiring two specific emphases when discussing television shows consumed by children: first, "childhood" itself is constructed through complex interactions between countless representations and their effects; and, second, interdisciplinary approaches are needed when assessing childhood and how it changes. Khan and Saltmarsh (2011) reinforce the first point in a few key ways, namely by grouping together cultural texts "that are produced for children or about them" (267). This helps one recognize how representations are more than just descriptive, but also constitutive. As a result, theorists have begun to consider "how representations of children and childhood in cultural texts contribute to shared understandings and normative discourses about children's place in the social world" (Khan and Saltmarsh 2011, 267). Such representations— both regressive and transgressive—emerge through literary, media, and popular texts according to Khan and Saltmarsh (2011), and "are a powerful means by which the broad category of childhood is constructed, maintained, protected and challenged" (267). In other words, within the logics and practices of childhood are depictions of this particular time period (or early phase of life) through various texts—those depictions in turn help to determine how "contemporary childhoods are imagined, produced and experienced" (Khan and Saltmarsh 2011, 267).

The second argument builds on the first by simply asserting the importance of everyday life and local, contextualized relationships to social norms. Daily rituals and media consumption matter, even if it is impossible to "grasp fully the nature of the socially and culturally constructed character of childhood, as it unfolds and changes in and through everyday life" (James and James 2004, 44). Thus, turning to the specifics of *Odd Squad*, it will be valuable to keep in mind the insights of critical pedagogy, in particular the give and take between representations of childhood and childhood itself, as well as the ability to provide counter-hegemonic challenges to larger ideologies through various texts.

An Odd-Based Youth-Centered Pedagogy

One such text, *Odd Squad*, is a children's television series produced by PBS Kids and created by Timothy McKeon and Adam Peltzman that has been running since late 2014. The "squad" in the show relies heavily on "agents" who all have names that start with an "O" and use math and humor to resolve strange happenings in the world. Each episode across 11 seasons offers valuable lessons into what children are capable of accomplishing when given the chance, in addition to developing a number of insights into parenting and trust. A single 30-minute show has two shorter episodes of about 12 minutes so the writers are hard-pressed to create depth in such a short time period, but they manage to do so. What is most significant in terms of *Odd Squad* overall is that it offers parents and children a world where girls are in charge, racial diversity is more than just shallow tokenism, adults are in need of saving and oversight, and technology is both dangerous and helpful, even if unpredictable. In part, these representations are internalized by viewers as possibilities and conceivable depictions of the world.

Let us take a look at two from 2017, one that is atypical (although these abnormal episodes occur fairly frequently—about every fifth show) and one that follows the formula to the letter. Season 8, Episode 1 ("Orchid's Almost Half Hour Talent Show") is unusual in that the "case" to solve is simply dividing Agent Orchid's 20-minute talent show into equal parts. An adult does appear briefly in this particular show, a villain named Music Man from an earlier episode, but only briefly as a talent show contestant who juggles 20 balls. The main plotline in the episode involves Agent Olympia attempting to secure a spot in the talent show by recruiting increasing numbers of contestants in order to divide 20 into equal segments. The Agents do not face a pending danger in the typical sense, but it is important for Olympia to both appear in the talent show herself as well as include everyone she has recruited along the way. It is instinctive for her to put herself last, so much so that something very interesting happens when she does perform.

Backing up briefly, Agent Olympia first needs to recruit a fourth contestant, which she does. The fourth act joins Orchid and Olympia as one of the many non-white Agents driving this episode: the black Agent Ocean who teaches a dragon to fly through a hoop. Agent Ocean is followed by a fifth Agent, also black, who does impersonations. Then, when Agent Orchid adds the Big "O" to the show, Agent Olympia finds four more guests to give each two minutes to perform. Eventually, Olympia has to find nine contestants in the spur of the moment in order to have 20 acts, including her own. What we see here involves children giving each other confidence and a space to perform. The only problem is that Agent Olympia forgets to plan her own act, the last one of the show. The ending scene has Agent Otis, Olympia's partner, encouraging her by joining her on stage for a musical act about not having a talent. Their rhyming and choreography is quite amazing—both nuanced and self-deprecating—showing that it is possible to turn the lack of a talent into an attribute through teamwork and practice. It is an impressive number, very catchy, and replete with a back-and-forth cadence that demonstrates trust and timing that seems to put a capstone on the talent show as a whole.

What is important in this episode, though, is something found across *Odd Squad* as a whole: the diversity of the cast and what that means for the viewers. Multiple studies have confirmed that more diversity in children's television shows has a positive impact on how children view those who are different and how they expect the world around them to look (Browne 1999; Dobrow, Gidney, and Burton 2018). Children can take a lot from the girl-power in this episode—both in terms of Orchid's firm but supportive leadership and from Olympia's perseverance and self-sacrifice—and parents can learn from the storyline that children can work through their own obstacles in a triumphant and organic way. Overall, the positive messages about each person having a worthwhile talent when given the chance are plentiful in this episode. However, the strongest emphasis focuses on the empowerment possible when girls are in leadership positions and meet the challenges necessary to overcome obstacles. *Odd Squad* will not change the patriarchal nature of the world, but it can make a difference, one step at a time. According to Dobrow, Gidney, and Burton (2018), contemporary television shows feature "female characters (who) account for just under one-third of all characters. Discouraging as this may appear, it's a significant improvement from the 1:6 ratio that F. Earle Barcus had previously found, and better than the 1:4 ratio that communications professors Teresa Thompson and Eugenia Zerbinos found in the 1990s." Not only are the ratios going up, but the same study, as well as other research, concluded that increasing female representation can encourage viewers to either resist or "contribute to the development of stereotypes, prejudice, and discrimination among children" (Brown 1999, 707). The show works by giving children an example to point to that both includes a diverse group of peers and shows how challenging situations can be effectively resolved through cooperation and teamwork, ensuring that the diverse individuals are crucial to decision-making and not just cardboard cut-outs.

Odd Squad's positive message is about teamwork and working together to generate confidence and success. Even though a talent show is inherently about individuals putting their own skills on display, Orchid's program is not only open to virtually anyone with a talent (as long as the total number of acts can be evenly divided into 20), and the acts are not ranked by judges, significantly eschewing the need for hierarchy or competition often present in the "search for talent." Additionally, the culminating moment and the final validation of Agent Olympia's problem-solving and determination is not about some flashy talent she might have. Instead, the real triumph is that she was able to find a way onto the show without excluding anyone, and that, together, she and her partner can support and riff off of each other (in some brilliant ways) to make the overall event a success. Children and parents alike can learn from the duo's catchy dialogue:

> AGENT OTIS: "If you're alone on stage, here's a piece of good news. Having nothing to show means having nothing to lose [...] Start with what you've got."
> AGENT OLYMPIA: "Well I have got this kazoo, but I'm light on skills."
> AGENT OTIS: "Don't worry, I've got a few."
> AGENT OLYMPIA: "Why don't we shake on this jam?"

Other episodes reinforce similar messages. In one of the more formulaic, yet profound episodes, the second half of Season 8's first show is called "The Perfect Score," and features Agent Olympia on a pilgrimage for self-validation and discovery. As a bonus, the episode also has a critical angle on grades and report cards that questions society's current obsession with the results of external assessment. The episode allows viewers to see through grading as arbitrary and to realize that self-motivation is superior to a focus on grades. The opening scene involves Agents Olympia and Otis going through the daily mail and "Report Cards" given to the Agents by various (adult) villains the squad has thwarted over the previous year. The villains anonymously rank the agents from 0 to 10 based on categories such as organization, effectiveness, and use of gadgets. Agent Olympia, clearly the perfectionist of the two, receives a few 10s and then comes across the unfathomable: a report card ranking her a 1 out of 10. How could that be? She is such a great Agent—or so she thought. In many ways, Agent Olympia represents the product of an education system (including parents, teachers, and administrators) that puts too much stake in test scores, grades, ranks, and other numerical forms of assessment. The National Council of Teachers of English (2014) discusses this tendency, concluding that these kinds of numeric indicators can limit learning—the "Perfect Score" is just an illusion.

Frustrated, Agent Olympia decides to track down the anonymous villain who has given her a 1 out of 10 in order to determine if she really is a bad agent. Despite the fact that the villains (all adults with the exception of "Baby Genius") are bound to a code of "no tattling," many of them still offer clues to Agent Olympia as to where she might find the villain who ranked her so harshly. The "villain" label is applied to many of the show's adults, indicating their one-dimensional natures as opposed to the child masterminds posing problems in other episodes. In this episode, Olympia begins to cultivate her own motivation rather than a concern for her report card. She does this incrementally and with purpose as she realizes that she can reason with the Mother of Baby Genius, that she can coax an address out of the notorious Tommy Two-Sie, and even that she can beat Freeze Ray Ray at his own game. The theme here is not an overt attack on standardized testing in any grand sense. It is simply the argument that children can overdetermine their own worth and constrain themselves through a fixation with numerical assessments.

Indeed, the interaction between Agent Olympia and Freeze Ray Ray is compelling not because Olympia can extract a ten out of ten from the villain, but because it emphasizes the power of a talented and committed child when faced with a tough challenge. The interaction also shows that adults can be overcome with a drive for domination and greed that risks subverting even the simplest of plans. Mr. Ray Ray thinks he can use Agent Olympia's perfectionism against her by luring her into the park, freezing her when she least expects it, and stealing her gadgets in order to control the world. These are the potential hazards of determining one's self worth based on an arbitrary report card, and the phrase "obsessed with tracking" in no accident in their dialogue:

> AGENT OLYMPIA: "Well, well, well. If it isn't Freeze Ray Ray. So, you think I'm a bad Agent?"
> FREEZE RAY RAY: "On the contrary, I think you're a great Agent!"
> AGENT OLYMPIA: "O.K. Then why did you give me a one out of ten?"
> FREEZE RAY RAY: "Because, I knew if I gave you a one out of ten, you'd become obsessed with tracking me down. And, now, I'm going to freeze you, steal your gadgets, and take over the world! *(Sinister laugh)* The perfect plan!"
> AGENT OLYMPIA: "Your plan is not perfect."
> FREEZE RAY RAY: "What?"
> AGENT OLYMPIA: "Your plan was, like, the worst! […] Your roommate had to give me another clue to get here because he does not like you very much so you might want to work on that. The only reason your plan did not work very well is because I'm such a good agent. *(With sudden recognition)* I'm a good agent! And it doesn't matter what you or any other villain says, or any other regular person like a baker or a crosswalk guard."

At this point, Freeze Ray Ray makes one last desperate attempt to fulfill his plan and decides to shoot a freeze ray at Olympia. All children, however, are equipped with the possibilities of self-motivation and validation and Olympia, being a good agent, has already equipped herself with her "mirror suit" that reflects any ray or bolt back on its source. Freeze Ray Ray cannot react in time and ends up watching it rebound back to encase his body in a box of ice. The scene ends with Agent Olympia getting Freeze Ray Ray's signature on the corrected report card indicating she is a "ten out of ten." The real perfect score, though, is not the ten of ten, but the recognition, by Olympia herself, that she is a good agent. On the flip side, the adult's greed is also his downfall, including his assumption that simply possessing the *Odd Squad*'s gadgets will allow him to "control the world." The child overcomes the nefarious plan through persistence and insight, offering important advice along the way, and discovering that validation comes from within, not from report cards.

What is truly astounding and serves as the beginning of a platform for a youth-centered pedagogy in *Odd Squad*, however, is the fact that the organization is exclusively run by children. In other words, children are both in charge and in training. They are making decisions and following instructions and are fully and completely in control of every aspect of the show. And they succeed! They thwart nefarious plans, protect adults from their absurd situations, and sustain a flexible and efficient organization. And, when compared to adults, the children are the capable and rational ones.

Is the argument that this is always the case, or if parenting should always be conducted based on this inversion of rationality? No, not at all. For one, the show is supposed to be a bit odd. More importantly, second, it is certainly the case, as effectively portrayed in many episodes of *Odd Squad*, that some situations involve decisions and actions made by very rational children in the face of bumbling or dishonest adults. Yes, the adults that typically appear in the show are one-dimensional characters without problem-solving skills that isn't the case in the real world. Nevertheless, contributing some representations where young people are more capable than adults is important. It is important because young people have to eventually learn to act on their own and because it is too totalizing to encourage children to always defer to adults.

Analyzing *Odd Squad* does not require immersing in child psychology and parenting literature, but there is a persuasive argument emerging from the show about the potential for children to make good decisions and resolve difficult problems, individually and collectively, when given the opportunity. These youth-centered opportunities may be in a context without adults present or even in a context involving opposition to adults acting in villainous ways, and parents would be remiss to ignore the inevitability of these situations. Do we encourage young people such as Ethan Lindenberger from Ohio to stand up against the anti-vaccination wishes of his Mother? *Odd Squad* would advise, "yes, definitely," for how else can we both check against the occasional flawed or nefarious pursuits of adults? It is just speculation, but Ethan Lindenberger must have absorbed some positive representations of independence and self-confidence earlier in his life. In addition, it is safe to contend that the type of executive functioning we are discussing has been found in young children, even younger than *Odd Squad*'s audience. Bernier, Carlson, and Whipple (2010) concluded that, "given the impressive range of child cognitive and socioemotional outcomes related to executive function, the search for the social contexts most likely to favor its development is an important task for future research" (336–337). Taking this information into account, not only is *Odd Squad* a compelling show and fun for children, it also presents significant messages to us all about child independence, creativity, and the ability to confront and overcome major crises.

Embracing the Odd

If we give *Odd Squad* the benefit of the doubt, we might be able to relate to our own children with more openness and trust. In some ways, "odd" is simply a matter of perspective and the best way to engage the imagination of a child is through respect, not paternalism. Certainly authority plays a role—the decrees made by Ms. O as the head of the Squad demonstrate that need—but "adult status" should not mean superior decision-making. On the contrary, when children with a purpose and leadership are given trust and responsibility, good things can happen for society as a whole. Scholars have referenced the need to give children independence for some time (Bowlby 1956). Furthermore, more recent work now explicitly contends that "there is a positive and significant relationship between parenting patterns with the child's independence" (Sunarty and Dirawan 2015, 111). Independence does not mean abandoning children to their own whims as much as a conscious and rigorous attempt to cultivate critical and self-aware thinking. As research on parenting models suggests, even the concept of parenting as a responsibility to impart autonomous and critical decision-making can bring about such results through the influence of social representations (Miguel, Valentim, and Carugati 2013). In short, "social representations are guides for action" (Miguel, Valentim, and Carugati 2013, 1163).

In some ways, *Odd Squad* is not as important for what it does and what it offers than for what it avoids: adult over-determination, the infantalization of child dreams and cooperation, and the trivialization of the decisions made and implemented by children. One of the ways *Odd Squad* avoids this common structure in children's programming is through an explicit hierarchy in the organization that does not rely on adults pulling the strings or otherwise manipulating the plotline or theme of the show. The talent show is run by children and Agent Orchid demonstrates she can maintain the talent show's time constraints yet still be fair to all the potential guests. Agent Olympia does not rely on other adults to achieve her understanding that she is a good Agent. Instead, she commits herself to tracking down the source of her low rating in order to dispel the myth that one villain can determine her self-worth. These spaces for youth autonomy are not unique to *Odd Squad* in that other PBS shows try to keep adults out of the picture (*Peg + Cat, Super Why, Word World,* or *Cat in the Hat*). However, it is still the case, even on PBS Kids, that the majority of the shows for children involve adults in oversight or lead roles (*Sesame Street, Electric Company, Caillou, Curious George, Sid the Science Kid,* etc.). The purely child-driven nature of *Odd Squad* is still quite rare overall, especially for programming involving actors and not cartoons.

The other transgressive move in the show is the way it not only offers a diverse set of characters in terms of race and gender, but that those non-white characters do not represent sidekicks or peripheral others with minor roles. Rather, they run the show by outsmarting the one-dimensional adults at every turn. As seen in the episodes discussed above, the few adults that do appear in the show are shallow villains and buffoons, incapable of any real sophistication and lacking any real character depth. The most challenging villains with the more complicated and nefarious schemes are other children (the disgruntled Agent Todd, for example). This means PBS is painting a world that is odd—not because of the bizarre scenarios confronted by the group, but because of the shattering of ageist and other norms in the show. When representations are diverse, tendencies to adopt racist or sexist views decline because it is easier to see differences as expected and valuable.

Steven Mintz (2012), a professor of history at the University of Texas at Austin, reminds us that our treatment of children and the education they undergo is "the true missing link: connecting the personal and the public, the psychological and the sociological, the domestic and the state" (17). More specifically, the lessons imparted throughout childhood, over time, tend to play "a crucial role in the intergenerational transmission and development of collective identities. Racial identity provides a particularly vivid instance of this process" (Mintz 2012, 21). The roles that non-whites and women play in the media representations that children consume are part of the struggle in a long-term battle against mainstream society rooted in economic, racial, and gender injustice. Mintz's point is well-taken and his argument urging a renewed analysis of the history of childhood in the United States has merit. On the other hand, he does not offer an explicit alternative approach to children's pedagogy that would help to reverse trends of discrimination and exclusion in society. *Odd Squad*'s messaging can fill in Mintz's gap. We need to start with a far more diverse array of experiences and role models, including women and children of color in leadership roles and a de-emphasis on white males in positions of authority.

New and different faces experiencing empowerment can show children that equality is not just an abstract ideal, but a principle that can actively resist white privilege at an early age. It is an uphill battle, but one that makes the instances of transformation more important to prioritize as part of the learning process: "U.S. society is extreme in the way that it individuates and color codes infants' gender. It is also distinctive in its age consciousness and its tendency to divide childhood into distinct stages and give each a precise label. And it is unusual in the way that it segregates children" (Mintz 2012, 23). Thus, what emerges here is a radically transgressive program hiding in the sheep's clothing of a PBS show for children. Not only does that mean, in simple terms, we should encourage the young people around us to watch *Odd Squad* when deciding between numerous options, it also sets up some crucial tenets for a youth-centered pedagogy that goes beyond the program itself. In sum, the show is portraying and expanding meaningful diversity in a multi-cultural world, portraying and expanding models of effective female leadership and empowerment, and portraying and expanding a nuanced form of interaction with technology. All of these valuable lessons are also significant in the context of young people making decisions and being in control without the paternalistic yoke of adult oversight.

We also need not rely on white males to ride to the rescue. Ms. O, also Agent Oprah, is the leader of the primary Odd Squad and, as a girl of color, offers a refreshing persona in charge. We need more powerful people of color, particularly females, as role models for our children that are inspiring leaders, not just "companions" or comical sidekicks. Dobrow, Gidney, and Burton (2018) assess the numbers of black characters in television programming and paint a stark picture of the need for more minority representation:

> Black characters account for 5.6 percent of our total sample of over 1,500 characters. (A study conducted in 1972 by researchers Gilbert Mendelson and Morissa Young for Action for Children's Television found that over 60 percent of the TV shows in their sample had no racial minority characters at all.) [...] It's important that children not only have a diverse universe of characters but also that these characters have diverse characteristics.

Children learn to internalize the types of bodies they generally see in positions of influence, generating a crucial multicultural impetus to put females and people of color in prominent positions of responsibility. If we are to change the hegemony of white males throughout Western society—as public officials, CEOs, and Oscar-winning actors—examples offered in shows like *Odd Squad* need to be highlighted and celebrated.

While it is difficult to determine what universal norms and values should be imparted to young people in various arenas, it is important to keep context and specificity in mind because every child and every family configuration is distinct. That said, we should look for some global lessons for our children that most of us would see as helpful to their progress and our collective future. Being kind, generous, and tolerant seem to be examples of such agreed upon lessons to impart. Rasmussen (2014) confirms:

> Parenting, like the rest of life, is a process of adjusting and readjusting. Adjustments are far easier when one has a philosophical center to adjust against. When using encouragement, as well as logical and natural consequences, and maintaining a democratic attitude, the philosophical center is teaching the child responsibility, cooperation, and respect and instilling the courage necessary to face life [112].

Rasmussen is certainly on to something, but it is easier said than done. We must work hard to find examples of such behavior and we need to augment his call with a sensitivity for diversity as well.

Odd Squad contains many of the lessons we need in order to develop a more inclusive youth-centered pedagogy. We know that at least some of the values conveyed in the media that children consume are instilled in their understanding of the world and the freedoms and responsibilities that are available. Given that observation, a show featuring empowered women and individuals of color deserves our attention. Moreover, when we see that the same show is all about the potential for children to organize and lead on their own, a larger picture begins to emerge. This picture is one with child autonomy and mutual respect for one another. When adults are not pulling the strings or otherwise asserting control, children can succeed. This does not mean adults will always fail or will fail to lead children, only that children are capable as well—and all types of children. Indeed, so-called "strange" children are actually the leading scientists charged with creating gadgets to help solve a series of cases. The children recognize that technology is not always what it seems and that flexibility is necessary to adapt to the inevitable flaws in the machines we use.

Respect and awareness of diverse identities, the promotion of a radical independence among our children, and the simultaneous deployment and suspicion of technological solutions all merge together in *Odd Squad* to represent a viable and compelling youth-centered pedagogy. Kesserling (2016) refers to "Poetic Shift" as representative of a youth-centered pedagogy that seeks "a platform by which youth can gain knowledge, practice and confidence in their written and oral language, to empower youth to 'engage in a process that moves them from student to teacher'" (111). When Agent Olympia realizes that she is a good Agent regardless of the opinions of the villains' ratings, it is easy for her to shield herself from the freezing bolt sent by Mr. Ray Ray because she can see his flaws: his inability to get along with others, his mistaken belief in the power of technology, and his overconfidence in his own plan. Those are lessons for us all and a means for teaching our children how to resist the unquestioned authority and misplaced objectives of villains of all kinds.

Notes

1. Much love and thanks to Hazel and Wesley for drawing my attention to *Odd Squad* and then patiently watching episodes over and over. May you stay odd in your unique and passionate ways.

WORKS CITED

Bernier, A., S. Carlson, and N. Whipple. 2010. "From External Regulation to Self-Regulation: Early Parenting Precursors of Young Children's Executive Functioning." *Child Development* 81(1): 326–339.

Bowlby, J. 1956. "The Growth of Independence in the Young Child." *Royal Society of Health Journal* 76: 587–591.

Coles, Tait. 2014. "Critical Pedagogy: Schools Must Equip Students to Challenge the Status Quo." *The Guardian*, Febuary 25, 2014. https://www.theguardian.com/teacher-network/teacher-blog/2014/feb/25/critical-pedagogy-schools-students-challenge.

Dobrow, Julie, Calvin Gidney, and Jennifer Burton. 2018. "Why it's so important for kids to see diverse TV and movie characters." *The Conversation*, March 7, 2018. http://theconversation.com/why-its-so-important-for-kids-to-see-diverse-tv-and-movie-characters-92576.

Freire, Paolo. 1970. *Pedagogy of the Oppressed*. New York: Continuum.

Giroux, H.A. and R.I. Simon. 1989. "Schooling, Popular Culture, and a Pedagogy of Possibility." In *Critical Pedagogy, the State, and Cultural Struggle*, edited by Henry A. Giroux and Peter McLaren, 217–236. New York: SUNY Press.

Giroux, Henry A. 1999. "Rethinking Cultural Politics and Radical Pedagogy in the Work of Antonio Gramsci." *Educational Theory* 49(1): 1–19.

Gordon, Thomas. 2000. *Parent Effectiveness Training: The Proven Program for Raising Responsible Children*. New York: Random House.

Graves, Sherryl Browne. 1999. "Television and Prejudice Reduction: When Does Television as a Vicarious Experience Make a Difference?" *Journal of Social Issues* 55(4): 707–727.

James, A. and A.L. James. 2004. *Constructing Childhood: Theory, Policy and Social Practice*. New York: Palgrave Macmillan.

Kesselring, J. 2016. "Making Transformative Space: Exploring Youth Spoken Word as a Site." Master's Thesis, Arizona State University. https://repository.asu.edu/attachments/170701/.../Kesselring_asu_0010N_16124.pdf.

Khan, Ummi and Sue Saltmarsh. 2011. "Childhood in Literature, Media and Popular Culture." *Global Studies of Childhood* 1(4). http://www.wwwords.co.uk/GSCH.

Luke, Carmen. 1994. "Childhood and Parenting in Popular Culture." *Journal of Sociology* 30(3): 289–302.

Miguel, I., J. Valentim, and F Carugati. 2013. Social Representations of the Development of Intelligence, Parental Values and Parenting Styles: A Theoretical Model for Analysis. *European Journal of Psychology of Education* 28(4): 1163–1180.

Mintz, Steven. 2012. "Why the History of Childhood Matters." *The Journal of the History of Childhood and Youth* 5(1): 15–28

National Council of Teachers of English. 2014. "How Standardized Tests Shape—and Limit—Student Learning." *Policy Research Brief*. https://www.ncte.org/library/NCTEFiles/Resources/Journals/CC/0242-nov2014/CC0242PolicyStandardized.pdf.

Nouri, A. and S. M. Sajjadi. 2014. "Emancipatory Pedagogy in Practice: Aims, Principles and Curriculum Orientation." *International Journal of Critical Pedagogy* 5(2): 76–87.

"Orchid's Almost Half Hour Talent Show." *Odd Squad*. Season 8. Episode 1, part 1. 2017. PBS Kids Programs.

"The Perfect Score." *Odd Squad*. Season 8. Episode 1, part 2. 2017. PBS Kids Programs.

Shih, Yi-Huang. 2018. "Rethinking Paulo Freire's Dialogic Pedagogy and Its Implications for Teachers' Teaching." *Journal of Education and Learning* 7(4).

Sunarty, Kustiah, and Gufran Darma Dirawan. 2015. "Development Parenting Model to Increase the Independence of Children." *International Education Studies* 8(10). http://dx.doi.org/10.5539/ies.v8n10p107.

Rasmussen, Paul R. 2014. "The Task, Challenges, and Obstacles of Parenting." *The Journal of Individual Psychology* 70(2): 90–113.

Lying Our Way to Truth

The Fun of Exploring Life with Calvin and Hobbes

Amar Singh

CALVIN: I'm writing a book about my life. It's called, "Calvin: The Shocking True Story of the Boy Whose Exploits Panicked a Nation."
HOBBES: Interesting title.
CALVIN: Thanks.
HOBBES: Specifically what exploits are you referring to?
CALVIN: That's the problem. Can you help me think of some I could do?

—Bill Watterson (2013b, 63)

Since its first appearance in November 1985, the adventures of Calvin and Hobbes have captured the imagination of masses. When comics as an art form was losing its battle against films, television, and video games there were three significant works that came out that inspired the recognition which seemed lacking so far. These works were *The Dark Knight Returns* (1986) by Frank Miller, *Watchmen* (1986–87) by Alan Moore, and *Calvin and Hobbes* (1985–1995) by Bill Watterson. The first two changed the way people started understanding superhero comics, not as a gimmick but as a genre meriting serious consideration because of how their stories could shape our understanding of the world. Geoff Klock (2002) argues, "Superhero comics do strange and wonderful things when exposed to literary and psychoanalytic theory" (1). He further elaborates that "if you read poetry, poetics or literary criticism, you will be surprised to find how superhero comic books fall in line, in an interesting way, with what you have been reading; you may also pick up a few new tricks to take back to poetry along the way" (Klock 2002, 1). *Calvin and Hobbes* did something different than these other two groundbreaking comics. It made its readers look at our ordinary lives in order to understand it as something extraordinary. To this end, Nevin Martell (2010) aptly sums it up, stating, "It's pretty mind-blowing to experience something that you expect to be nothing more than ordinary, only to find that it is changing the way you look at the world. [...] Calvin and Hobbes was intended to transcend the funny pages, but no one could have guessed just how far" (para. 3).

As parents, *Calvin and Hobbes* can function as an aperture that provides us with insight into the psyche of our children. Through reading the comic strip *Calvin and Hobbes* parents can develop an understanding of what their children might be going through. The thrust of this essay lies on comprehending the perspective of children who have created their own imaginary world in the same way Calvin has made an imaginary world for himself. Ultimately, going through the pages of Watterson's comic is an emotional experience in itself—an intense one that not only puts a smile on our face but also gushes out subdued feelings that rehash our appreciation for life. Through this rehashed appreciation it can be possible to build better parent-child connections and appreciate the imaginative possibilities that lie within the real world of adults, once seen through the child's eye.

Reading *Calvin and Hobbes* is also an aesthetic experience. On one hand the comics may evoke the sense of mirth at first, but on the other hand they also trigger philosophical probings that can lead one to question the very essence of happiness. The comics persuade us to imagine what it would be like to come across a child whose best friend is a stuffed toy with whom the child has created an imaginary space. For the child this toy is a real being, with whom he shares his emotions and discusses the philosophy of life. Calvin sees Hobbes as an extension of himself. Such a sight would surely trigger a certain amount of concern in parents towards that kid. For some parents this could lead to the belief that it was just a phase of childhood development. Whereas other parents might simply ignore *Calvin and Hobbes*, brushing it aside as merely a fictional cartoon strip created solely for reader's amusement. In fact, this is the tension that Bill Watterson intended to stimulate when creating both these characters. This can be evidenced through the consistent breaking of the fourth wall by characters in order to interact with the readers. This suggests the *fictionality* of their strips, despite Watterson never choosing to do so. Watterson (2005a) believed that to make Calvin's imaginary world believable, it would be an error "to remind readers that the whole strip is a bunch of artificial drawing" (12). One of the reasons for the success that *Calvin and Hobbes* has enjoyed over the years is its interaction with the readers.

The reason why Calvin becomes so important for parents is because of the fact that the personality of Calvin is a collective reservoir of childhood, an archetype of infancy that is fermented with anxiety, inquisitiveness, thoughts of rushing towards adulthood, and the puzzlement of going through emotions that are overwhelming. Calvin even personifies ADHD children who believe in their own imaginary world. Lawrence C. Rubin (2008) in *Popular Culture in Counseling, Psychotherapy, and Play-Based Interventions* attempts to explain the compulsion of needing a transitional object that serves an important purpose in shaping our personality. He muses over the idea of D.W. Winnicot who describes transitional objects as "things, people, and places that anchor us during developmental struggles and the integration of new experiences" (Rubin 2008, 46). Thus, given the definition, transitional objects could be anything—say from music to stories to characters to even stuffed toys. In the case of Calvin, the stuffed toy Hobbes can be considered as a transitional object that serves in the process of personality development for both Calvin and his readers. We encounter the similar experience when reading *Winnie-the-Pooh*, where the stuffed Pooh serves as a transitional object not only for Christopher Robin but also for generations (Rubin 2008, 47). This explanation provides us with an understanding of why children's literature frequently employs the technique of fusing human attributes to animal characters. Doing this makes it easier for children to grasp the so-called moral responsibility of being human through an entertaining and engaging way. Hobbes and Pooh in continuing such lore, perform a similar task, but then they grow up to be much more. Pooh for Christopher Robin is the link in-between innocence and maturity, a workshop where he goes back to position himself against the teachings of the world, to test his wisdom among his imaginary friends, to seek confidence. However, Hobbes' orientation with Calvin is different. Hobbes is not Calvin's escape but rather a part of his reality in the real world. Calvin's wisdom not only grows with him but also through him.

> Because of Calvin's ability to imagine, Hobbes is able to assist Calvin by bolstering— sometimes providing—courage to explore the world, take on challenges, recover from disappointments, and generally move psychologically forward. Without Hobbes the world may seem too scary, lonely, or meaningless to meet challenges necessary to move him along his development [Rubin 2008, 54].

Another major difference is that Christopher Robin acts as an arbiter who gets into the world of his fiction to restore order into the ensued chaos. It is not Christopher Robin that seeks our attention but Pooh. Yet for Calvin it is his imaginary buddy Hobbes who supports him, by being the *raison d'être* of his conscience.

> CALVIN: Hobbes, what should I do when Moe comes to beat me up in gym class?
> HOBBES: Well, you can always do what tigers do when a rhino charges.
> CALVIN: What's that?
> HOBBES: We scramble like maniacs for the nearest tree.
> CALVIN: That's your advice? To sit in a tree all day?
> HOBBES: It doesn't impress the girls, of course, but there's no sense impressing them and then getting killed, my dad used to say [Watterson 2013a, 107].

Tigers and Childhood Development

> My brothers, why is the tiger required by the spirit? [...] To create new values—not even the tiger is capable of that: but to create freedom for itself for new creation—that is within the power of the tiger.
>
> —Nietzsche (2006, 17)

One of the first questions that should be addressed is, why a tiger and not any other animal? Watterson's choice was obviously influenced by his cat Sprite in his creation of Hobbes (Watterson 2013, 12). However, but if we go by Calvin's world itself, the answer seems to be even more profound. On a metaphysical scale, Calvin seems to be a child carved out of the imagination of Nietzsche's Zarathustra. Taking a cue from one of Zarathustra's speeches ("On the Three Metamorphoses") where he explains the necessity of the three metamorphoses of the soul, from a camel to a lion to a child, Calvin's personality seems to be sutured alongside Hobbes. This dichotomy appears to help him understand the ways of the world before he can fully immerse himself into this world: "But tell me, my brothers, of what is the child capable that even the lion is not? Why must the preying lion still become a child? The child is innocent and forgetting, a new beginning, a game, a wheel rolling out of itself [. ....] The spirit wants *its* will, the one lost the world now wins *its own* world" (Nietzsche 2006, 17).

Furthermore, parental supervision plays a crucial role in the development of child's personality. In the absence of parental supervision children might try to seek the same attention from other available resources. Some children engross themselves with animals, toys, or video games. The more children engage themselves with toys instead of parents, the more they connect with them and start personifying them. As such, children begin to feel more and more association with them. Such is the case with Calvin. He believes that Hobbes understands his feelings and Hobbes can advise Calvin on the serious matters. Children, and even parents, often look toward imaginary friends and toys to foster good learning habits and moral values. Many parents also play along with the imagination of their children and consider the toy as a living being. Tea parties with dolls and putting stuffed animals to sleep are examples of this. Such tricks employed by parents can prove helpful in the child's development by giving children the understanding that their parents appreciate their feelings and imaginative worldview. As these things happen, the boundary between the real and imaginary starts to blur.

According to Schultz (2011), "Children who experience learning disability, especially Nonverbal Learning Disability, […] struggle to arrange their thoughts together. Their verbal skills may be fine but the moment they are asked to arrange their thoughts sequentially, comes the struggle" (58). An intervention in such cases is needed from the parent's side. If such children are continually overlooked, the situation can get worse. The child may develop an alternative space to cope with the scenario if society doesn't meet their needs. In such scenarios when the transitional object integrates with the psyche of a child and the process is healthy, "the object is not repressed, mourned, or forgotten, but integrated throughout the psychic field where the object loses meaning with the course of time. But when the attempt at integration is unhealthy the focus of the child on the object can develop into fetishes, addictions, or obsessional rituals" (Rubin 2008, 46).

To put it simply, it is imperative that parents seek through the meanings behind the strange activities of our children rather than rejecting them altogether as child's play. For instance, in a comic strip appearing on December 7, 1986, Calvin's father wants to engage him with "Readings on Dialectical Metaphysics" as a bedtime story (Watterson 2013a, 190). Against that Calvin offers to read him a story, "Goldilocks and the Three Tigers," which he claims was written by Hobbes. In the story a young girl named Goldilocks went into the forest and saw a cottage. Upon entering, she saw three bowls of porridge—big bowl, medium bowl, and a small bowl. Before she tasted the porridge the three tigers came home and "quickly divided Goldilocks into big, medium, and small pieces and dunked them in the porridge" (Watterson 2013a, 190). This horrifies his father, who is filled with both shock and awe, and who quickly bids Calvin a goodnight. Being stunned and perplexed by the outcome, Calvin says agitatedly to Hobbes, "He didn't even look at our illustrations." This particular comic gives readers and opportunity to glimpse inside a deeper meaning than just the surface level joke. There is a father who wants to mold his son with the "language" that he has accustomed himself to, and there is a child who is reformulating his father's lessons that replaces his rationalizing discourse with a world of wonders. That is why, like Aristotle who "uses geometry as an example of knowing," Calvin too uses illustrations for what his father misses (Desmond 2012, 6). William Desmond (2012) in his book *The Intimate Strangeness of Being* ponders over, "Why do we sometimes chastise the child, or more mellowly, indulge him or her" (6)? He quickly responds to this himself, "Because we have this inveterate tendency to think that to be is to be intelligible, and that to be intelligible is to be determinate. [...] Moreover, this movement from the indefinite to the definite is often seen as a progressive conquering of the indeterminate, and hence a progressive process of leaving behind the original astonishment" (Desmond 2012, 6). The father is drenched into the confidence of having perfected the "powers of knowing," which Desmond (2012) refers as "barbarism of reflection" (260). In short, rather than indulging Calvin by facilitating his wonder to a more concentrated understanding, the father abandons him. The son, therefore, in an effort to grasp the viewpoint of his father, chooses to take refuge in his delusion of Hobbes. Robert Greene (2018) in his book *The Law of Human Nature* tries to simplify the idea of Heinz Kohut, the renowned psychoanalyst, and explains why children are drawn to imaginary figures. In his words:

> In our first months, most of us bonded completely with our mother. We had no sense of a separate identity. She met our every need. We came to believe that the breast that gave us food was actually a part of ourselves. We were omnipotent—all we had to do was feel hungry or feel any need, and the mother was there to meet it, as if we had

magical powers to control her. But then slowly, we had to go through a second phase of life in which we were forced to confront the reality—our mother was a separate being who had other people to attend to. We were not omnipotent but rather weak, quite small and dependent. This realization was painful and the source of much of our acting out—we had a deep need to assert ourselves, to show we were not so helpless, and to fantasize about powers we did not possess.

Hobbes for Calvin is the *metaxu*, the in-between that do not call for choosing an "either/or" from the choice (Desmond 2012, xvii). Calvin is not ready to choose the choice in-between; maybe he does not want to and he does not even need to. The sign that he shows suggests his desire to grapple both the desire of his parents' attention and his understanding with Hobbes. This, in turn, functions as an "ontological exploration of the immanent between of finitude and metaphysical transcending to what cannot be determined in entirely finite terms" (Desmond 2012, xvii). The Kierkegaardian sum of absolute that comes in the form of choosing and not choosing which Calvin encounters in the manner of either/or. The choice that is posited to him is that "either" he listens to his parents "or" he face their abandonment, which is seen when the father does not want to listen to Calvin's story. With this choice "all the esthetic returns, and you will see that only thereby does existence become beautiful, and that this is the only way a person can save his soul and win the whole world, can use the world without misusing it" (Kierkegaard 2000, 76). But till Calvin can make the choice, by not losing himself into his parents, Calvin needs an alternate "object of desire" who understands him and works more like an extension. This is where Hobbes comes into play.

Should the Truth Be Exposed?

The question of whether the truth about Hobbes being a figment of Calvin's imagination should be exposed is an important one. Would it not be better just to expose the truth and tell Calvin that Hobbes is a just a toy? Hobbes cannot talk or write a story, and ultimately in truth Calvin is just imagining things. Should the parents shatter the imaginary and creative world of Calvin? Should his parents kill the imaginary power of a child by molding his/her imagination according to their understanding? Or should parents play along with the imagination of their children to make them understand the real world? It is not that Calvin's parents are oblivious of his situation. They occasionally raise the issue (strips of December 16, 1985) and try to make him aware of the truth (strips of May 26, 1986). However, they go along with the idea of playing the role of acknowledging Hobbes as real because for Calvin he is the only friend who is out there and who is, while "somewhat peculiar, a good companion, in a weird sort of way" (Watterson 2013a, 380).

If parents are to follow the moral maxim that truth should be told no matter what then the danger of adulterating the sequence of fate that was taking shape on its own behest, stands in front of the parents. Now, the outcome, good or bad, shall bear the marks. Even a good outcome cannot be justified because it is not organic, it is ultimately adulterated and so will be part of every future event that shall consequently take place. Jennifer Jackson (1993) theorizes that the moment we lie we "manipulate others into making choices we think appropriate (in which case we *may* be interfering with their rights of self-determination)" (186). But Jackson (1993) makes a case for non-lying forms of deception—such as in some cases where doctors try to protect their patients from certain cruel truth—that she believes cannot be considered analogous to lying (186). Whether a breach of trust takes place in deception, cannot be settled *a priori* (Jackson 1993, 185). If one goes by the moral maxim, the whole act of justifying any synonym of a lie is worthless and inadmissible. But here emerges the question, should it be?

Let us interpret it by positioning a case from the film *Lars and the Real Girl* directed by Craig Gillespie. The character Lars in the film witnesses a similar situation to that of Calvin. Lars fantasizes a partner which in reality does not exist. In the film, Lars comes across as a person who, though adorable and likable, is eccentric and likes to live by himself. One day he comes across the news of his sister-in-law's pregnancy, and with this news disturbing memories from his childhood rush back to him. Next, he is shown gripped in his delusion as he takes out a human-sized doll that he has ordered from an adult website. He introduces his doll to people of his town as his girlfriend Bianca. His family doctor, Dagmar, suggests to Lars' brother that he should act as if Bianca is a real person. She suggests that this delusional shift in Lars has happened because of some unresolved issues that Lars is now coping by creating this imaginary girlfriend. The whole town comes to the rescue and everybody treats Bianca as Lars' partner. As the story unfolds we get to know about the repressed guilt that he has about his mother's death and the subsequent aloofness that he experienced from his father. As he confronts those issues and reaches for a resolution, Bianca starts to get sicker. She ultimately dies, which brings Lars back to the real world.

Now, what is appropriate in a situation like this? On one hand there is the maxim that we must tell the truth in any scenario. But on the other hand, in scenarios like Lars and Calvin, exposing truth for others acts as a hindrance in figuring out the truth for themselves. Rather than being exposed to the light of the sun, the truth is being figured out by itself through the shadows of lies. In fact, who out there can claim to know the truth? If, as Plato's allegory goes, we are a slave to the unreal then it is all about defending "my truth being better than your truth." In such a situation when a lie is uttered, it is not done to outweigh the truth, but to help discover it. Therefore, if the truth is the greatest principle by law, lying (in these exceptions) is equally justifiable since the lie is meant to bring about truth. The exposition of truth will make such characters prone to a psychological scar that may never heal. As suggested by Joseph Margolis (1963), the tautological principles that require no justification are similar to non-tautological principles that require one (416–17). It is all speculative, everything lies here in-between the maybe and maybe not. The interference and the demand to assert our own version of the truth is similar to a violent act that will only produce a normalization of what constitutes reality. However, if not, then the "action is irreversible, and a return to the *status quo* in case of defeat is always unlikely. The practice of violence, like all action, changes the world, but the most probable change is to a more violent world" (Arendt 1970, 70).

Conclusion

The above discussion suggests that going through *Calvin and Hobbes* can turn out to be a reflecting process on one's own life as well as the lives of their children. In strip after strip one meanders through philosophical inquires while learning valuable parenting skills and getting laughs along the way. With each new turn of the page, we see Calvin dismantling and recreating himself again and again. It is not just the metamorphosis that he undergoes but metamorphoses. Why Calvin does that, or for that matter why anyone imagines dismantling and recreating their world, is something that no single answer can explain. However, the thing that one can be sure of, Hobbes is not just a figment of Calvin's imagination, an apocryphal; it is *him* and he is very much real. He is as real as Calvin's mom and dad, and the fact is, his parents know this as well. Deriving cues from Calvin's experience one can say that children who are perceived as different or aloof could be a groundswell of new ideas and fun. If catered well, these children can be beneficial for the progress of the society. Tobin Sieber (2003) suggests, in his essay on *What Can Disability Studies Learn from Culture Wars*, that there is an acute need of revision of "asthetic ideal on the healthy and able body as well as an appreciation of alternative forms of value and beauty based on disability" (182). Instead of being over determined for their disability, parents need to play along with the imagination of the child with ADHD, autism, or any number of mental disabilities and let their world grow. Rather than taking the imagination of a child down or compartmentalizing their imagination as an excuse to protect the child, parents should strive to organize their own imaginations in coherence with their children. It should not be about killing (exposing the truth) or curing (enforcing normalized lessons) on children's imaginations and disability. It should be about embracing these alternative orientations of the world and gleaming from them the mind wondrous alternative possibilities. Doing so will help bridge the gap of communication and understanding between children and their parents. Parents need to adapt to these children and cater to their imaginations.

This is not to say that parents shouldn't intervene in the case of disability. However, it is to say that intervention must not be taken as purely dogmatic where the parent ruthlessly asserts what is real and what is unreal. Rather, the interventions we need are ones that develop the self-confidence in children so they can believe in their imaginations without being disparaged. In the same way in which Lars' community assists him, and the father helps Christopher Robin by giving him Pooh, Calvin's parents provide him Hobbes as a way of learning and discovering himself. Calvin's father reading him "Readings on Dialectical Metaphysics" as a bedtime story could be seen as his method of intervening to prepare his child for complex and abstract thoughts at an early stage, so that later in life he may not be discombobulated by abstract imagination. Thus, when we see the parents providing support to Calvin's "imagination," it is not the lie that they are supporting but the potential of the child's mind. This lie is a way for Calvin to explore new ideas, to position himself into this world, to place among fictions that will become a staple for the future course. Ultimately in *Calvin and Hobbes*, the parents accept the fact that Hobbes is out there for Calvin in their absence and he will be there unless Calvin decides otherwise. Together they provide an alibi to lie, and the more we love them, the more we come in acquaintance with the fact that a lie can be an asset to discover the truth. To deny a lie to a child, therefore, is to deny their very truth itself.

Works Cited

Adelizzi, Jane Utley, and Diane B. Goss. 2001. *Parenting Children with Learning Disabilities*. New York: Bergin & Garvey.

Arendt, Hannah. 1970. *On Violence*. New York: Harvest Books.

Bakhurst, David. 1992. "On Lying and Deceiving." *Journal of Medical Ethics* 18(2).

Desmond, William. 2012. *The Intimate Strangeness of Being: Metaphysics After Dialectic*. Washington, DC: The Catholic University of America Press.

Girard, René. 2017. *Things Hidden Since the Foundation of the World*. London: Bloomsbury.

Greene, Robert. 2018. *The Laws of Human Nature*. New York: Viking.

Inside Out (film). 2015. Written and directed by Pete Docter, et al. Distributed by Walt Disney Studios Motion Pictures.

Jackson, Jennifer. 1993. "On the Morality of Deception: Does Method Matter? A Reply to David Bakhurst." *Journal of Medical Ethics* 19(3).

Kierkegaard, Søren. 2000. "Either/Or, a Fragment of Life." In *The Essential Kierkegaard*, edited by Howard V. Hond and Edna H. Hong. Princeton, NJ: Princeton University Press.

Klock, Geoff. 2002. *How to Read Superhero Comics and Why*. New York: Continuum.

Lars and the Real Girl (film). 2007. Written by Nancy Oliver. Directed by Craig Gillespie. Distributed by MGM.

Margolis, Joseph. 1963. "'Lying Is Wrong' and 'Lying Is Not Always Wrong.'" *Philosophy and Phenomenological Research* 23(3).

Milne, A.A. 2005. *Winnie-the-Pooh*. New Delhi, India: Puffin Books.

Nietzsche, Friedrich. 2006. *Thus Spoke Zarathustra*, edited by Adrian Del Caro and Robert Pippin. New York: CUP.

Rubin, Lawrence C. 2008. *Popular Culture in Counseling, Psychotherapy, and Play-Based Interventions*. New York: Springer.

Schultz, Jerome J. 2011. *Nowhere to Hide: Why Kids with ADHD and LD Hate School and What We Can Do About It*. San Francisco: Jossey-Bass.

Shea, Sarah E., et al. 2000. "Pathology in the Hundred Acre Wood: A Neurodevelopmental Perspective on A.A. Milne." *Canadian Medical Association Journal* 163(12).

Siebers, Tobin. 2003. "What Can Disability Studies Learn from the Culture Wars?" *Cultural Critique* 55: 182–216.

Swain, Carol. 2014. *Gast*. Washington, DC: Fantagraphics Books.

Warburton, Nigel. 2006. "Plato *The Republic*." *Philosophy: The Classics*. 3rd edition. New York: Routledge.

Watterson, Bill. 2013a. *The Complete Calvin and Hobbes*. Kansas City, MO: Andrews McMeel Universal.

Watterson, Bill. 2013b. *The Complete Calvin and Hobbes*. Kansas City, MO: Andrews McMeel Universal.

What Is Beauty, What Is Beast?

The Edutainment Value of
Condon's Beauty and the Beast

Debaditya Mukhopadhyay

Being a parent gives birth to an immense responsibility tagged intimately with the lives a parent raises. The American Psychological Association lists the "three major goals" of parenting as "ensuring children's health and safety, preparing children for life as productive adults and transmitting cultural values" (Parenting). As parents it is important to give both physical and intellectual nourishment to children. The delicate anatomy human babies are born with creates the need for fulfilling the first major goal. Though the fulfillment of this first goal is essential for the sheer survival of the child, it is ultimately the next two that have a greater claim on parents' time and energy. Since these goals can mostly be fulfilled by spending time with children talking, this intellectual training of kids by parents is very important to the entire notion of parenting. If children are predominately dependent on parents for obtaining physical nurturing and trainings for surviving physically, they are no less dependent on them when it comes to receiving intellectual nurturing as well. The problem begins if this dependence is mistaken for inferiority by the parents. A neglectful or intimidating attitude from parents can have huge ramifications. It is normal for children to appear obtuse early on, particularly while learning intellectual lessons. However, it is incorrect to rectify that by assuming the child is inferior.

The intellectual training in question, therefore, should look less like an authoritarian session of learning and more like a playful conversation between a parent and child. Since the operative term here is "playful" it is important to have a look at some significant definitions of the same. Johan Huizinga (1949) observes that "play constitutes a training of the young creature for the serious work that life will demand later on" (2). The opinion of Sarala Chazan (2002) is that "play occupies a realm outside of everyday events. It has to do with imaginings and trial action. Anything is possible" (19). Combining these two significant observations, it can be argued that for a healthy, relaxed, and enriching conversation to successfully transfer important cultural, social, and ethical values into children that it requires a particular type of medium. In order to be entertaining and educational, this domain must not look like the world of daily life and yet needs to have the ability to contain important elements of it. Film and television in particular offer entertaining scopes for discussing serious issues that can help children learn fully, while not feeling dictated by their parents. This essay will offer a discussion exploring the possible ways Bill Condon's film *Beauty and the Beast* can be used for this purpose. As suggested by Monique Wonderley (2009), "pre-adolescents have philosophical capacities" that are important for imbibing intellectual training (5). In fact, "these natural capacities" in children can be nourished by "(1) developing children's senses of empathy and (2) improving children's moral reasoning abilities" (Wonderley 2009, 5). This essay will pay particular attention to the references to classic literary works featured in the film because they seem to make a commendable attempt at displaying the importance of developing reading habits in children. Lastly, the potential of the film to serve as an introduction to children about complex ideas like Foucault's theory of discourse will also be analyzed in order to demonstrate the need to utilize popular culture as a starting point for parenting and critical engagement with the world.

On the basis of Debra Danilewitz's (1991) take on the importance of fairytales, it seems these timeless tales can indeed be the medium that can help bring parents and children together in productive ways. According to Danilewitz (1991):

> Adults wishing to make contact with a child will have to do so through the means of play—in the realm of imagination, in the transitional zone. Though it is difficult for children to know how to invite adults into this place (and sometimes frightening for adults to return to). In a shared story a child and an adult can contribute what each does best, the child's ability to move from the concrete world to the created one, adults capacity to move up and down the rungs of their experience [89].

In fact, fairy tales are likely to be more effective when told by parents because these tales should be "told by someone close, warm, observant, caring, slowly enough to leave room for reactions. They are seldom told in a nursery school setting to a group of children because of this need for intimacy when telling the fairy tale" (Danilewitz 1991, 90). One might still interject that the prioritizing of parents telling stories instead of children reading stories themselves is problematic. Danilewitz (1991) answers such objections by pointing out reading these stories alone is not as rewarding because of the compulsory happy ending they often have. What can actually make these useful and enriching is a discussion that allows the readers to realize that these magical portraits are reflections of their own world. In short, "the essence is in the telling of the tale, it is the interaction and dialogue between parent and child that is of importance. The child in turn is able to dialogue with the story itself so as to work through and master certain inner developmental issues" (Danilewitz 1991, 88).

Verbal storytelling is certainly useful for these purposes but there are reasons to look for a better alternative as well. Danilewitz (1991) emphasizes the importance of "telling" the story in an impactful manner and, if that has to be done verbally by the parent, the whole process becomes a little more difficult. Stories are used to initiate discussion and this discussion can be more effective if a parent can focus his/her mind more on the discussion and less on narrating. Verbal storytelling has limitations because it does not give a parent this opportunity of investing his or her entire focus on discussing and teaching things. Carrying out the process by asking the child to read classic stories by themselves might apparently seem to be feasible but even this has its pitfalls. No doubt, "stories may be capable of sending moral messages, most children are not capable of receiving them" (Wonderly 2009, 3). This article suggests that learning through reading comprehension is not likely to take place for many children without engaged conversation. To this end, Darcia Narvaez claims "that, on average, third graders grasped the intended moral messages of stories only 10% of the time" (quoted in Wonderly 2009, 6). In short, "one might tell the child stories with didactic lessons in order to elicit favourable behaviour and to discourage unfavourable behaviour. Such stories often adhere to the ideal that children are empty vessels to be filled or inculcated with specific moral values" (Wonderly 2009, 3). Put simply, "films are useful tools for moral educators. In order to gain the most from them, children should approach movies from an educational standpoint. Teachers and/or parents should prime children for issues that they will confront in the films and discussion should immediately follow them" (Wonderly 2009, 7). Ultimately, even if "reading a book is educationally superior to viewing a film […] this does not change the fact that the children's film genre is an effective instrument of moral education and moreover, one that has several advantages over children's literature" (Wonderly 2009,7).

Some serious objections at this method of using films for educating children is very much in vogue. Wonderly's (2009) article briefly touches on this issue, saying: "Many theorists who advocate moral instruction through children's literature have expressed doubts about film"(7). For instance, Amanda Cain (2009) believes the filming of stories diminishes their educational value because films are governed by "mass marketing forces that favour profit over moral education" (6). Ian Wojcik-Andrews (2000) concurs, arguing that the production process of a Disney film is quite similar to any product of the mass-market. Furthermore Jim Taylor (2010) notes:

> In a recent survey, three-fourths of parents believed that materialism and the negative influences from television, movies, and music were a "serious problem" in raising children. Over 85 percent of parents believe that marketing contributes to children being

too materialistic, sexual content leads children to become sexually active at a younger age, and violent content increases aggressive behaviour in children.

Though highly insightful, the post seems to homogenize popular culture when it defines it, saying: "popular culture used to reflect our values. No longer. Now it is a voracious beast of materialism, celebrity, and excess that shapes those values to meet its own greedy needs." All the objections mentioned above are logical but at the same time they have their limitations. By viewing components of popular culture only as commodities, they seem to use an oversimplified view of popular culture. In order to counter this essentialist approach, an overview of the varied definitions of popular culture is needed.

The six definitions offered by John Storey (2014) seem apt for the purpose. Storey (2014) offers the following features of popular culture: (1) It is a culture "that is widely favoured or well liked by many people"; (2) Since it is liked by the masses and has an obvious antinomic relation with class, popular culture is "the culture that is left over after we have decided what is high culture"; (3) It is "mass-produced for mass consumption. Its audience is a mass of non-discriminating consumers"; (4) It is "the culture that originates from 'the people'"; (5) In the political sense, it appears to be "a site of struggle between the 'resistance' of subordinate groups and the forces of 'incorporation' operating in the interests of dominant groups"; and (6) It comprises of those components that have achieved a "postmodern culture [...] that no longer recognizes the distinction between high and popular culture" (5–12). These definitions of popular culture, in aggregate seem to define popular culture as something that has evident commercial purposes for serving lucid content that either genuinely or illusively speaks to everyone. Hence, it is improper to associate the popularity of popular culture with their marketability. Branding of such components does accelerate their acceptance but it cannot do so with something that has no potential for popularity.

Wonderly (2009) contends that children's films are comparatively more useful than other tools in carrying on engaged conversation with children. She comments:

> Selecting "Be kind to others" from a list of five possible moral lessons does not indicate that a child will come to respect or obey this imperative. However, identifying with a fellow being, experiencing his pain and reasoning to the conclusion that causing such pain is wrong might very well result in genuine moral growth. The proper instructional role of narratives is not to inundate children with moral maxims, but rather, to advance the aims identified in the previous section: educating the sense of empathy and developing moral reasoning skills. Children's films can serve both of these ends [Wonderly 2009, 5].

All these features of popular culture, particularly the first and second, are frequently endorsed by fairy tales that are adopted by popular culture. While behind many selections, commercial motives prevail, this adoption can still enable rustic folklores and fairy tales a welcome touch of sophistication that helps to increase their acceptance, if executed properly. Both folklores and fairy tales are said to be manifestations of the contents of primordial and universal forms that lie at the unconscious level of the mind. This explains these tales' capacity to appeal to humanity in general along with their wisdom imparting nature. Bruno Bettelheim's (1976) comments illustrate this aspect of fairy tales, saying:

> Through the centuries (if not millennia) during which, in their retelling, fairy tales became ever more refined, they came to convey at the same time overt and covert meanings—came to speak simultaneously to all levels of the human personality, communicating in a manner which reaches the uneducated mind of the child as well as that of the sophisticated adult. Applying the psychoanalytic model of the human personality, fairy tales carry important messages to the conscious, the preconscious, and the unconscious mind, on whatever level each is functioning at the time. By dealing with universal human problems, particularly those which preoccupy the child's mind, these stories speak to his budding ego and encourage its development, while at the same time relieving preconscious and unconscious pressures. As the stories unfold, they give conscious credence and body to id pressures and show ways to satisfy these that are in line with ego and superego requirements [5–6].

Another objection regarding fairy tales that seems important is their unrealistic nature. One writer for instance calls them "often far removed from reality" (Danish 2013). She notes, "Many women end up waiting out for their man that fits the image of 'Prince Charming' and who will ride in on a steed and rescue them—whereas the reality is often a beer-guzzling sports fan" (Danish 2013). This is an objection raised against the overuse of "happy endings" in fairy tales. In order to counter these views, it is important to show how and why the presence of the fantastic is integral for fairy tales' happy endings. Fairy tales are mostly centered upon the fantastic and this reliance serves the plots of these tales in a very interesting way. In the conflict between good and evil that forms the base of almost all fairy tales, elements of fantasy play a crucial role. Evil may raise the stake as high as it wants but the resolution in a fairy tale generally has evil defeated. Another important aspect of fairy tales is their connection with myths. To quote Atterbery (2014): "Fantasy provides new contexts, and thus inevitably new meanings, for myth. Fantasy spins stories about stories. That is the cultural work it performs" (3). To this end, fantastic narratives are "engaged in solving a problem or a set of problems specific to the time in which it was written" (Atterbery 2014, 3).

Having justified the utility of children's film, it now makes sense to begin exploring the applicability of Bill Condon's 2017 *Beauty and the Beast*. As mentioned in Wonderly's (2009) article, parents are to "prime children for issues that they will confront in the films and discussion should immediately follow them." Indeed, this essay is meant to serve as a guide to parents intending to use this film as an educational medium. What the film itself offers is known as edutainment, a term popularized by Walt Disney himself. As explained by A. Bowdoin Van Riper (2011), this term signifies "films designed to educate as well as entertain: to actively convey factual information about the real world, while using it as a backdrop for comedy or drama that, in turn, leavened the educational elements of the production" (2). Disney Studios, according to Van Riper (2011), has been consistent at producing such films for years. Though productions made by Disney himself were mainly limited to using "whimsical narrative elements even in the most serious of documentaries" that mingled entertaining narratives with educating documentaries (Van Riper 2011, 4). Van Riper (2011) proposes to extend the applicability of this term by arguing that edutainment value is present in "all Disney productions that deliberately interwove documentary and narrative elements—the realistic and the fantastic—in order to educate the audience" (4). Though not a documentary, Condon's film makes a conscious attempt to mix realistic and fantastic elements by refusing to use the medium of 2D animation, which certainly makes its amalgamation of the real and the fantastic a vivid one. In an interview the director himself comments that he wanted all the characters "to become human beings [… and to] translate everything into something that feels more real [… and] more grounded in a specific moment" (*Screen Crush* 2017).

As mentioned previously, the film's edutainment value will be explored at first by pointing out its potential for imparting lessons on empathy. Empathy enables the self to feel for the "other." The Other is defined as "anyone who is separate from one's self" and whose "existence [...] is crucial in defining what is 'normal' and in locating one's own place in the world" (Ashcroft 2009, 169). In the words of Jacques Lacan, the "other" "designates the other who resembles the self, which the child discovers when it looks in the mirror and becomes aware of itself as a separate being" (Ashcroft 2009, 170). The problem with such developments lies in the simultaneity of the rise of this sense of superiority and the imposition of an equivalent amount of inferiority upon the "other." Parents can draw their children's attention to this process and its ramifications by using the very beginning sequence of the film in discussion. The film begins with showing the selfishness of the prince and his punishment. An enchantress, in the disguise of an old and ugly woman comes to the luxurious castle of the prince seeking help and in return offers a rose. The prince gets "repulsed by her haggard appearance" and refuses to help her. He is repulsed because the woman embodied the Other for his rich, male, handsome, and young "self." The enchantress warns the prince by saying "beauty is to be found within" but the prince mocks her. As a result, the enchantress decides to punish the prince by giving him an inhuman appearance. She also cursed the whole castle and its inhabitants by turning them into objects. The enchantress gave the cursed prince the rose that he laughed at and asked him to win the love of another person before the last petal of the rose fell down to break the curse.

The curse of the enchantress seems to offer a strong cautionary message against othering. In fact, considering the heterogeneity of humanity all over the world, it is unjust to hate people who have different physical features. Beauty has its ethnic varieties and therefore is relative. In short, one needs to see beyond those apparently loathsome features and feel the situation of people who look different. Since the prince was incapable of doing so, the enchantress decided to teach him a lesson. The entire sequence of "Mob Song" in the film shows this in a vivid manner. A portion of this song that attests this hatred of the Other, reads: "We don't like what we don't understand. In fact, it scares us. And this monster is mysterious at least."

The prince is otherized and presented as a monster by Gaston because Gaston had ulterior motives. He wanted to use the crowd for slaughtering the prince. Gaston's motives should be highlighted by parents in order to warn their children about the vicious politics of othering. Paul Koudounaris' (2016) explains how the Other is often depicted with an imposed burden of monstrosity. He writes:

> Monstrosity has always been more concept than reality. Accusations of monstrous appearance have been a traditional means of defining an outsider, and have long served as a part of a basic system of alterity that separates the Self—being one's social, ethnic, political, or religious group—from the Other, who represents the opposition. By using a simple strategy of polar inversion, the Self claims superiority by appropriating an ideal set of virtues, while projecting corresponding vice onto the Other [Koudounaris 2016, 44].

Moral reasoning develops the ability to decide what is right and wrong in a given situation. Along with showing the impact of positive moral decisions by characters like Belle, the film also shows people, particularly Gaston, making immoral choices. Attention should be drawn to these wrong decisions to help children learn the negative consequences of othering. The repulsion of characters toward the prince alienates him and causes him to become the very monster they fear. This can serve significantly in teaching children how wrong it is to hate, bully, and ostracize people for being different. Children from countries with ethnic diversities can be especially encouraged to view an Other not as a threat or inferior by using Condon's film as something more than just entertainment.

After explaining how not to behave with people who look different, parents can start discussing the importance of being friendly. A large part of the narrative is about Belle and the prince's interaction. In order to free her father from the prince's castle, Belle decides to offer herself as the prince's prisoner.

This begins Belle's stay at the castle. Initially, they both fail to connect with each other because of their differences. Both are shown to be unwilling to open up. The prince does not want to reveal his suffering to Belle. Belle too refuses to share her suffering with the prince. Their first meeting makes him appear as a heartless being to her. To him, she remains just the daughter of a thief. The west wing of the palace contained the enchanted rose, which was basically the most important secret of the prince. His anger at seeing Belle come near it shows how unwilling he was to let her know about his world. Ultimately, Belle helps break the curse but not until after Gaston leads the townspeople to storm the castle. The prince could have certainly benefited by letting Belle know everything about him. Instead he abuses her when he finds her lurking around the rose and that leads to Belle's escape. The escape endangers Belle's life as wolves attack her, but it also compels the prince to show his human nature. He saves Belle and gets seriously injured. His intervention, risking his life, moves Belle and she starts caring for him. She deliberately returns to the castle for saving him. This sequence can demonstrate to kids how the characters could have easily avoided the discomfort they caused each other by opening up and trusting each other despite their differences and fears.

Children can understand the importance of opening up to others when they see how the film celebrates the growing friendship between the two. The film uses the song "Something There" to depict their growing admiration for each other and its lyrics reflects Belle's amazement at realizing that their first impressions were wrong. Belle sings: "There's something sweet, and almost kind, but he was mean and he was coarse and unrefined, and now he's dear, and so unsure, I wonder why I didn't see it there before." Despite his looks the prince starts appearing adorable to Belle and the "something" the song refers to is Belle's changed outlook. The most impactful revelation about the prince is shown in the scene where he sets Belle free without any condition. He even apologizes to his servants for not being able to do the same for them. Belle returns to him a second time because she realizes that physical appearance has nothing to do with beastliness. She identifies Gaston as a monster for his behavior despite his good looks.

At the end, Belle returns to the prince voluntarily out of love and breaks the curse. Belle ultimately finds in him a suitable companion, despite his shockingly different appearance because through her consecutive interactions with him and Gaston she realizes the importance of looking beyond physical appearances. She finds unconditional love in the prince whom she initially feared as an Other by exploring his world and contrasting him with Gaston. In an interview with Amon Warmann, Condon is questioned on whether "the film touches on issues like freedom and fear of the Other, which is very relevant right now" to which he firmly replies: "Absolutely, and that definitely resonates more now. But I had other reference points before Donald Trump came along. There are plenty of other examples of that both in my country and around the world" (*FlickeringMyth.com* 2017). In another interview with E. Oliver Whitney, Condon agrees that he consciously had "more people of color in the cast" because he wanted to imply "that they're all individuals" (*Screen Crush* 2017).

The film is important for parents for its display of both ideal and faulty parenting too. Three different parents are shown in the film, namely the prince and his father, Belle and her father Maurice, and Mrs. Potts and Chip. The prince's father, though hardly depicted at all, is shown to be the root cause of all the trouble. As Mrs. Potts explains to Belle, in the middle of the song "Days in the Sun," after the young Prince lost his mother "his cruel father took that sweet innocent lad and twisted him up to be just like him." The prince was taught to be selfish, abusive, and boastful by his father. The prince is shown to be completely incapable of performing even the most basic daily activities like brushing teeth, combing hair, etc. Put simply, the prince had become beastly long before getting cursed due to the way he was parented. The way this film depicts a direct relation between the prince's shocking looks, and his father's flawed parenting, warns parents how bad behaved children are easily subjected to otherizing. The prince's father encouraged his son to indulge in luxury and lavishness without making him aware of ethical and moral values. This can indeed be a message to parents who rely solely on costly toys for keeping their children happy.

Juxtaposed to this is Maurice, who also lost his wife. He is shown as a successful father, albeit in an unconventional way. He seems to have shared his world and ideals of simple living and high thinking with his daughter. Maurice, however, regrets about being over-protective about her daughter. He tells Belle: "I have always tried to protect my little girl. Probably too much," before letting her go to the prince, whom he still considered a dangerous beast. This too is a significant message for parents. Just like Maurice, they must also let their children grow up by facing the world as it is, instead of always trying to draw them away from the harshness thinking they are too young. Belle had learnt lessons of self-respect and self-reliance from Maurice and his acknowledgment of Belle's maturity makes her growth complete. She is shown making good decisions on her own. Maurice protected her as long as it was possible and stopped intervening when she was mature enough to make them on her own. Mrs. Potts and Chip are examples of a parent and child going through a difficult time. Her disciplining of Chip shows the importance of maintaining the process of parenting even in the most hopeless situation. Her hard work pays off. Chip does not get spoiled during his cursed stage as a teacup. The prince's father, Maurice, and Mrs. Potts have all raised their children basically as single parents in the film. While the men lost their wives, Mrs. Potts lost the company of her spouse due to the curse. Despite this similarity, the prince's father fails while the other two succeed. This distinction in the film serves to prove that it is the quality of parenting that matters, not following conventions of wealth.

The film's depiction of the importance of books is worth discussing, especially as books are being increasingly neglected in modern times (Dredge 2013). The film's association of charm and even magical powers with books seems certainly like a welcome gesture under such circumstances. For Belle, reading books is her ticket to wonderlands. The charm of book reading comes out when she tells a librarian in town how she had managed to get away from her daily life's mundane routine through a story set in Italy. In the wonderful library of the Beast's castle there is an unnamed book that has magical powers. The Beast tells Belle it is a book "that truly allows you to escape." With the help of the book, Belle and the Beast get teleported to Paris, inside the room where Belle was born. One cannot help appreciating this symbolic portrayal of a book's power that enables an ardent reader to transcend both space and time. In an engaging scene from the film, Belle does something very interesting while reciting the poem by Sharp:

> The air is blue and keen and cold,
> With snow the roads and fields are white
> But here the forest's clothed with light
> And in a shining sheath enrolled.
> Each branch, each twig, each blade of grass,
> Seems clad miraculously with glass:
> Above the ice-bound streamlet bends
> Each frozen fern with crystal ends.

She then looks at the surroundings that perfectly echo the images of the poem as she adds the following lines on her own:

> For in that solemn silence is heard
> In the whisper of every sleeping thing:
> Look, look at me,
> Come wake me up
> For still here I'll be.

What this little yet beautiful improvisation by Belle manages to convey to the viewers is the charm of literature and creativity. As children are expected to identify with Belle, with a little encouragement from their parents about these habits it could enable children to develop a deeper interest in books.

As mentioned before, this film also has a significant potential for priming young minds for advanced critical thinking. To people who might express doubts about the capacity of children's minds in learning more nuanced ideas, it seems important to refer to Wonderly's (2009) article again:

Philosopher, Gareth Matthews, reported several observations of philosophical thinking among children. For instance, he mentions the Cartesianesque inquiry of one six-year old: "Papa, how can we be sure that everything is not a dream?" (1980, p. 1). Anecdotal exchanges between curious youngsters and their parents say fairly little about the philosophical capacities of children; however, Matthews (1984) also engaged small groups of elementary students in extended ethical discussions, in which the children explored various moral dilemmas and considered possible solutions (p. 92). It is important to note that many college-level philosophy courses largely proceed in this way [3].

The film can give rise to some important questions in children's minds, including why it is so easy for people like Gaston to still play the hero in the real world and why it is uncommon to be an individual like the prince or Belle. If parenting needs to prepare children for survival in the world, it must not engage a young mind only with utopias. Providing a reality check is also important for preparing the children to face the world as it is.

In such context, thinkers like Michel Foucault, who managed to bring significant changes in the worldview of humanity, can play a very important role. Foucault explained why it is important to question even things considered absolutely indubitable like truth itself. In his seminal lecture "The Order of Discourse," Foucault (1981) comments

in every society the production of discourse is at once controlled, selected, organised, and redistributed by a certain number of procedures whose role is to ward off its powers and dangers, to gain mastery over its chance events, to evade its ponderous, formidable materiality [52].

Paul A. Bové (1995) observes that the Foucauldian use of the word discourse "allows us to understand that: 'the "self-evident" and "commonsensical" are those ideas that have the privilege'" of being backed up by "unnoticed power," which produces "instruments of control"(54). Parents can encourage children to consider how such viewpoints explain the supremacy of masculinity, which Gaston endorses, or the socialization of violence against an Other in the film. During the sequence of the "Gaston" song, Gaston, the obnoxious, egoistic and narcissistic antagonist is praised by the crowds unanimously. Condon shows the "materiality" of this paean of praise by showing how slyly LeFou, Gaston's minion, passes coins to the crowd and literally coaxes the song out of them. The song praises him saying: "No one's big like Gaston," "No one fights like Gaston," "No one hits like Gaston," and so on. This ultimately projects Gaston as a typical embodiment of toxic masculinity. The scene shows how LeFou, who clearly has a vested interest in pleasing Gaston, artificially produces this praise without questioning it. People like Gaston dominate, bully, kill, colonize, and control openly. Yet they are socialized as proper because through them the unnoticed power structures of society operate. They are indeed "instruments of control" and yet their true nature remains hidden to the public.

After the film ends, parents can ask their children to think why Gaston is killed and not exposed as a villain to everyone? His death generates a narrative of an accidental or even heroic death and does not expose him as a manipulator who sustains the power structure by disciplining and punishing anything that rivals him. Discussion can be initiated regarding the immediate rage of the crowd against the Beast. Parents can ask children what they think about the reaction of the crowd. They are wrong to react that way indeed but they are also reacting in "expected" ways. Presence of the Other is to be always put under control by the power structures. The Other is not to be understood, it is to be institutionalized, just like the madmen Foucault talks about in his lecture (1981, 53). Such observations will certainly take time for young minds to understand but they will also teach children how to read between the lines and to question the obvious.

The film discussed in this essay can help children imbibe many positive qualities, even if they view it without any discussion with the parents. The procedure explained above, however, can increase this impact. Firstly, the discussion with the parents about the various aspects of the film will help strengthen children's relationships with their parents through being co-participants in interpretation. Secondly, appreciation of the children's proper reasoning abilities from parents during the discussion can increase the confidence of the children significantly. Thirdly, it is not possible for children to always successfully read between the lines or scenes themselves. For attaining this surplus of meaning, discussion with parents can help immensely. This essay offers a model example for doing these through its exploration of the possible usage of a film about the meaning of beauty and beastliness. As the film shows, none of these qualities have any intimate link with physical appearances. By discussing these aspects of the film with children before, after, and during the viewing, the imparting of a few basic values about life in general should become easier. Let the exploration and utilization of tales "as old as time" begin!

Works Cited

American Psychological Association. n.d. "Parenting." https://www.apa.org/topics/parenting/index.aspx.html.

Ashcroft, Bill, Gareth Griffiths, and Helen Tiffin. 2009. *Post-Colonial Studies: The Key Concepts.* New York: Routledge.

Atterbery, Brian. 2014. *Stories About Stories: Fantasy and the Remaking of Myth.* New York: Oxford University Press.

Beauty and the Beast (film). 2017. Screenplay written by Stephen Chbosky and Evan Spiliotopoulos. Directed by Bill Condon. Distributed by Walt Disney Studios Motion Pictures.

Bettelheim, Bruno. 2010. *The Uses of Enchantment.* New York: Knopf.

Bové, Paul A. 1995. "Discourse." In *Critical Terms for Literary Study* 2nd edition, edited by

Frank Lentricchia and Thomas McLaughlin, 50–65. Chicago: The University of Chicago Press.

Chazan, Sarala E. 2002. *Profiles of Play: Assessing and Observing Structure and Process in Play Therapy.* London: Jessica Kingsley Publishers.

Condon, Bill. 2017a. "Bill Condon on the Beast's New Song in 'Beauty and the Beast' and the Modernized 'Be Our Guest.'" Interview by E. Oliver Whitney. *Screen Crush*, March 14, 2017. https://screencrush.com/bill-condon-beauty-and-the-beast-interview.html.

Condon, Bill. 2017b. "Interview—Beauty and the Beast Director Bill Condon." Interview by Amon Warman. *Flickering Myth.Com*, March 7, 2017. https://www.flickeringmyth.com/2017/03/interview-beauty-and-the-beast-director-bill-condon/html.

Danilewitz, Debra. 1991. "Once Upon a Time... The Meaning and Importance of Fairy Tales." *Early Child Development and Care* 75: 87–98.

Danish, Elizabeth. 2013. "Influence of Fairy Tales on Children." *Health Guidance*, August 30, 2013. https://www.healthguidance.org/entry/15745/1/Influence-of-Fairy-Tales-on-Children.html

Dredge, Stuart. 2013. "Children's Reading Shrinking Due to Apps, Games and YouTube." *The Guardian*, September 26, 2013. https://www.theguardian.com/technology/appsblog/2013/sep/26/children-reading-less-apps-games.html.

Foucault, Michel. 1981. "The Order of Discourse." In *Untying the Text: A Post-Structuralist Reader*, edited by Robert Young, 48–78. Boston: Routledge and Kegan Paul.

Huizinga, Johan H. 1949. *Homo Ludens a Study of the Play.* London: Routledge & Kegan Paul.

Koudounaris, Paul. 2016. "The Monster in the Mirror." In *Guillermo Del Toro at Home with Monsters: Inside His Films, Notebooks, and Collections*, edited by Britt Selvesen et al., 43–60. San Rafael, CA: Insight Editions.

Rice, Louis. 2009. "Playful Learning." *Journal for Education in the Built Environment* 4(2): 94–108. https://doi.org/10.11120/jebe.2009.04020094.

Storey, John. 2014. *Cultural Theory and Popular Culture an Introduction*, 6th edition. New Delhi, India: Pearson.

Taylor, Jim. 2010. "Parenting: Know Your Children's Enemy." *Psychology Today*, January 25, 2010. https://www.psychologytoday.com/us/blog/the-power-prime/201001/parenting-know-your-childrens-enemy.html.

Van Riper, A. Bowdoin. 2011. "Introduction." In *Learning from Mickey, Donald and Walt: Essays on Disney's Edutainment Films*, edited by Bowdoin A. Van Riper, 1–14. Jefferson, NC: McFarland.

Wojcik-Andrews, Ian. 2000. *Children's Films History, Ideology, Pedagogy, Theory.* New York: Garland.

Wonderly, Monique. 2009. "Children's Film as an Instrument of Moral Education." *Journal of Moral Education* 38(1): 1–15. http://dx.doi.org/10.1080/03057240802601466.

The Mediation of Scientific Neutrality

She-Ra's *Warning of Erring Toward Evil Through Disinterested Inquiry*

JL Schatz

Scientific progress, and indeed science in general, is often understood as neutral in its pursuit. No doubt, given that science reveals what is true about the world, progress in science is often upheld as a noble goal since it will help us better understand the universe around us. However, as is quite obvious, science has been used to help create any number of great atrocities from nuclear weapons to eugenics to the sophisticated technological efficiency that produces factory farms and enables the trains to run on time. Nevertheless, many within the scientific world claim that these horrors are not the result of science in of itself. Instead they believe the fault lies on how science is used or falsely reproduced when, in fact, nothing is further from the truth (Gastonne 2015). At the very least, human understanding of science is always mediated through politics, culture, and language. As Anabela Carvalho (2007) writes,

> Public perception and attitudes with regard to those domains are significantly influenced by representations of scientific knowledge conveyed by the press and other mass means of communication (Wilson, 1995; Krosnick et al., 2000; Corbett and Durfee, 2004). Like any other dimensions of reality, science is reconstructed and not merely mirrored in the media [223].

This is why two different groups of scientists can look at the same scientific data and can reach different meanings and conclusions (Duhaime-Ross 2015). This is to say nothing about the many times scientists have disagreed with each other's methods for study and how future science has proved the past truths of science wrong. In short, there is no scientific progress that can be understood as fundamentally neutral and uninformed by human constructions surrounding truth, and often power. Because of this, approaching science under the pretense that it is a disinterested mode of inquiry can have disastrous consequences.

Netflix's remake of the popular 1980s cartoon *She-Ra* can be an effective warning against approaching scientific investigation into how the world works as unbiased, demonstrating how such pretenses risk producing ev-er-greater threats to existence. In the show, the Horde, run by Hordak, is an intergalactic colonial power that invaded the planet Etheria, ruthlessly killing the kingdoms ruled by the Princesses. While initially it appears that the Princesses fight using magic, and the Horde uses advanced technological weapons, the show reveals that the power of the Princesses' magic comes from indigenous technology within Etheria, which is every bit as powerful as the science the Horde commands. In the real world, colonialist empires often employ their weapons to subdue indigenous populations whose ways of life are considered too primitive to survive, often due to their supposed lack of a proper understanding of the world (Maddison 2013; Glenn 2015). So too in the real world it has become clear that indigenous systems of knowledge production were as advanced as the forms of world-making tools brought by colonists, whether that be scientific or religious (Semali and Kincheloe 1999). In *She-Ra*, through both the characters and plotlines, these parallels become increasingly obvious as the knowledge of how Etheria works is revealed to both the heroes and the antagonists. At the same time, the show deliberately focuses on how the characters come to understand that knowledge in order to complicate what makes one a Princess or a member of the Horde in the first place.

I stumbled upon Netflix's remake of *She-Ra* when looking to find something to watch with my 9- and 11-year-old kids either before or immediately after school. I remembered that I enjoyed watching the original when I was around their age while waiting for the morning bus. I had rewatched some of the older 1980s *She-Ra* with them when they were younger but eventually stopped when we lost interest. In the original, She-Ra the character was a much more scantily clad and powerful version of her human-self Adora. In almost every episode she would transform from Adora into She-Ra by holding her sword and proclaiming, "For the honor of Grayskull," and then subsequently beating back the Horde. In the episodes where she didn't save the day and needed help, it was often her cousin He-Man who swooped in at the last moment to rescue her. There is no Princess Alliance or much mention of any population outside of the Whispering Woods, which is a particularly magical region of Etheria where the rebels hold out against the Horde. Unlike the original, in Netflix's version He-Man is non-existent and when Adora transforms she is significantly less sexualized, and not every episode needs her to become She-Ra to save the day. In fact, if were it not for the title and the names of characters, locations, and calling upon the honor of Grayskull to transform it would be an entirely different show. Fortunately, both myself and my kids found Netflix's remake to be an entertaining family watch, as well as significantly more complex and interesting than the original.

While watching *She-Ra* with my kids I used many of the strategies suggested by other authors in this book, particularly by those essays in the first part. And, while I also talk with my kids about what they're hearing while listening to NPR in the car, it is worth repeating the value of fiction in talking about real world politics. This fact is particularly true when dabbling in questions of science and science-fiction since the two are often intertwined with real world scientists looking toward the fictions of their childhood for ideas of scientific discovery (Schatz 2009, 1–17). Similarly, science-fiction looks to known science in order to create a believable technological chain of events to produce the currently unimaginable universes the imaginary characters find themselves in (Schatz 2009, 87–110). These fictions—along with the horrors and paths to salvation depicted within them—inform the viewers of how science can be used and which technologies human civilization chooses to pursue. No doubt, the same companies that make robotic vacuum cleaners for the home also have military contracts that utilize that same technology to make killing increasing efficient (Hellström 2012, 2). Meanwhile, all these technologies along with their beneficial and destructive possibilities appeared in novels, film, and television long before they ever became reality. By using the science-fictions of today to begin contemplating the science of tomorrow we can better prepare humanity to avert the worst of technology's applications while steering us toward their best. At the same time, by looking at how science-fiction imagines the future it can reveal more about ourselves at the present to better understand how the horrors of tomorrow can be so readily imaginable.

To be clear, none of this is to say that science is not without its merits or that all scientific progress should be halted unconditionally. Rather, it is to say which science we put our belief behind matters and that no progress should be taken as intrinsically desirable without first scrutinizing the cost to get there and its applications once we do. To put it another way, just because animal testing, which kills more than 100 million animals per year, can give us a new scientific breakthrough for eyeliner or soap says nothing to the morality of that killing for that knowledge (PETA; NAVS). Likewise, even though things like funding space-based laser weapons systems would produce an incredible amount of technological and scientific breakthroughs it says nothing on if that progress is worth the risk of the targeted mass killings that would come with it (Helwich 2001). To put it bluntly, to even use the rare earth materials necessary to produce the computing systems that helped bring this book to publication doesn't speak to the question of the deadly mining practices that poisons the environment (Bontron 2012). In each instance, unpacking these often untold consequences is necessary for understanding the way science participates in political, economic, and social relationships rather than seeing it as a noble and neutral pursuit. Once stripped of its supposed neutrality it becomes possible to appreciate other systems of knowledge production and work to avoid many of science's insidious applications and methods.

The False Dichotomy Between Good Princesses and the Evil Horde

As mentioned previously, Netflix's *She-Ra* takes place on the planet Etheria where the inhabitants of the Princess kingdoms are being hunted down by the Horde, who are intergalactic colonists and base their operations in the Fright Zone. The show's focus is on the character Adora, who was previously a force captain of the Horde. She defected to the Princesses once she learned about the Horde's true ambitions, after discovering her power to turn into She-Ra in the first two episodes of season one. The sword she uses to transform is a piece of what various characters call "first one's tech," tying it to the now extinct first peoples of Etheria who left these artefacts behind. She-Ra's sword is by no means the only piece of ancient technology the characters encounter. Many episodes feature the Princesses racing against the Horde to obtain various technological artefacts, which are oftentimes more powerful than the magic the Princesses currently possess or the current military weapons the Horde commands. In so doing, the show sets up a dynamic where indigenous science is valued and where its application can be used for the forces of good or the forces of evil.

It is worth noting here a few things before getting into the question of science. First, the fact that Adora believed that the Horde was good until she witnesses some of their military tactics firsthand indicates that the bright line between good and evil is often only a matter of perspective. This is further supported by the fact that, as the show progresses, the viewers learn that the Horde also has several former Princesses in their midst who left the Alliance because of how they were treated, and who ultimately found a home in the Fright Zone. Second, while the Horde is definitely traditionally portrayed as the villains in the show, the majority of characters in the Horde are given a certain amount of depth that demonstrates how their motivation isn't just to kill innocent civilians. In fact, part of the reason the Fright Zone has its name is because it causes individuals worst fears to come into existence, which then propels them into committing violence against the Princesses. Third, much of the show's plot revolves around how the planet is to be managed and whether the Princesses or the Horde should be the stewards of it because of their knowledge of the ecosystems and the Universe's design. To this end, part of Hordak's colonial ambitions for Etheria is to terraform it into a planet that could be habitable for his people.

Taken together, the above points demonstrate how threat construction between good and evil functions in order to increase hostilities against those who are deemed threatening. This is especially true in the case of environmental managerialism and international politics where doing what one wants with one's own country is a nationalist right, and where telling other countries what to do is taken as a sign of global leadership. As Paul Trenell (2006) writes,

> By focusing attention on the threats posed by outsiders, national elites found that the domestic populace could be more easily homogenized and managed. […] There is a danger that a security framework could import this type of "us versus them" thinking into the environmental realm to detrimental effect. By searching only the external realm for the causes of insecurity "our complicity in evil is erased" (Campbell, 1993: 3) and the faults in our own actions are overlooked. […] Therefore, casting an issue in security terms puts the onus of action onto governments, creating a docile citizenry who await instructions from their leaders as to the next step rather than taking it on their own backs to do something about pressing concerns [17–18].

Unfortunately, the characters in *She-Ra* often fall into this precise trap as they continually demonize the other side by thinking only of their own needs for security and what they understand to be a habitable environment. It is also why both sides find it so easy to recruit others to fight for their cause since they create the message that failure to do so will threaten life itself. They do this despite several characters changing sides and coming to agree with the politics of the other, more than their own.

While the Horde is much more explicit in its claim to violence, throughout the show the history of the Princess Alliance and the means they used to secure itself is also fraught with a similar proclivity towards exclusionary practices. What is perhaps most telling to this end is that the regions ruled by the Princesses—which in the show refers to a race of magical entities more so than just to a royal title—doesn't just contain Princesses but rather a vast array of species. While most are humanoid in nature, some are not. Most notably is She-Ra's steer, Swift Wind, who throughout the show continues to complain about how horses are treated throughout the kingdoms and advocates for their equality to the more human-like creatures. Meanwhile, the Fright Zone contain many citizens who aren't from the planet Hordak is invading from; but from a collection of species from both worlds, several of which are Princesses from Etheria. And, while many of these individuals are also human-like, their degree of humanness vary greatly with many having a combination of human and other animal traits. Overall, there isn't a whole lot that on face distinguishes who are with the Princesses and who is with the Horde. Nevertheless, the two sides are maintained by constructing alliances to their respective leaders through the creation of identities centered on being either a Princess or a member of the Horde, which doesn't necessarily require actually being a Princess or from the planet Hordak originates from.

While in the show these dynamics serve to create a level of depth that often isn't seen in children's animated programming, in the real world it functions to securitize populations into national identities wholly independent from whether that state serves the individual's best interest or not. To this end, David Campbell (1992) writes,

> As an imagined community, the identity of a state is the effect of ritualized performances and formalized practices that operate in its name or in the service of its ideals. Discourses of danger and the multifarious ethical powers of segregation [...] establish a geography of evil that inscribes the boundaries of inside / outside. [...] In each of these foundational moments, [...] a fictive paragon has been presented as a regulative ideal by which to make judgments. [...] In each case, the exclusions effected by foreign policy are occluded, for all interpretations that seek to expose identity as a representation that should be historicized and problematized have themselves to be excluded in order for a contingent identity to be rendered secure [143].

As a result, *She-Ra* helps produce a discourse of political identity formation that sustains real world identities out of the social constructions of citizenship through providing a representational foundation for good and evil. In both cases, the fear of survival and the artificial construction of us versus them sustains a certain militancy against the other instead of seeking alternative arrangements of power and international cooperation.

One major exception to being motivated out of fear is Adora herself, who continues to have sympathy for her former Horde companions and friends. Throughout both seasons, as much as the plot revolves around having She-Ra battle the Horde, the plot also remains centered on Adora getting her friend Catra to see the unrestrained violence of Hordak's invasion of Etheria. Catra almost always retorts that the Princesses are no different, and that she is aware of the Horde's use of fear. Furthermore, the characters under Catra's command understand what they are doing but likewise compare it to the violence of the Princesses, which they fear is even worse. Most notably, is the Princess Scorpia, who is a scorpion-human hybrid who pines after Catra and joined the Horde because she didn't feel wanted by the Princesses. Given that Scorpia is the only animal-hybrid depicted as a Princess and is the only explicit portrayal of lesbian interest, one can readily guess at why Scorpia didn't fit with what the Princess Alliance was fighting to preserve. When learning more about her own origin, Adora learns that the power of She-Ra is the title of a warrior, and that the last She-Ra failed by placing her individual friendships before her mission to protect Etheria. She learns this in season one, episode 11, where the warning she receives while training parallels her desire to peacefully reach out to Catra instead of fighting. Taken together, Adora decides that while she will align with the Princesses that she will also continually look for another way than violence to win the war. Conversely, those characters motivated out of fear from the Horde or the Princess Alliance are consistently more prone to suggest violence than Adora is.

Science, Magic, and the Dangers of Neutrality

Returning now to the question of science, with the construction of political identity in mind, it is apparent how technological progress and scientific knowledge production gets bound up with securitizing forces throughout the show and in the real world. Certainly science is used to sure up political consensus for action as much as technology is used to forcefully carry out that consensus while appearing neutral in its call. As Douglass Kellner and Jeff Share (2007) write, "The current religion of science and technology propagate the myth that information is objective, thereby making the social and historical construction of knowledge disappear and hiding the mechanisms of hegemony and power" (64). Within *She-Ra*, this myth of scientific neutrality becomes clear through Princess Entrapta. Unlike the other Princesses in the show who use magic, when Entrapta is asked by another character what her power is she says nothing, and then references her knowledge of science and the first one's tech. Throughout most of season one, Entrapta's technological skills help the Princesses further unlock She-Ra's powers and understand how to use the ancient artefacts the Princesses are searching for in their war with the Horde. Together, they learn that the first one's tech serves as the basis for the Princesses' magic—even though they don't understand fully how they make use of it. For Entrapta, understanding how the technology works is her only ambition in order to learn more about how Etheria functions. In fact, Entrapta's main reason in agreeing to become part of the Princess Alliance is because they had more first one's tech to experiment with. And, once joining, Entrapta's biggest worry is about moving over all of her equipment, not the risk of the Horde. As a result, even as she sides with the Princesses in season one, her motivation was always for science itself rather than the mantle of the Princess Alliance and its calls for justice against the Horde.

While Entrapta's desire for discovery appears neutral at the onset, the fact that her advances in understanding science help the Princess Alliance achieve some pretty decisive victories against the Horde in season one shows that its production was anything but. Naturally, early on it appears her research on the first one's tech is desirable because the only alternative presented is the Horde, which threatens all of Etheria. In this way, Entrapta's work is upheld as politically neutral because she's in it for the sake of science, and positively since its application is to fight an objective threat. This supports the illusion that disinterested science will work for the greater good and allows lines like "I would be honored to […] provide weapons" in season one, episode six, to appear desirable. In fact, the threat of the Horde is established to be so great that in season one, episode four, Princess Perfuma joins the Alliance because they were literally poisoning her land and preventing her from using her powers of making plants grow (sometimes into fighting monsters). In fact, despite Perfuma and Entrapta having an at-odds but friendly relationship with each other, it is clear that Perfuma is only willing to tolerate Entrapta's antics because Etheria depends on it. In this way, like in reality, "security language has been characterized in terms of an objectivist epistemology [… often requiring] the authority of science to demonstrate the existence of 'objective' threats. […] Even in the context of real material dangers, the invocation of environmental security threats is fundamentally about socially constructed risks" (Liftin 1999, 365).

Once again, it is worth returning to how the media figures into this real-world equation between science and neutrality. While *She-Ra* does an excellent job at opening up conversation above how technological advancements can be harnessed for political purposes, the media at large often mediates what people take away from science and whether it's being harnessed for the purposes of good or evil. As Anabela Carvalho (2007) writes,

> The media are key elements in the mediation of the "relations of definition" (Beck, 1992) between science, the public and the political spheres. The notion of science as an "ivory tower," exempt from public exposure and debate, is increasingly inadequate. As our "risk society" (Beck, 1992) generates new problems that require scientific interpretation but affect us all, science is asked to "come out to the street" and to be the basis of political decisions. Policy-makers often expect scientists to provide answers to problems that are debated in the media and other public arenas, and make a variety of public uses of science to legitimize action or inaction. Scientific knowledge is also utilized by a number of other social actors, including business and activists, to justify particular programs [224].

As this happens, it is not only the application of science that lacks neutrality. Rather, it also calls into question the very means by which science generates truth itself. "In the media, as in other arenas, there is no such thing as 'pure facts.' Instead, 'truth claims' are embedded with certain worldviews, judgments and preferences" (Carvalho 2007, 225). As science becomes understood and known through the media, the language of science itself becomes embedded with the biases that its transmission holds, ensuring that its production is never purely a neutral endeavor.

Within *She-Ra*, the morality of Entrapta's scientific neutrality comes increasingly into question toward the end of season one and throughout season two. After a semi-botched mission to rescue Princess Glimmer from the Horde, Entrapta gets left behind—thought to be dead by the other protagonists—and immediately continues her work in advancing the first one's tech that the Horde possess. Despite initially being Catra's prisoner, Entrapta quickly rises in the ranks of the Horde and becomes Hordak's favorite due to the technological breakthroughs she keeps willfully producing. In fact, in season two, episode two, when Catra reveals to She-Ra and the other Princesses that Entrapta was alive and wasn't being held captive, they explicitly ask if Entrapta is working with the Horde. Entrapa responds, "I'm on the side of science. But I am living at the Fright Zone now and the Horde is supplying me with tools and materials for my work. So, yes, I guess? […] But don't worry about me. I love it here. I've made unbelievable progress in my research. And the Horde has been so supportive." To Entrapta her choice continues to feel politically neutral because she has always just been on the side of science and her only question was always just where it was best conduct her experiments from. However, to the other Princesses and the Horde, Entrapta's choice is very much political since where she does her research could tip the scales of the war. No doubt, the Alliance begins to suffer an increasing number of defeats by the Horde after using the technology and weapons Entrapta creates for them. At the same time, whenever the Horde experiences a setback like in season two, episode five, while Catra bemoans their defeats, Entrapta consistently says things like "A scientist never returns empty-handed. There's always data." Because Hordak recognized that the greater pursuit of knowledge over Etheria would give the Horde more power than any single military victory Catra could provide, he increasingly favors Entrapta over Catra during the course of season two.

While the evil misapplications of Entrapta's science is obvious in the show as it wreaks havoc over Etheria, and literally threatens to let Hordak terraform the planet to be inhospitable to most life there, in reality the misapplications are often harder to identify. Given the existence of threats in the real world it appears obvious that individual nations would develop weapons to protect themselves, which subsequently must become increasingly more sophisticated as other nations and potential threats develop better technology themselves. Throughout history, scientists were often happy to go to work for both the Allies and the Axis, the United States and the Soviets, and so on since access to those budgets meant better resources and the ability to further their scientific discoveries (Lewis 2016). Naturally some scientists adamantly believed in the positive value of the nuclear weapons their work helped to produce because they were necessary to stop the existential threat the other side posed. However, "few scientists involved in the [United States' Manhattan] project thought deeply about the long-term implications" of their work (Colglazier 2018). No doubt, there is a whole contingency of scientists and philosophers to this day who believe that the application of science is not their immediate responsibility because their job is only to adhere to the empiricism of the natural world (Ruphy 2006). To them, questions of how that knowledge is used should be left up to politics. Sadly, this belief ignores the fact that the dissemination of science is never fully impartial. To put it simply, "science is always contextual and contingent. It is bound by political, institutional and personal factors and relies on a set of assumptions that are often questionable" (Carvalho 2007, 238). Therefore, the production of science should never be regarded as completely neutral since doing so risks writing off the lives that are lost as an acceptable collateral for scientific discovery.

As a result, there is a need to not prioritize scientific pursuit and progress without limits or take for granted that any and all knowledge production is good regardless of the social, political, and geographical location it takes place within. To this end, Simon Dalby (1998) builds on a tradition of other scholars, writing that

> modes of "knowing" the world and their political specification of peoples and societies as "threats" or in need of "management" are not merely technical issues requiring research [... because] knowledge is not neutral but appears in various forms of power/knowledge used by protagonists in the politics of environment[. ...] This is not to suggest that environmental problems [...] do not in some sense "exist" in the real world. Forests are being cut down and people displaced. The potential for disruptions as a result of climate change needs to be taken seriously. [...] But, [...] how these issues are described and who is designated as either the source of the problem, or provider of the potential solution to the problem, is an important matter in how environmental themes are argued about and in who gets to make decisions about what should be done by whom [Seager 1993, 179–180].

This ability to claim ownership over the truth, and to prioritize that truth over even who is speaking it, ignores the way supposedly objective science is put to work in defense of planetary existence. This is especially true at the point that, while

> the world exists independently of language, [...] we can never know that (beyond the fact of its assertion), because the existence of the world is literally inconceivable outside of language and our traditions of interpretation. In Foucault's terms, "we must not [...] imagine that the world turns toward us a legible face which we would only have to decipher [... to] dispose [...] the world in our favour" [Campbell 1992, 6].

In turn, we can't expect any science alone to solve our problems without understanding the conditions from which it arises and is put to task to solve. By focusing our attention to these discursive underpinnings of science, instead of just the truth of what can be discovered, we can better ensure positive technological developments while avoiding the "us versus them" thinking that often serves as the foundation for scientific research and development through military spending. To this end, "academics have an important responsibility in fomenting media literacy on science issues and in advancing the tools for a critical deconstruction of science communication" (Carvalho 2007, 240).

Fortunately, there is another path to take. This can be seen in several of the characters who come to deeper realizations during the course of season two. To a large extent, Entrapta defecting to the Horde forced many of the protagonists to believe they could just reach out to her and get her to understand in much the same way Adora believes she can for Catra. No doubt, once they individually knew someone who was part of the Horde, it ruptured their initial way of thinking because it was one of "us" that became a "them." Throughout the show, viewers got to know even some of the lower henchmen in ways that made it hard to just root against the villains as in most children's animated programming. In these moments, the conclusions to these episodes often ended up more cooperative and required the Horde and Princesses to work together to overcome an obstacle (often accidentally unleashed by Entrapta while doing her research) instead of requiring She-Ra to use her sword. It is telling that as the show continues, She-Ra learns to develop her sword into a shield and a rope, discovering new ways to attack problems without needing to cut them down.

In the real world, we too can think about global dangers and others differently. As David Campbell (1992) writes,

> were those possibilities explored, then the boundaries of American identity and the realm of "the political" would be very different from that which currently predominates, for the distinction between what counts as "normal" and what is thus "pathological" would have been refigured. Besides [...] even the differences in the interpretation of danger [...] demonstrates how even those articulations with the most affinity do not mechanically reproduce a monolithic identity [256–257].

Indeed, within discussions of immigration, citizenship, and national identity who counts as an "us" or a "them" is often very difficult to determine with any amount of precision. This is why even United States citizens can be threatened with deportation in the attempt to stem the supposed threat of illegal immigration (O'Kane 2019). It is also why the race to fear the other because of the threat they supposedly pose results in a violent securitization at the complete expense of all those who aren't included in its protection. No doubt, the whole history of mass incarceration and deportation has been fraught with so much racialized violence and bias because of constructed threats to the social, economic, or political order (Davis 2003). However, by reframing the question of danger and identity away from the alleged objective threat, it can be possible to reach cooperative solutions that would be better suited to actually solve planetary problems. This requires going beyond one's own knowledge base and opening oneself up to different kinds of knowing than just the calculative logic of threat construction.

All of the above is even more true in the world of advancing science and the rampant growth of technology. As individuals and politicians get a hold of, fund, or suppress scientific studies they do so for a particular purpose in mind. And, even when the scientist isn't thinking about its actualized applications, they are in part producing them in reality. Whether Entrapta or Einstein are responsible for the weapons their knowledge produced is secondary to the reception of that knowledge by others. When these representations manifest into existential threats, science can be readily called in as the solution to sanitize the problem by objectively exterminating the disease—even when that includes whole populations. Reorienting our understanding of science from neutral to political would better equip us to discover new ways to confront threats because it will enable us to understand how even scientific truth comes with its conditions and limitations. Looking past just the data to comprehend the world that data represents makes us better suited to seeing beyond just what one's told to take as a given. The perception of neutrality will never aid in this pursuit since it will only cause a more fervent attachment to one's own truth and knowledge of who or what is evil. Whether by technology or magic, Princess or Horde, science or fiction the way we understand this discourse matters since its dissemination is never neutral. Like media, there is a need to deconstruct the representations in order to unpack the lessons that we should be taking away from even animated programs like *She-Ra and the Princesses of Power*.

Works Cited

Bontron, Cécile. 2012. "Rare-earth Mining in China Comes at a Heavy Cost for Local Villages." *The Guardian*, August 7, 2012. https://www.theguardian.com/environment/2012/aug/07/china-rare-earth-village-pollution.

Campbell, David. 1992. *Writing Security: United States Foreign Policy and the Politics of Identity*. Minneapolis: University of Minnesota Press.

Carvalho, Anabela. 2007. "Ideological Cultures and Media Discourses on Scientific Knowledge: re-reading news on climate change." *Public Understanding of Science*, 16(2): 223–243. https://www.ssoar.info/ssoar/bitstream/handle/document/22420/ssoar-2007–2-carvalho-ideological_cultures_and_media_discourses.pdf.

Colglazier, E. William. 2018. "War and Peace in the Nuclear Age." *Science & Diplomacy*, January 19, 2018. http://www.sciencediplomacy.org/editorial/2018/war-and-peace-in-nuclear-age.

Dalby, Simon. 1998. "Part Four: Introduction." In *The Geopolitics Reader*, edited by Gearóid Ó Tuathail, Simon Dalby, and Paul Routledge, 179–186. New York: Routledge.

Davis, Angela. 2003. *Are Prisons Obsolete?* New York: Seven Stories Press.

Duhaime-Ross, Arielle. 2015. "Scientists Can Draw Very Different Meanings from the Same Data, Study Shows." *The Verge*, October 7, 2015. https://www.theverge.com/2015/10/7/9469845/different-meanings-from-same-data-research-science.

Gastonne Philippe. 2014. "The Myth of Scientific Neutrality." *The Daily Bell*, April 14, 2015. https://www.thedailybell.com/all-articles/news-analysis/the-myth-of-scientific-neutrality/.

Glenn, Evelyn. 2015. "Settler Colonialism as Structure: A Framework for Comparative Studies of U.S. Race and Gender Formation." *Sociology of Race and Ethnicity* 1(1): 54–74. https://www.asanet.org/sites/default/files/attach/journals/jan15srefeature.pdf.

Hellström, Thomas. 2012. "On the Moral Responsibility of Military Robots." *Ethics and Information Technology*. http://www.diva-portal.org/smash/get/diva2:558749/FULLTEXT02.

Helwich, David. 2001. "Missile Defense: Trans-Atlantic Diplomacy at a Crossroads." ISIS Briefing on Ballistic Missile Defense 6. http://www.isisuk.demon.co.uk/0811/isis/uk/bmd/no6_paper.html.

Kellner, Douglas, and Jeff Share. 2007. "Critical Media Literacy: Crucial Policy Choices for a Twenty-First-Century Democracy." *Policy Futures in Education* 5(1): 59–69.

Lewis, Danny. 2016. "Why the U.S. Government Brought Nazi Scientists to America After World War II." *Smithsonian Magazine*, November 16, 2016. https://www.smithsonianmag.com/smart-news/why-us-government-brought-nazi-scientists-america-after-world-war-ii-180961110/.

Liftin, Karen. 1999. "Constructing Environmental Security and Ecological Interdependence." *Global Governance* 5: 359–377. http://faculty.washington.edu/litfin/research/litfin-constructing.pdf.

Maddison, Sarah. 2013. "Indigenous Identity, 'Authenticity' and the Structural Violence of Settler Colonialism." *Global Studies in Culture and Power* 20(3): 288–303.

NAVS. n.d. "The Cruelty and Waste of Animal Experimentation." *National Anti-Vivisection Society*. https://www.navs.org/the-issues/the-cruelty-and-waste-of-vivisection/.

O'Kane, Caitlin. 2019. "18-year-old U.S. Citizen Detained by Border Officials Said Conditions Were So Bad He Lost 26 Pounds, Almost Self-deported." *CBS News*, July 26, 2019. https://www.cbsnews.com/news/us-citizen-detained-by-ice-francisco-erwin-galicia-border-officials-conditions-bad-almost-self-deported/.

PETA. n.d. "Animal Testing 101." *People for the Ethical Treatment of Animals*. https://www.peta.org/issues/animals-used-for-experimentation/animal-testing-101/.

Ruphy, Stephanie. 2006. "'Empiricism All the Way Down': A Defense of the Value-Neutrality of Science in Response to Helen Longino's Contextual Empiricism." *Perspectives on Science* 14(2): 189–214

Schatz, JL. 2009. *The Technological Narrative of Biological Evolution.* Ann Arbor, MI: ProQuest, UMI Dissertation Publishing.

Semali, Ladislaus, and Joe Kincheloe. 1999. "What is Indigenous Knowledge and Why Should We Study It?" In *What Is Indigenous Knowledge? Voices from the Academy*, edited by Ladislaus Semali and Joe Kincheloe, 3–58. New York: Falmer Press.

Trenell, Paul. 2006. "The (Im)possibility of 'Environmental Security.'" Master's thesis, University of Wales. https://studylib.net/doc/8529766/-im-possibility-of—environmental-security-.

About the Contributors

Anne **Bialowas**, Ph.D., is an associate professor in the Department of Communication at Weber State University. She teaches undergraduate courses in communication theory, media studies, and gender in addition to graduate courses in advanced presentations, team building, and facilitation. Her research interests encompass sport communication, popular culture, rhetoric, and gender studies.

Mike **Catello** is a teacher and writer who lives in the suburbs of Pittsburgh with his wife and two children. He is an adjunct English instructor at South University and author of "Self-Muzzling in a Clickbait World That Never Could Have Spawned the Sex Pistols Without the Kinks," published in *Atticus Review* in 2015.

Ryan **Cheek** is an instructor in the Department of Communication at Weber State University. He is also a doctoral candidate in Technical Communication & Rhetoric at Utah State University. He teaches undergraduate courses in communication theory, communication law, interpersonal and small group communication, and argumentation studies. His research interests encompass political rhetoric, masculinity, and argumentation studies.

Amber E. **George**, Ph.D., teaches undergraduate courses in philosophy and sociology at Galen College. She has coedited several books including *Education for Total Liberation* (2019); *The Image of Disability* (2018); *The Intersectionality of Critical Animal, Disability, and Environmental Studies* (2017); and *Screening the Non/Human* (2016). She is the editor-in-chief of the *Journal for Critical Animal Studies* (*JCAS*).

Charity **Gibson** received a Ph.D. in literature and criticism from Indiana University of Pennsylvania. Her dissertation focuses on issues regarding motherhood and the mother-daughter relationship. In her research and scholarship, she continues to write on contemporary issues related to motherhood and parenting. She serves as an assistant professor of English at the College of the Ozarks, teaching literature, composition, and critical theory.

Jacob E. **Gindi** is not only a passionate leader and mentor within the banking sector but also a devoted dad of four children. His skills as a facilitator of critical thinking have been put to good use with expanding social justice themes and the horizons of his children. In his spare time, he enjoys playing guitar, studying the stock market, and engaging anyone in critical debate.

Kevin D. **Kuswa**, Ph.D., earned his degree in communication studies from the University of Texas at Austin. He has published work in argumentation, cultural studies, and critical pedagogy, his most recent piece appearing in the *Quarterly Journal of Speech*. He has also been coaching debate for more than two decades and is the head of debate and a member of the History Department at Berkeley Preparatory School in Tampa, Florida.

Debaditya **Mukhopadhyay** is an assistant professor of English at Manikchak College, affiliated with the University of Gourbanga. Popular culture, myth, adaptation, and theatre are his areas of interest. He has forthcoming articles on *Indiana Jones and the Temple of Doom* and *The Shawshank Redemption,* to be published with McFarland and Palgrave Macmillan, respectively.

JL **Schatz**, Ph.D., is the director of debate at Binghamton University, where he teaches courses on media and politics out of the English Department. He has several edited book collections on critical animal studies, disability, and gender in the media, and he has published numerous articles on science-fiction and technology. He has also served on the executive board of the Institute for Critical Animal Studies and the Central New York Peace Studies Consortium.

Rae Lynn **Schwartz-DuPre**, Ph.D., is a professor of communication studies and women, gender, & sexuality studies at Western Washington University. Her research interests include postcolonial, rhetoric, media, and gender studies, and the ways in which (re)presentations rhetorically constitute knowledge and to what effect. Her edited collection *Communicating Colonialism* takes up the relationship between communication and postcolonial studies.

Amar **Singh**, Ph.D., is an assistant professor of English at Banaras Hindu University, India. His research interest lies in the area of popular culture, film studies and cultural studies. His doctorate research at Bergische Universität, Wuppertal, Germany, is on hyperrealism and Christopher Nolan's cinematic texts.

Ryan **Vaughan** is a professor of English at Binghamton University where he earned his Ph.D in 2006. He identifies as a pop culture maven trying to use his knowledge for the forces of good. Kind of like Batman, but his tool belt is loaded with obscure if not enlightened connections between sitcoms and culture, instead of grappling hooks and Batarangs.

Index

www.ingramcontent.com/pod-product-compliance
Lightning Source LLC
Chambersburg PA
CBHW031137270326
41929CB00011B/1661